MAPPING
AMERICA

Septentrionalissimas Americæ partes, Groenlandiam puta, Islandiã et adjacentes, quod Americæ tabulæ commodé comprehendi non potuerint, peculiari hac tabella Spectatoribus exhibendas duximus.

AMERICA SEP TENTRIONALIS

FRAN CIA

MAR DE

OCEANUS ZUR PERUVIANUS PACIFI

Tropicus Capricorni

AMERICÆ nova Tabula.
Auct. Guilielmo Blaeuw.

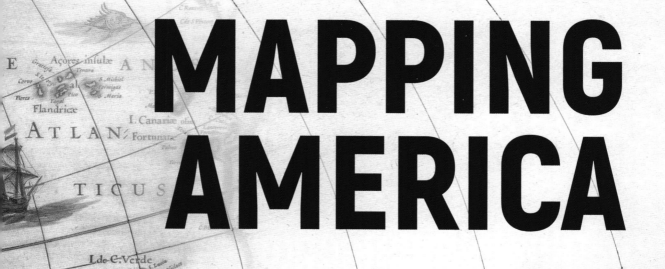

MAPPING AMERICA

THE INCREDIBLE STORY AND
STUNNING HAND-COLORED
MAPS AND ENGRAVINGS THAT
CREATED THE UNITED STATES

**NEAL ASBURY AND
JEAN-PIERRE ISBOUTS**

APOLLO
PUBLISHERS

Mapping America: The Incredible Story and Stunning Hand-Colored
Maps and Engravings that Created the United States
Copyright © 2021 by Jean-Pierre Isbouts and Neal Asbury

All rights reserved. No part of this book may be used or reproduced in any manner
whatsoever without the written permission of the publisher, except in the case of brief
excerpts in critical reviews or articles. All inquiries should be sent by email to Apollo
Publishers at info@apollopublishers.com. Apollo Publishers books may be purchased for
educational, business, or sales promotional use. Special editions may be made available
upon request. For details, contact Apollo Publishers at info@apollopublishers.com.
Visit our website at www.apollopublishers.com.

Published in compliance with California's Proposition 65.

Library of Congress Control Number: 2020942966

Print ISBN: 978-1-948062-76-3
Ebook ISBN: 978-1-948062-77-0

Printed in the United States of America.
Second printing.

CONTENTS

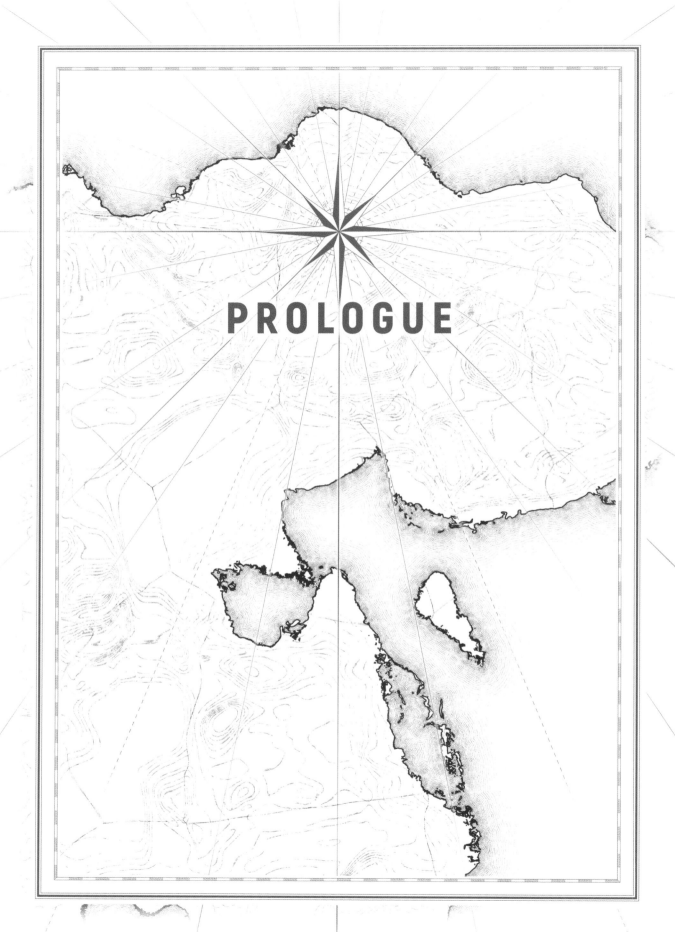

PROLOGUE

SUNDAY, OCTOBER 28, 1618: IT WAS SHORTLY AFTER DAYBREAK, around 6:30 a.m., when the gate to his cell was opened and the condemned man was served his final breakfast. Though much of the city was still asleep, he was wide awake, having spent much of the night listening to the sounds of hammering and sawing in the courtyard below. After all, what man would want to spend his last night on earth asleep? Better to stretch out on the straw of his cot and relive the memories of all the great voyages of his life. And how marvelous they had been, those long months upon the vastness of the ocean, steering his ship with a steady hand and a stout heart. Ask any number of Londoners and they would tell you that he was a hero, a swashbuckling explorer who had thumbed his nose at the Spanish and Portuguese and stolen a march on them to the New World. There had been a moment, not too long ago, when his name was on the lips of every Englishman, a symbol of English pride and prowess. Why, then, did he find himself in this cell? Where were the fame and wealth that was his due? Why was he sitting in this dungeon, listening to the sounds of the workmen building his scaffold?

It was a question he had often asked himself these past few years: why did King James hate him so much? Was it because his book *The Historie of the World* had slighted him in some way? Or was it because James—the Catholic son of Mary, Queen of Scots—had always been envious of his predecessor, the Protestant queen Elizabeth I? Was James jealous of the many glories that Sir Walter Raleigh had bestowed upon her reign? Didn't the king know that it was Raleigh who had charted the first English maritime route to the New World? That it was he who had ordered the creation of the first English settlement on the Atlantic coast? True, this settlement—the "Lost Colony" of Roanoke—was

FIG. 1. William Segar, *Portrait of Sir Walter Raleigh*, ca.1598. Painted at the height of his fame, the portrait includes a map of Cádiz in the background.

eventually abandoned, but that didn't take away the fact that it was he, Raleigh, who had provided England with the strategic toehold that surely would grow and launch a new and glorious era.

But now, all those great triumphs lay in the past. Instead, Raleigh had been dragged in front of a special tribunal known as the Commissioners. King James had been at pains to avoid a public trial for fear it might provoke riots. He knew that Raleigh was popular in England, and this was only heightened by his reputation as a buccaneer who had given the Spanish a run for their money. The king made sure that the so-called "trial" was actually a hurried, carefully scripted exercise lasting fewer than four hours.

That had not prevented Raleigh from confronting his accusers head-on, forcefully denying the charges levied against him: that he had engaged in acts of piracy; that he had attacked a Spanish settlement without authority to do so; that he had betrayed the trust of his sovereign; that he had engaged in a plot to overthrow him. In the end it didn't matter. The outcome was a foregone conclusion. No one was surprised when, at the end of the proceedings, Lord Chancellor Anthony Bacon stood up and duly declared that Sir Walter Raleigh was found to be a traitor and therefore deserved the punishment of death.

Still, a hush fell over the room as soon as the verdict was read. Some closed their eyes and crossed themselves. Everyone knew what that meant, *a traitor's death*. First, Raleigh would be strung up until he was near death from asphyxiation. Then, he would be strapped to a table and methodically disemboweled, with his intestines and sex organs thrown to the dogs. And then, if he was still alive, he would suffer the pain of having his limbs and then his head cut off, one by one.

But then, two days later, came a small remission: the king had decided to show mercy, given the prisoner's past service to the Crown. The sentence of being hanged, drawn, and quartered was commuted to one of beheading. Not a pleasant prospect either, but a good deal less onerous than being strung up and seeing one's intestines ripped from one's body.

With the sentence thus confirmed, the petitions began. Raleigh's son Carew, a precocious thirteen-year-old, wrote to beg the king to remember "the many great places of command" given to his father "by the most worthy Queen Elizabeth," a reminder that may have done more harm than good.[1] Others pleaded with the Crown that the execution of so prominent a mariner, so marvelous a hero of the age, for perceived offenses against the despised Spanish Empire, could only rile public sentiment. It might set people's hearts against any future dealings that James could want to have with the Spanish.

Next came Raleigh's wife, the beautiful Bess, former maid of honor to Queen Elizabeth, to beg for her husband's life. Her entreaties met with a stone wall of indifference. As the attorney general summed it up, "He hath been a star at which the world has gazed; but stars may fall, nay they must fall when they trouble the sphere wherein they abide."[2] The Crown conceded only to allow Bess to have supper with her husband on the eve of his execution, and to take possession of his corpse after the ax came down.

Now the king's consort, Queen Anne, entered the fray, even though she was bedridden at Hampton Court and was prompted to intervene only by a passionate letter from Raleigh himself. In it, he had poured out his gratitude to the queen, certain in the knowledge "that you have beheld my affliction with compassion."[3] Moved by this eloquent plea, she, too, beseeched her husband to show mercy, but to no avail. The king's mind was made up, and he would see Raleigh to the scaffold if it was the last thing he did.

Thus Sir Walter found himself transferred to the Gatehouse Prison on the eve of his execution and locked in a cell that had once formed part of the fourteenth-century monastery of St. Peter, close to Westminster Abbey. That day, as he was led across the courtyard, in full view of his scaffold, he had chanced upon an old friend, Sir Hugh Beeston.

"Will you be present at the great show tomorrow, Sir Hugh?" Raleigh asked cheerfully.

His friend, thunderstruck, stammered that he would indeed try to be there, "if he could find a place in the crowd," for all of London was expected to come and pay tribute to the hero of the high seas.

Raleigh smiled and said, "Aye, I don't know what you may do for a place. You must make what shift you can." And he added with a smirk, "But for my part, I am sure of one."[4]

There were others who also reported being amazed by the fact that the condemned man was in such high spirits—almost as if he had been delivered of a great burden. One witness, a man named Francis Thynne, warned him that he shouldn't "carry it with too much bravery, lest your enemies take exception." Raleigh brushed such scruples away. They had condemned him to death; what more could they do? If anything, he was now free to think and say what was on his mind. "It is my last mirth in the world," he replied; "do not grudge it to me."[5]

The Reverend Robert Tounson, the priest who attended Raleigh on this final day, was equally surprised. "He was the most fearless of death that ever was known," he later wrote, "and the most resolute and confident, yet with reverence and conscience." Indeed, as Raleigh chattered the hours away without a care in the world, the chaplain grew alarmed. Had the great hero taken leave of his senses? But Raleigh laughed and said that "he'd never feared death" and would certainly not start now. As to the manner of his execution, "he had rather die so, than of a burning fever." Indeed, during the last few days he had been tormented by a high fever, though he knew that he would soon be cured of it.

Then evening fell, and at long last, his wife, Bess, was allowed into his presence. They hugged and whispered, held hands, and supped together, lingering over the meal prepared by the kitchens of nearby Palace of Westminster. When the bells of the abbey struck at midnight and the warden came to escort Bess out, she embraced her husband and clung to him with all her strength. That was when she told him through a veil of tears that she had permission to give him a proper burial, rather than to endure the shame of having his corpse exposed for all to see. It was the custom of the day to place the head of a traitor on a spike at London Bridge, where it would slowly decompose as a warning for others. Raleigh would not have to suffer that final indignation.

"It is well, dear Bess," he said jokingly, "that thou mayst dispose of it dead that hadst not always the disposing of it when it was alive."[6]

One final kiss, and then the heavy door was shut, the candle flame flickered, and he was alone with his thoughts. Seated at the rough-hewn table, Raleigh remembered a love poem he'd written for Bess many years ago, before they were married. He took a pen, dipped it in the inkpot, and wrote it down from memory, the lines more moving and apt than ever before: "Even such is time, that takes in trust / Our youth, our joys, our all we have / And pays us but with earth and dust." He paused, then added two lines: "But from this earth, this grave, this dust / My God shall raise me up, I trust."[7]

The final hours slipped by. Outside it had begun to rain. He tried to sleep on his bed of straw, but it was to no avail, and he was wide awake when the priest came at 5:00 a.m. to give him his final Communion. Already he could hear the sounds of Londoners converging on the square below, children in tow, so as to secure a good spot. They were soon joined by maids and shopkeepers hoping to do good business, selling hotcakes, sausages, and warm ale. Within the hour the courtyard was packed with people, jostling for a view of the scaffold.

Inside, much to the surprise of his jailors, Raleigh was enjoying a hearty breakfast. Why waste a perfectly good meal? He finished with a satisfying pull at his pipe, undoubtedly using some of the tobacco from the queen's own fields of Virginia. He then stood and took great care with his wardrobe, choosing a "hair colored" (i.e., tan) doublet, black taffeta breeches, silk stockings, and, finally, a black embroidered waistcoat. Someone handed him a cup of wine for fortification, which he drank with relish.

Outside, the sky had turned a dark metal gray, which some found rather suitable for the occasion. A steady drizzle, whipped by the wind coming down the Thames, ensured that everyone was cold and miserable. Some of the guards lit a fire to provide a modicum of warmth for the notables who were now taking their seats around the scaffold. The cream of English nobility had come to see their great rival and sometime friend dispatched to another world: William Compton, the Earl of Northampton; the Earl of Oxford, son of Raleigh's great nemesis; Lord Percy, brother of Northumberland; and John Pym, a member of Parliament and a vocal critic of King James, whose arrest by King Charles I, many years later, would spark the English Civil War. Another eyewitness, the recently knighted Sir John Eliot, soon to be appointed Vice Admiral of Devon, watched in awe as Raleigh climbed the steps to the scaffold. "Guards and officers were about him," he later wrote; "the scaffold and the executioner, the axe, and the more cruel expectation of his enemies."

And how was the prisoner himself? Amazingly, he looked as if the whole thing left him utterly unperturbed, "as if already [his mind] had been freed from the cloud and oppression of the body." While this was sure to disappoint those who had hoped to see their great rival trembling with fear, "it filled all men else with emotion and admiration."[8]

Silence fell over the crowd as Raleigh now turned toward them for his final oration. Several accounts have survived, which all suggest that he spoke for nearly three quarters of an hour with great eloquence and authority. Point by point, he refuted the king's charges and all the slanders that had been heaped upon him.

And then it was time. Raleigh kneeled to pray, then stood up to shake hands with all the noblemen and officials lined up around the crowded scaffold. As he embraced his friend Thomas Howard, Earl of Arundel, who had supported his ill-fated voyage to Guyana, he said, "I have a long journey to go and therefore I will take my leave."

He then turned to the executioner and, on impulse, bade him to show him the axe. The executioner hesitated; never before had a condemned man wished to see the instrument of his death. But at last he relented and produced the hatchet. Raleigh raised his eyebrows and inspected the blade with a practiced eye, running his finger along the edge as if to test its bite. Satisfied, he nodded and smiled. "This is a sharp medicine," he said, "but it is a physician for all diseases."[9]

He kneeled one last time, put his head on the block, and stretched his arms—the agreed signal that he was ready for death. The crowd held its breath. Even the birds were quiet; not a sound was heard. The executioner raised the axe, then hesitated.

"For God's sake, man, strike!" Raleigh cried. "Strike!"

And then the blade came down, once, and a second time, hard, before the noble head was finally severed from the body. It toppled to the scaffold's wooden floor and lay still, its lips still moving.

It was done. Sir Walter Raleigh, England's greatest explorer, was dead. With him ended an era that had seen three glorious expeditions to the New World on behalf of his patron, Queen Elizabeth I, led by a man who in 1617 had only escaped death by promising her successor, King James I, to find the gold of the lost city of El Dorado. Alas, no gold was found in Guyana. What the expedition did produce was a diplomatic spat with Spain, after some of Raleigh's men attacked a Spanish outpost, against orders. Thus, upon Raleigh's return to England, King James had ordered his death sentence, for no other reason than to placate the Spanish ambassador, Count Gondomar, and avoid war with the Spanish Empire.

England would soon have cause to regret Raleigh's untimely death. Had it not been for him, England might never have had settlements in Virginia; might never have had its laws and democratic ideals planted on American soil; and might never have had its tongue—English—become the language of the United States. Indeed, the backlash against his execution was not long in coming. Many in England were outraged that such a prominent person had been butchered on such a flimsy pretext. The public outcry became so fierce that within a matter of weeks, the king was forced to defend himself in a seventy-two-page pamphlet that documented Raleigh's "great and heinous offences." The book had the opposite effect, and Raleigh's popularity only grew in the decades to come.[10]

In many ways, then, the story of Sir Walter is a fitting start to the birth of America. Time and again the fate of the United States and the dream of a republic based on freedom and equality would hang in the balance, solely on the strength of bold and courageous men and women. At times it seemed that only a stroke of luck, or a stunning twist of fate, saved that dream from being utterly extinguished. It is only because of people like Sir Walter Raleigh and so many other heroes, now known and forgotten, that the dream of America became a tangible reality.

In his *New York Times* review of Rick Atkinson's masterful book *The British Are Coming*, historian Joseph J. Ellis wrote that the American Revolutionary War was "a distant world where there are no witnesses to interview, no films of battles, or photographs of the dead and dying."[11] Ellis was writing about the contrast between the Revolutionary War and the wars of the twentieth century, and in that sense he was right. But then he erred when he wrote, "Visually, all we have are those paintings by John Trumbull, Charles Willson Peale and Gilbert Stuart." That is not true, and it reveals the blind eye that many authors and historians have long turned toward the greatest mass medium of the eighteenth century: the printed map. In an age of tremendous exploration and expansion, maps brought home the boundless thrill of undiscovered lands beyond the horizon. For the first time in human history, maps and engravings captured the majesty of the earth's continents and the stars of the firmament, making them tangible for everyone, from kings and noblemen down to the maids and merchants in the art of Vermeer.

Indeed, while much of the early exploration was initiated by the Portuguese and the Spanish, it was the Dutch, the leaders of maritime trade in the seventeenth century, who would create the Golden Age of Cartography. The Dutch—Calvinists through and through—believed that cartography served the public interest, and they published whatever maps they found without any concern for intellectual ownership. The Spanish were the exact opposite: they considered their discoveries (including any potential sources of gold) proprietary knowledge that amounted to state secrets, therefore rarely published in map form. Only in the eighteenth century did the center of European cartography shift from Holland to France and England as both these nations became colonial powers in their own right. Maps now gained a political imperative, to clearly delineate spheres of influence in the hotly contested territories of North America.

When the Revolutionary War began, it was maps that illustrated the glory and the carnage, the triumphs and the defeats, in breathless newspaper accounts on both sides of the Atlantic. The first thing Lieutenant General Thomas Gage did while preparing for the great British invasion of New York was to send out reconnaissance parties "capable of taking sketches of the country" and drawing maps to "mark out the roads and distances from town to town." And when the final order for the attack came, as in the case of Lieutenant Colonel Francis Smith's planned assault on Concord, such orders were accompanied by detailed maps illustrating all of the key geographical features, including hills, ridges, rivers, bridges, and towns.[12] These, in turn, served to illustrate the after-action reports that were carried by fast schooner to London, there to be engraved overnight in the form of maps to be presented to King George III.

In an age before photography, film, or video, it was maps that informed and guided British war policy, that kept all of Europe in thrall, and that ultimately inspired the farmers and fishermen of the New World to defeat the greatest empire on earth.

That is why this book will tell the full story of America, from the Age of Discovery through the Revolutionary War, in a way that has rarely been done before: through the art of mapmaking. It is these maps that give us an unprecedented look at the ambition, struggle, and glory that attended the exploration of America and the birth of our nation.

FIG. 2. A fifteenth-century map of the world based on Ptolemy's *Geographia* by the German cartographer Leinhart Holle (1482)

I

THE DAWN OF THE
RENAISSANCE

SHE WAS A THREE-MASTED, SQUARE-RIGGED GALLEY, OF THE TYPE that had sailed the waters around Palos de la Frontera since Roman times. With a length of just over seventy-seven feet and a beam of twenty-six feet, displacing little more than two hundred tons, she was unremarkable in every aspect, down to the worn sails, the frayed ropes, and the warped wood of her stern, bleached white by salt spray and the sun. She was what mariners referred to as a "carrack," a ship built around a wooden frame called a "carvel" that made her sufficiently sturdy for long-distance travel in blue waters. Unlike other vessels of the era, she also boasted an unusual combination of square-rigged sails on the foremast and lateen-rigged sails on the mizzenmast, which gave her the uncanny ability to tack fore and aft, with a sail set along the full length of the keel, into the prevailing wind. Portuguese seamen had been quick to exploit this innovation to their advantage, notwithstanding the carrack's limited cargo capacity. That is why at the close of the fifteenth century, Portugal was dominating the first phase of European exploration, a position she would tenaciously defend until well into the sixteenth century.

But on this day, as she strained against the ropes on the quay of Palos de la Frontera, she hardly looked like a vessel that was about to change the face of the world. In fact, the two ships that were scheduled to sail with her looked even more worn and disheveled than she was. Unlike the carrack, they were smaller vessels known as "caravels," a design originally credited to Prince Henry the Navigator, the third son of King John I of Portugal. There was a good reason for their poor repair. Both ships had been forcefully requisitioned by the Crown, much against the wishes of their owners, who had therefore neglected their maintenance. Once, when their sails were still trim and their wood was still

FIG. 3. A replica of Columbus's flagship, a carrack known as the *Santa María,* built in 1492

fresh in varnish, they had carried the lofty names of saints, as was customary in Spain. But now they were simply known as the *Pinta* and the *Niña,* the feminine version of the owner's surname, Niño.[13]

Both caravels were considerably smaller than the mother ship they were destined to accompany. The square-rigged *Pinta* had a length of sixty feet and drew just seven feet for a capacity of no more than fifty-eight tons of cargo, as did the *Niña.* The latter was still lateen-rigged, but there were plans to make her square-rigged—using square-shaped sails positioned at right angles to the length of the ship—as soon as she reached the first stop in the Canary Islands. If they made it that far. Caravels were not oceangoing craft; they were designed for coastal traffic, always staying within sight of land. But both boasted bow-sprits set at rakish angles, as if to defy anyone who claimed they were not ready and eager for deepwater seas.

Their seaworthiness was the least of Christopher Columbus's problems. His flagship, now rechristened *Santa María*, had originally sailed these coastal waters as *La Gallega*, with a full complement of experienced crew, most of whom he had retained. But were they trustworthy? Would they stick with him through the long and dangerous voyage ahead? He was, after all, not Portuguese but a man from Genoa, an Italian.

Many noblemen at the court of Castile had asked themselves the same thing. Why should he, Cristoforo Colombo, be entrusted with such a risky voyage? Worse, he had been married to Filipa Moniz Perestrelo, a member of the Portuguese aristocracy, and everyone knew that Portugal was already contesting Spain's command of the seas. Why would anyone put their faith in this man?

Not surprisingly, the same question had been on the mind of Spain's Queen Isabella and King Ferdinand when they initially rejected Columbus's proposal. The royal couple were in the final stages of ejecting the Muslims from Al-Andalus, Moorish Spain, and had other things to worry about. They were not the only ones. Other princes of Europe had also dismissed Columbus's idea of finding a westward route to the silk and spices of the East—or "the Indies," as Asia was known—as hopelessly unrealistic.

That such a new route was urgently needed, everyone could agree. Throughout the fourteenth and fifteenth centuries, the European population had grown exponentially. To feed them, the European ports of Venice, Genoa, Antwerp, and others had developed a flourishing business with the East, including India and China, by using a land passage known as the Silk Road. These "Indies" produced spices such as mace, cloves, nutmeg, and pepper that not only improved the taste of meat but could also act as preserving agents, allowing for the distribution of pork, beef, and other perishable foodstuffs throughout Europe. What's more, the East produced many other desirable goods, including silks, jewels, and gold.

Originally developed in the second century by the Chinese Han dynasty, the Silk Road had long offered European caravans a relatively safe route from China to the Mediterranean Sea across northern India, Persia, and the Byzantine Empire. It was these caravans that had introduced Europe to Chinese innovations such as paper and gunpowder, as well as a host of other products. But after the breakup of the Mongol Empire, and the conquest of Constantinople by the Ottoman Turks in 1453, that land route was suddenly cut off or, at the very least, fraught with danger. The obvious solution, then, was to see if a sea route to the Indies could be found—one that would bypass the Ottoman Empire entirely and remain safe from marauding vessels. The Portuguese believed that such a maritime route should run eastward, around the southern tip of Africa and into the Indian Ocean, even though there were many who insisted that these faraway seas were filled with "boiling waters" and the most horrific monsters.

Columbus, however, had a different idea: to sail westward, where he believed he would in due course make contact with the Asian continent. It was this rather revolutionary concept that he proceeded to pitch to the various courts of Europe.

The Earth Is Not Flat

Regardless of the maritime route, very few people in the fifteenth century still believed that the earth was flat. The century had experienced an explosion of new ideas, largely as a result of a movement we now call the Renaissance. This is a French translation of a word first coined by the sixteenth-century author Giorgio Vasari, namely *rinascità*, or "rebirth." As Vasari described it, at the dawn of the fifteenth century, the Quattrocento—a group of Florentine artists, scholars, and scientists—had decided to break with medieval ideas that had restrained creative and intellectual endeavor for so long. The result was a veritable rebirth of Western knowledge and learning, inspired by the great models of antiquity.

Of course, Vasari's view was an exaggeration. As early as the thirteenth century, a movement called Scholasticism had inspired scholars such as Thomas Aquinas and John Wycliffe to study the works of Greek philosophers such as Plato and Aristotle, even though these sages had lived and worked in a pagan world before the embrace of Christianity. Aristotle, whose writings had been preserved in the Muslim libraries of Córdoba and Grenada, and subsequently in monasteries throughout Europe, particularly appealed to the medieval mind because of the practical and tangible quality of his ideas.

One intriguing idea, first postulated by the Greek philosopher Pythagoras, was that the world was *not* flat as suggested by other ancient sources including the Hebrew Bible. For example, Thomas Aquinas wrote in his *Summa Theologiae* that the earth was round because of "the movement of heavy bodies toward the center." By the fifteenth century, this idea had become universally accepted despite Church teachings, as evidenced by the use of an orb to symbolize a king's temporal power on earth.

Scholasticism percolated into almost every aspect of medieval intellectual endeavor, from ethics to physics, from music to poetry, and from political theory to rhetoric and logic. Using Latin as their common language, these scholars would lay the foundation for the great humanists of the Renaissance, including Marsilio Ficino, Thomas More, and Erasmus.

FIG. 4. A thirteenth-century depiction of a spherical earth with the four seasons, from *Liber Divinorum Operum* ("Book of Divine Works")

But it was in Florence that the movement suddenly burst into public view. In 1401, the Florentine Guild of Cloth Merchants, known as the *Arte di Calimala*, announced a competition to design a new set of bronze doors for the Baptistery of St. John, located opposite Florence's Cathedral. The very idea of having a competition for a sacred work of art was new, and it reflected the fact that Florence had become a wellspring of many talented artists and sculptors. The cloth merchants wanted to make sure they got the best for their money. All competing artists were asked to submit a design for one of the bronze door panels, depicting Abraham's sacrifice of Isaac. Seven competitors did so, but only the work of the winner and the runner-up has survived. Both were young, aspiring goldsmiths: the twenty-four-year-old Filippo Brunelleschi and the twenty-three-year-old Lorenzo Ghiberti. Shockingly, both sculptors openly modeled their saintly figures on pagan Roman art. Brunelleschi went as far as to include a copy of a Roman sculpture, *Boy with a Thorn*, in his composition.

In a previous era, they might have been denounced as heretics and

FIG. 5. Filippo Brunelleschi, *The Sacrifice of Isaac*, competitive panel, 1401. A copy of *Boy with a Thorn* is shown at the bottom left. This competition is usually considered the start of the Florentine Renaissance.

condemned to the stake. But this time, surprisingly, neither the Church authorities nor the wool guild objected. They rallied around the declared winner, Lorenzo Ghiberti, since his submission was technically superior: he had cast his design in one piece.

Most historians mark this moment as the beginning of the Renaissance. In due course, it would revolutionize all fields of human endeavor, including art, music, sculpture, architecture, science, engineering, and literature. While the thirteenth-century Scholastics still sought to reconcile the fruits of antiquity with Christian dogma, the humanists of the Renaissance believed that only an uninhibited, empirical investigation of nature would validate ancient treatises and reveal the boundless creativity of the divine. In sum, the Renaissance inspired humankind to pursue freedom in all its forms: freedom of expression, freedom of choice in government, and freedom to pursue happiness in whatever enterprise one chose. That new focus on the value of the individual also unleashed long-simmering resentment against a Church that had become self-absorbed and beset by corruption, igniting the Reformation.

Vasari described the Renaissance as a revolutionary movement that fundamentally broke with the past. But it is doubtful that men like Leonardo da Vinci, Michelangelo, or Donato Bramante saw themselves in that vein. More likely, they considered themselves the descendants of great precursors such as the fourteenth-century painter and architect Giotto di Bondone, just as Columbus fashioned himself after the thirteenth-century explorer Marco Polo. But the rise of the Renaissance did produce entirely new aspiration: the discovery and exploration of new worlds beyond the medieval horizon. Through this and other endeavors, the Renaissance would ultimately produce the Age of Enlightenment, the principles of which would guide the Declaration of Independence and the US Constitution.

Italians played a major role in fostering the Renaissance, but we should also remember something that is often ignored in modern history books: Florence, Venice, and Rome were the beneficiaries of a massive "brain drain" from the Byzantine Empire, after the fall of Constantinople to Sultan Mehmet II in 1453. Scores of musicians, poets, astronomers, writers, architects, mapmakers, librarians, scientists, and artisans fled to the West, making an incalculable contribution to the flowering of the Italian, and later European, Renaissance. By the sixteenth century, the population of Greek refugees in Rome had grown so large that Pope Gregory XIII was compelled to establish the Greek Pontifical College, welcoming all Eastern refugees who were prepared to embrace the Latin rites.

A Thirst for Knowledge

All this led to an unprecedented thirst for knowledge, and for access to knowledge that was previously the exclusive province of the elite. The greatest catalyst in that process was the invention of a machine known as the printing press. Until 1487, books were essentially bound, handwritten originals, copied laboriously from a source, as had been the case since before antiquity. Today we know that the first attempt to mechanize the book-copying process actually took place in

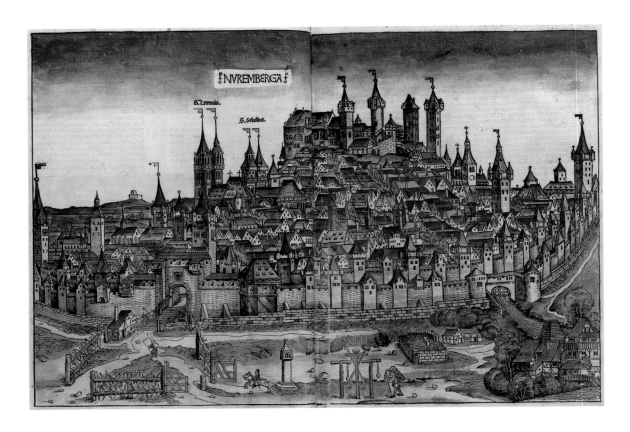

FIG. 6. "The city of Nuremberg," a hand-colored woodblock print from the *Nuremberg Chronicle*

China, where Bi Sheng experimented with various movable woodblock techniques during the Han dynasty (206 B.C.E.—220 C.E.). In the West, however, the printing press was first created around 1450 in the workshop of Johannes Gutenberg. Gutenberg was not a bookbinder but a goldsmith who developed a special hand mold to rapidly produce movable metal type in a uniform style—what today we call a typeface. Gutenberg's typeface was designed by Peter Schöffer, who created a font of 202 characters inspired by the German Gothic style of script. Other regions soon developed their own type styles. In 1470, for example, Venetian typographers developed the Roman typeface—predecessor of one of the most popular fonts used in word processors today.

For the first time, the printing press broke the monopoly on learning among the titled classes and revolutionized the distribution of ideas throughout Europe. For example, it is very doubtful that without the printing press, the Reformation of the sixteenth century would have spread as quickly as it did, propelled by books and pamphlets written by Martin Luther, John Calvin, and many others. Some historians have estimated that by 1500, some twenty million printed books were already in circulation.

The Gutenberg Bible is often cited at the first major product of the printing press, but another book of equal significance was the *Nuremberg Chronicle*, also known as the *Liber Chronaricum*, or "Book of Chronicles." Not many people are familiar with this book today, but in many ways it was the first encyclopedia of its kind. Of course, specific details about the world outside Europe were still sketchy, since the great age of exploration had yet to begin. Thus, the authors of the *Nuremberg Chronicle* based their "history of the world" on the Bible as well as other contemporary sources, including the highly popular book *Cronicha de tuto el monde vulgare* ("Chronicle of the Entire Modern World") by the Augustinian monk and scholar Giacomo Filippo Foresti, published in 1483.

The *Chronicle* organized its history in seven major chapters, each focused on key figures in the Judeo-Christian Bible. For example, the first chapter, entitled "The First Age," covered the earth's prehistory from the Creation to the Great Flood. According to the *Chronicle*, the Creation as described in Genesis occurred in the year 4000 B.C.E., which was a commonly held belief at the time and would not be challenged until the mid-nineteenth century.

FIG. 7. "The Fifth Day of Creation" from the *Nuremberg Chronicle*

Chapter 2 took its readers from Noah's descendants to the age of Abraham, while Chapter 3 described the events up to the foundation of the Kingdom of David. Only by Chapter 6 did the book enter the modern era, starting from the birth of Christ to the late fifteenth century; not surprisingly, this was by far the largest chapter. Among others, it told the story of Pope John VIII, who turned out to be a woman. The final chapter offered its readers a look into the future, based on sources such as Revelation, up to the day of the Last Judgment. The last few pages of the book are blank, for it was here that the reader was expected to add any developments in the future—right up to the End of Times.

As a literary enterprise, the *Chronicle* was an immense intellectual and commercial tour de force. It was also a very expensive one, costing upward of a thousand Rhenish guilders (around $75,000 in today's currency) for paper, printing costs, and the distribution of the book. More importantly, the book involved the collaboration of authors, artists, and technicians in a way that had never been done before. While Hartmann Schedel was the principal researcher and author, the project also involved several painters, including Johann and Willibald Pirckheimer and Michael Wolgemut; the geographer Hieronymus Münzer; the printer Anton Koberger; and finally, the foremost German artist of the time, Albrecht Dürer.

Published in 1493, the *Nuremberg Chronicle* became the first fully illustrated printed book in history, boasting no fewer than 1800 woodcut illustrations. Many of these were then painstakingly colored by hand to produce "deluxe" editions.

FIG. 8. A page from the *Nuremberg Chronicle* with a hand-colored illustration of Constantinople. The *Chronicle* was the first fully illustrated book to be printed after the development of the printing press.

The First Maps

Hand in hand with the growing understanding of the modern world went a desire to explore the boundaries of that world and chart these lands in ways that could be published and distributed for eager buyers throughout Europe. Thus was born the age of cartography—of mapmaking. Maps opened a window on unknown worlds as no other medium had ever done, unlocking the farthest, most exotic locations on earth. In the years to come, cartography would stir the imagination of people around the world, regardless of language, culture, or ethnicity, uniting them in a common desire to discover territories that no European had ever witnessed before.

The problem was that the medieval understanding of geography was still very rudimentary. Since antiquity, few people had actually endeavored

FIG. 9. A mid-fifteenth-century map of the world, based on Ptolemy's *Geographia*. The landmass of Sinae, or "Cina," is shown at the far east.

to try to depict the earth in all of its far-flung beauty and detail.

In response, many Renaissance explorers—including Christopher Columbus—turned to the only authoritative geographical sources available: those from antiquity. Just as the works of Roman authors like Juvenal and Virgil inspired the development of Renaissance epics and novels such as Boccaccio's *Decameron*, so, too, did Renaissance geographers have a great model in the work of the second-century Greco-Roman geographer and mathematician Claudius Ptolemaeus, commonly known as Ptolemy. Though he wrote several books on mathematics and astronomy, Ptolemy's greatest work was the *Geographia*, which documented the known world from the Atlantic Ocean to China in 180 degrees of longitude, and from the Arctic to Africa in 80 degrees of latitude. Translated into Arabic, it was preserved in the libraries of the Umayyad Empire, including the Library of Córdoba, and ultimately resurfaced in a Latin translation in Florence in 1406.

Originally written in 150 C.E., Ptolemy's book drew from several Greek and Roman sources, including the works of a Phoenician explorer known as Marinus of Tyre. While Marinus's books are now lost, it is clear that Ptolemy greatly prized his predecessor's discoveries—such as the idea of assigning to each place a unique latitude and longitude.

Among others, Marinus established his zero meridian along the Canary Islands—many centuries later, the jumping-off place for Columbus's great westward journey—and judged that the earth was a sphere with a circumference of 180,000 stadia, which corresponds to around 20,700 miles. Since the actual circumference is 24,901 miles, that was an astonishingly accurate estimate for the time.

Marinus was also the first ancient author to identify the continent of China, or "Shera," later adopted in Ptolemy's atlas. Some historians believe that Marinus arrived at these startling insights because of the immense trade network that the Phoenicians had built from the seventh century B.C.E. onward, using their base in what is today Lebanon and northern Israel.

Ptolemy incorporated Marinus's data in a set of eight books, the last of which was intended as a proper "atlas" in the modern sense of the word. This book contained a large projection of the world as antiquity knew it, followed by more detailed regional maps. The set that would survive into the Renaissance had twenty-six such maps: ten of Europe, four of Africa, and no fewer than twelve maps of Asia. In this, both Ptolemy and Marinus must have relied not only on written sources but also on reports from sailors and merchants who had plied those shores. That is the only way to explain how Ptolemy could produce such startlingly detailed maps of places like the Gulf of Thailand, the Bay of Bengal, and northern Vietnam, all of which were reportedly based on the eyewitness reports of merchants who had actually sailed to those places.

After the fall of the Western Roman Empire, Ptolemy's *Geographia* would have been lost were it not for the zeal of Muslim scholars to capture and preserve the knowledge of Greco-Roman times. During the reign of the tenth-century Umayyad nobleman 'Abd-al-Rahmān III in what is now the Spanish region of Andalusia, for example, Al-Andalus attracted an array of artists and scientists from all over Europe, regardless of their faith. The city of Córdoba became a major center of learning after the establishment of the University of Córdoba

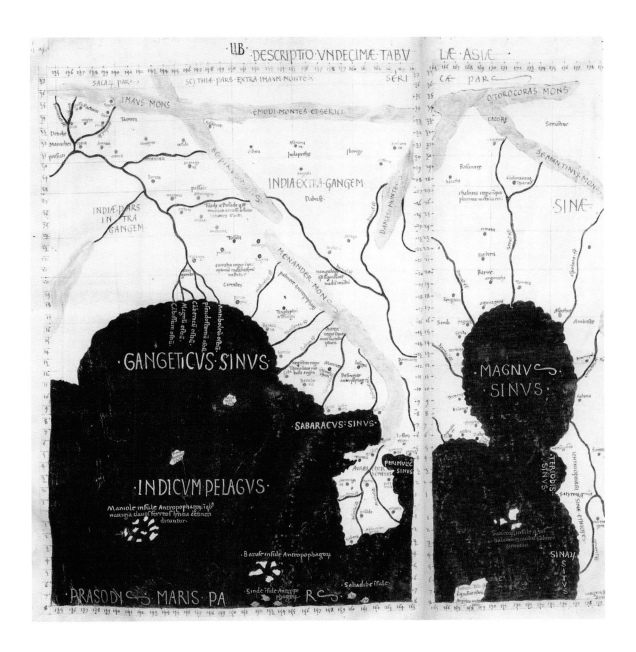

FIG. 10. The eleventh map of Asia from Ptolemy's *Geographia*, depicting India beyond the Ganges (*India extra Gangem*) and the land of *Magnus Sinus*, the South China Sea (fifteenth-century edition)

by 'Abd al-Rahmān's son, Al-Hakam II. His agents scoured the bookshops of Alexandria, Damascus, and Baghdad in search of books for Córdoba's rapidly growing library, which ultimately grew to four hundred thousand volumes with works by Plato, Aristotle, Archimedes, and other Greek scholars that otherwise would have been lost.

More than five thousand calligraphists were employed in copying the works, so as to ensure their continued distribution through the Islamic world. This included Ptolemy's *Geographia*, which in the ninth century inspired a Muslim scholar, the Persian author Āl-Khwarizmī, to publish an Arabic edition that also featured maps of the Nile and the Black Sea. Āl-Khwarizmī's works would have a major influence on medieval science in the West. Among others, it was he who developed the decimal position system that we still use in mathematics today.

The Arabic version of Ptolemy's *Geographia* was translated into Latin in the twelfth century as Europe was emerging from its turmoil during the Dark Ages. This may have been the edition that the Italian explorer Marco Polo consulted before he set out in 1271 on his long journey over what became known as the Silk Road to the Far East. Other translations in both Greek and Latin followed, notably in Constantinople, just fifty years before the fall of the city to Ottoman forces. From that point on, the *Geographia* entered the bloodstream of the Renaissance, thanks to the recently developed printing press. Its first printed edition was issued in 1477 in Bologna, the site of one of the oldest universities in Europe, and included a set of printed maps using the woodcut technique. This was followed in 1478 by a Latin edition printed in Rome, and in 1482 by editions printed in Ulm, in today's Germany, and one in Rome edited by the Italian humanist Francesco Berlinghieri.

Quite possibly it is the 1478 Rome edition of the *Geographia* that Columbus consulted as he began to plot his great voyage in the early 1480s. One thing that must have fascinated him was Ptolemy's tantalizing depiction of a stretch of ocean that led from the Canary Islands—known as the *Fortunatae Insulae*, the "Fortunate Islands"—to the eastern shore of *Magnus Sinus*, what today we call the South China Sea. Here, on paper, was the ultimate challenge, the great leap into the unknown, first drawn by a mind that had turned to dust almost fifteen hundred years ago. If Ptolemy believed that by crossing the great

Atlantic Ocean he would be able to reach China via its back door, so to speak, then clearly it had to be so. Of course, the real challenge was to convince others of its feasibility as well.

In 1485, Columbus decided to present his plans to the first monarch on his list. This was King John II of Portugal—not an unreasonable choice, given that Portugal had taken the lead in exploration with its discovery of West Africa. In brokering this meeting, Columbus must have relied on the connections of his wife's family. Her father, the Portuguese knight Bartolomeu Perestrelo, had been a member of the household of the *Infante*, better known as Prince Henry the Navigator. Sure enough, Columbus was given an audience in Lisbon and delivered his pitch. The king was intrigued, and Columbus, now encouraged by the king's rapt attention, added that it would only be proper that he, Columbus, should be promoted to "Great Admiral" so as to raise the profile of this great endeavor. Come to think of it, he said, it was only fair that he should also be appointed as the governor of whatever new lands in Asia he might be able to discover. And as far as sharing in the profits was concerned, would a 10 percent share of any future proceeds be acceptable? Here, as in so many other aspects, Columbus revealed himself as not only a Renaissance explorer but also a shrewd and ambitious businessman.

King John pondered the map that Columbus had spread before him, scratched his head, and decided to refer the matter to his councillors. Unfortunately, these courtiers took one look at Columbus's plans and rejected them out of hand. Their response may have been motivated by politics rather than by scientific considerations; after all, what this Genoese proposed was bound to be fantastically expensive, involving no fewer than three ships for an expedition of more than a year. That was certain to drain resources from other, more practical things that His Majesty might wish to undertake.

Three years later, Columbus returned to the Portuguese court once more. Again, King John listened attentively, but this time Columbus's proposal was upstaged by new developments: the Portuguese explorer Bartolomeu Dias had just succeeded in rounding the Cape of Good Hope on the southern tip of Africa. This was clear evidence that an *Eastern* maritime route to Asia was practical and viable, rather than a pie-in-the-sky idea to reach the Indies by going westward.

A lesser man might have given up at this point, but one thing we know about Columbus is that he was exceedingly strong-willed and convinced of the plausibility of his ideas. Thus he humbly retraced his footsteps back to his hometown of Genoa, there to petition the Milanese governor. Unfortunately, the city had just fallen under the sway of the Duke of Milan, none other than Ludovico "Il Moro" Sforza, the patron of Leonardo da Vinci. Flushed with victory, the House of Sforza had other things on its mind and sent Columbus packing. The would-be explorer then traveled to Venice to present his case to the doge—only to be rebuffed once more. Meanwhile, his brother Bartholomew Columbus had reached London to propose the venture to the English king, but Henry VII, too, had other fish to fry. In the end, both returned to Portugal empty-handed.

There remained only one other option: to petition the Spanish Crown once more in a last, desperate gambit. As it happened, King Ferdinand and Queen Isabella had finally succeeded in evicting the last Emir of Granada in 1492. Many of the local Muslims and Jews, heirs of the great period of the *Convivencia*, were forced to choose between conversion to Christianity or swift expulsion from Spain. Many chose the former, though it would make little difference; during the subsequent heyday of the Spanish Inquisition, many of these *Moriscos* would be singled out for persecution.

Columbus was a canny observer of the human psyche and believed that the Spanish royal couple, in their moment of victory, might now look more kindly on his plans. He seized on their successful religious cleansing campaign as the perfect motive to fund his journey eastward. "As it was in this year of 1492 that Your Highnesses concluded the war with the Moors who reigned in Europe," he later wrote in his log, no doubt echoing the presentation he made to the Spanish royals, "I saw the royal banners of Your Highnesses placed by force of arms on the towers of [the formerly Moorish palace of] the Alhambra."[14] What better way, then, to continue this crusade for Christendom but to expand it westward? His mission, as he saw it, was to go "to the regions of India, to see the princes there and the peoples," so as to better assess "the measures to be taken for their conversion to our Holy Faith."

It was a very smart spin on the whole endeavor, and this time, it worked. "Therefore," Columbus proudly continued, "after having banished all the Jews

FIG. 12. *(Opposite page)*
Vesconte Maggiolo, *Portolan
Chart*, sometimes referred to as
the "Map of Columbus," 1510

from all your Kingdoms and realms, during this same month of January Your Highnesses ordered me to go with a sufficient fleet to the said regions of India." As the icing on the cake, Isabella and Ferdinand agreed to give him what he had so strenuously sought from the Portuguese Crown. "For that purpose I was granted great favors and ennobled," he could not resist adding, overjoyed at finally joining the nobility that had previously thumbed their noses at this Italian arriviste. "Henceforth," he wrote with glee, "I might entitle myself *Don* and be High Admiral of the Ocean Sea and Viceroy and perpetual Governor of all the islands and continental land that I might discover and acquire." For all intents and purposes, he had succeeded in his great matter.

There was only one problem. He actually had to deliver on the promise of a westward route to the fabulous riches of the Indies.

THE DISCOVERY
OF THE AMERICAS

AT 6:30 A.M. ON AUGUST 3, 1492, JUST HALF AN HOUR BEFORE sunrise, the newly minted admiral of the Spanish Navy stood on the aftcastle of the *Santa María* and surveyed his small flotilla. It was Friday, and the dock was filled with people who had come to gawk at the three small ships that were about to sail into the unknown. Above him, the first breath of wind brushed the sails, as if probing their fitness for the long journey. Even at this early hour, the air already carried the heady smell of polished wood, fish offal, and salt—the unmistakable scent of a ship about to sail. Around him, his crew scurried to their assigned tasks, tending to the buntlines, the clew garnets, and the topsails, while stevedores strained under the weight of the last barrels being carried on board. He wondered whether they would be enough, these provisions, but that was the least of his problems.

Foremost on his mind was the reliability of his ships and the crew that had been tasked to sail them. He was well aware that the owners of the *Pinta* and the *Niña*, Christoval Quintero and Juan Niño de Moguer, deeply resented being forced to relinquish their vessels against their will and had tried to delay the journey in any way possible. It was not a good omen, and sailors were very superstitious about such things. That was also why he wasn't sure about the loyalty of the captains who were in command of these ships: Captain Martín Alonso Pinzón on the *Pinta* and his brother Vicente Yáñez Pinzón on the *Niña*, each supervising a crew of about twenty-six men.

Above all, he worried about the many unknowns that awaited him on the journey ahead. It all depended on how one read Ptolemy's—or, better, Marinus's—calculations about the actual distance between Spain and the eastern coast of Asia. Ptolemy had written that the landmass comprising both Eurasia and Africa occupied 180 degrees of the terrestrial sphere. Marinus, however, believed that the oceans were much smaller and that the ratio of landmass to sea mass was 225:135. According to Marinus's calculations, the distance between Spain and Japan was just 2,000 nautical miles—a huge error, since as we know today, the actual distance is 10,600 nautical miles. Fatefully, Columbus had based the route of his voyage on Marinus's measurements. There was not a single vessel in fifteenth-century Europe that could carry sufficient water and provisions for a journey of over ten thousand miles. It was not until the development of the behemoths of the seventeenth century, the British galleons and the Dutch *fluyt*s, that men would succeed in covering such huge distances.

Another mistake Columbus made was equally catastrophic: he was using charts prepared by the ninth-century geographer and astronomer Al-Farghani, known in the West as Alfraganus, and had mistaken an Arabic mile (1.18 modern international miles) for Italian—Roman—miles (roughly 0.8 miles today). This prompted him to underestimate the actual distance even more. On top of that, Columbus lacked the navigational instruments that the eighteenth century would take for granted, such as the Davis quadrant and the sextant. The only instruments that Columbus had at his disposal were a cross-staff, a rudimentary device to measure the altitude of the sun and the stars; a plain quadrant with a plumb line, used for calculating longitudes and latitudes; an astrolabe, another device for calculating latitude at sea depending on the altitude of celestial bodies; and a compass, used for dead reckoning.

But Columbus rarely used cross-staffs and astrolabes. Instead, he put all his faith in his compass, the bearings of which he scrupulously plotted as straight lines on his charts. And last but not least, Columbus worried about the wind—the trade winds, to be precise. By the end of the fifteenth century, it was well known that the prevailing wind in the southern Atlantic was a strong easterly that blew westward. It would probably carry them to the Indies, but it was doubtful that his caravels, designed for coastal traffic, would be able to turn around and return to Spain, fighting this headwind all the way.

By rights, then, this whole venture should have ended in failure—with the inevitable deaths of all hands in the middle of the ocean, deprived of food and potable water. But, as if by a miracle, that is not what happened.

A Journey Against All Odds

At 8:00 a.m., at high tide, Columbus ordered the lines cast and the *Santa María*, the *Pinta*, and the *Niña* slowly edged away from the quay, while the crowd along the shore waved and the sails snapped taut in the breeze. Once out of the mouth of Palos de la Frontera, he led his convoy past the confluence of the Odiel and Tinto rivers, hoping that the tide would carry their seven-foot draft vessels over a treacherous sandbar known as Saltes. "The wind is strong and variable," Columbus wrote in his logbook that night, "and we had gone 45 miles to the south by sunset." Then, after a careful study of the compass, "I altered course for the Canary Islands, to the SW and south by west."

He had barely traveled three days when disaster struck. The rudder of the *Pinta* slipped from its socket and broke. Columbus immediately suspected sabotage by the ship's owners. Fortunately, Captain Martín Pinzón reacted quickly and ordered the rudder secured with strong ropes, with which they were able to limp into the Grand Canary. Despite Columbus's earlier misgivings, he was impressed with Martín's rapid response and praised him for his presence of mind. Perhaps, he mused, he could trust the Pinzón brothers after all. He decided he could leave both captains in charge of supervising the repairs of their vessels—a new rudder for the *Pinta*, and square sails for the *Niña*—while he sailed his caracca to the island of La Gomera for victualing.

Unfortunately, all of this took a lot longer than he had hoped. So it was nearly a month before Columbus could finally lead his small flotilla into the open Atlantic. Already it was September 6, the storm season was due to begin soon, and the anxiety of the crew was palpable. None of them had ever sailed so deep into blue waters, so far from home. Columbus sensed it, and to assuage their feelings he decided to keep two books: one that recorded their progress in much shorter distances, to create the impression that they were close to home, and one that accurately tracked the lengthening miles of their journey.[15]

FIG. 13. An astrolabe attributed to the German goldsmith Hans Dorn from 1483

There were other things to worry about, too. Just before he sailed from the harbor of Gomera, heading due west, he was told that some people on the island had spotted a Portuguese naval squadron of three caravels. He immediately surmised that the purpose of this flotilla was to try to stop him from leaving the Canary Islands. He knew that King John II of Portugal was incensed that Columbus had "gone over" to the Spanish side. Apparently, the king was under the impression that Columbus was going to chart a new route to West Africa, so that the Spanish could challenge Portugal's control of that territory. It seemed plausible, then, that the king had ordered his ships to stop Columbus from leaving the Canary Islands.

There was no time for him to verify whether rumors of the Portuguese force were true, but neither could he take the chance. The only thing he could do was urge his crew to greater speed, desperate to create as much distance between him and the Portuguese vessels as possible. But here, too, he was stymied; maddening though it was, there was very little wind on that day and the next, so they made only modest progress. All through those anxious days Columbus stood on the aftcastle, peering toward the Spanish coastline for any sign of his pursuers.

Finally, on Sunday, September 9, the sails stirred and billowed, the tackle pulled taut, and the carrack woke from its slumber, steadily moving westward. By the afternoon, he was relieved to find that they were no longer in sight of land, but that feeling was certainly not shared by his crew. As he wrote in his logbook that night, many sailors "sighed and wept for fear that they would not see it again for a long time." Columbus, however, was elated. He could feel the pounding swell of the waters underneath the keel, while the midmast groaned and creaked under the powerful force of the wind. They were under way at last! Propelled by the steady breeze, the ship sailed at a steady clip of seven and a half knots, and by the end of the day they had covered 90 miles. The next day, Monday, was even better; they covered as much as 180 miles, though as he wrote, "I only recorded 144 miles in order not to alarm the sailors if the voyage is lengthy."

And lengthy it was. The sun rose and set, day after day, only to be replaced by the storm clouds of autumn and a steady drizzle that made it feel as if "it was April in Andalucía." As the days passed into weeks, the sailors began to

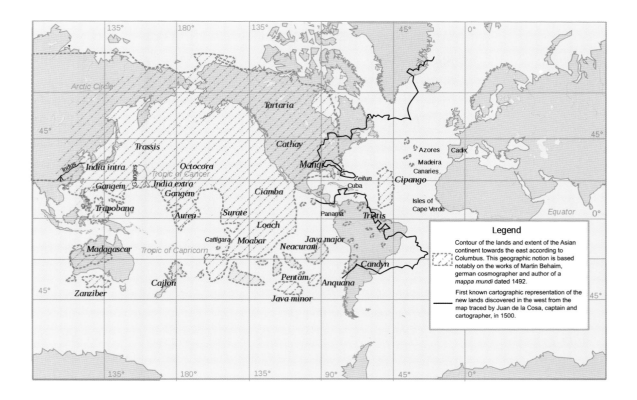

Legend

Contour of the lands and extent of the Asian continent towards the east according to Columbus. This geographic notion is based notably on the works of Martin Behaim, german cosmographer and author of a *mappa mundi* dated 1492.

First known cartographic representation of the new lands discovered in the west from the map traced by Juan de la Cosa, captain and cartographer, in 1500.

grumble. Where were these Indies? Shouldn't they have reached them by now? Wasn't this supposed to be a journey of no more than two thousand miles?

The Pinzón brothers felt the same way. On October 6, Captain Martín came over to Columbus's flagship to argue that perhaps it would be better to steer southwest by west, for according to the ancient charts the island of Japan should now be very close.

Columbus heard him out but then firmly ordered that they continue due west, "until we reach the mainland"—meaning the mainland of Cathay, or China. "Later we can go to the islands on the return voyage to Spain," he added hopefully, once again in the mistaken belief that Japan and China were much closer to Europe than they really are. "My decision has not pleased the men," he wrote ruefully in the privacy of his cabin, but "despite their grumbling I held fast to the west."

Fortunately, the next day, October 7, brought great excitement: some of the crew thought they had spotted land. The *Niña,* the fastest ship in the convoy, raced ahead to see better and joyously fired a cannon shot while running up a

FIG. 14. Columbus's concept of Asian geography, based on Ptolemy, overlaid over an actual map of the world (Source: Mindriot)

flag. This was the agreed signal that "land had been sighted." Alas, as the day wore on, no land was seen in any direction, and Columbus faced the fact that the sighting had simply been an illusion. The crew was devastated.

But later that night, Columbus wrote by the flickering light of a candle that "God did offer us a small token of comfort: many large flocks of birds." There are no birds in the middle of the Atlantic Ocean. It was unmistakable proof that land, though not yet visible, could not be far away. What's more, Columbus sniffed the air and found it balmy and fragrant, more evidence that land was near. "It was," he wrote, "a pleasure to breathe it" after so many weeks on the ocean.

Rather than putting their minds at ease, however, these tantalizing signs only increased the apprehension of the crew, many of whom were at the end of their tether. No one in modern history had ever sailed so far for so long without ever seeing land. Were they lost? Had their captain made a miscalculation? Was he steering them *away* from land, rather than toward it? Some became so agitated that for the first time in the voyage there was a sense of mutiny in the air. And yet, still more telltale signs drifted by the ships: a cluster of reeds, a small wooden plank, a branch. Every sailor who wasn't working stood at the railing of the ship, eyes glued to the horizon.

To buck up the spirits of his crew, Columbus gave them some welcome news: the "Catholic Sovereigns" had agreed to pay the first man to sight land a special bounty of 10,000 *maravedíes* (roughly $540), while Columbus himself promised to give that man a "silk doublet."[16] But that evening, as the sun slowly sank into the great expanse of water, Columbus himself became impatient. He tried to divine the direction that the birds had flown from, made a slight adjustment to his course, then retired to his usual spot on the aftcastle. He stayed there, legs spread against the swell, and watched the light slowly fade from the sky.

The hours passed. Then, at long last, a glimmer of hope. At 10:00 p.m., he thought he saw a light. It was, he remembered later, like a "little wax candle bobbing up and down." *Could it be the torch of a fisherman, or perhaps a campfire on a faraway beach?* he wondered. Or was the dark of the night playing tricks on him? Finally, he called for Pedro Gutiérrez, a representative from the Spanish court who had insisted on accompanying him, and asked him whether he could

FIG. 15. John Vanderlyn,
The Landing of Columbus, 1847

see it, too. Gutiérrez peered into the distance while Columbus held his breath, and then cried "Yes!" He, too, had seen the light. Excited, Columbus summoned another officer, but by then the light had disappeared. Ahead of them was nothing but darkness. They watched as the moon rose in its third quarter, while the ships plowed on at a steady nine knots. The excitement ebbed, and all was quiet once more. Gutiérrez smiled apologetically and went down to his cabin; eventually Columbus retired as well. Shortly thereafter, the hourglass moved past midnight, and it was Friday, October 12, 1492.

Then suddenly, BOOM! A cannon shot. Columbus bolted upright in his bed, grabbed his robe, and ran upstairs to the forecastle. This time, there was no mistake: the *Pinta* had sighted land, just six miles to the west. *Land!*

The next day, accompanied by the Pinzón brothers, Columbus stepped ashore with the royal banner and the standards of Aragon and Castile. After offering a prayer of thanksgiving, he solemnly declared the island to be the possession of Their Highnesses, King Ferdinand and Queen Isabella, and named it "San Salvador."

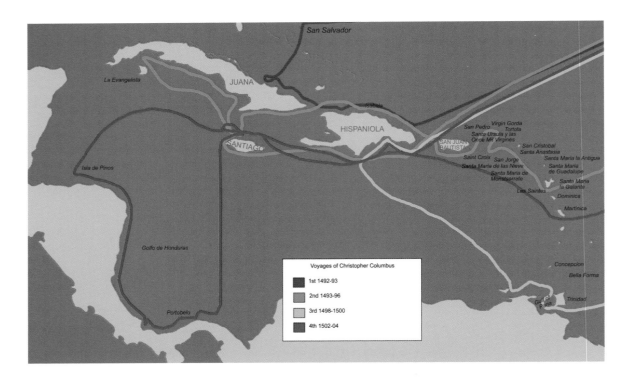

San Salvador
La Evangelista
JUANA
Isabela
HISPANIOLA
SANTIAGO
Isla de Pinos
Golfo de Honduras
Portobelo

Virgin Gorda
San Pedro Tortola
Santa Ursula y las
Once Mil Virgines
SAN JUAN
BAUTISTA San Cristobal
Santa Anastasia
Saint Croix San Jorge Santa Maria la Antigua
Santa Maria de las Nieve Santa Maria
Santa Maria de de Guadalupe
Montserrate Santa Maria
la Galante
Las Saintes Dominica
Martinica

Concepcion
Bella Forma

Gulf of
Paria Trinidad

Voyages of Christopher Columbus

1st 1492-93
2nd 1493-96
3rd 1498-1500
4th 1502-04

FIG. 16. Map of Columbus's voyages between 1492 and 1504

In hindsight, it was a miracle that the winds had nudged these fragile vessels toward the Bahamas—or the Turks and Caicos, as some believe. Had they drifted further north, in the direction of North America, the crew might well have mutinied, or they simply might have died from lack of water and food. Furthermore, the entire 3,670-mile journey had lasted only six weeks, an astonishingly short time given that well into the eighteenth century, bigger and faster ships would often need between eight and ten weeks to travel between Britain's Portsmouth and Boston, a distance of at least 3,250 nautical miles.[17]

To the end of his days, Columbus believed he had reached one of the outlying islands of the Indies. After his arrival in the Bahamas he continued to travel from one island to the next, hoping to see well-dressed Chinese or Indian mandarins but instead meeting a variety of nude or half-clad Carib, Taíno, or Guanahatabey people. These natives greeted the European travelers warmly, but when queried about the presence of spices or precious metals, such as gold, they were dumbfounded. As the days wore on, this became an acute problem, because finding a shorter route to these commodities was the primary reason why the Spanish Crown had financed the enterprise. Even after Columbus

moved farther west to explore the northeast coasts of Cuba and Haiti, there
was still no evidence that he had established a new route to Asia. Worse, on
December 25, 1492—Christmas Day—his flagship, the *Santa María*, ran
aground and had to be abandoned. Just three weeks later, the party set sail for
home. They left behind thirty-nine sailors who had agreed to stay and build a
newly founded settlement, La Navidad.

Severe winter storms flayed the two fragile caravels as they battled the
foaming seas, but on February 15 they reached the Azores and one month later
made it to Barcelona. On March 15, 1493, Columbus formally made his report
to Ferdinand and Isabella. Contrary to the truth, he assured them that he had
reached an island off the coast of China, which he named Hispaniola. He also
added, rather disingenuously, that "there are many spices, and great mines of
gold and other metals" to be found there.[18]

FIG. 17. Emanuel Gottlieb
Leutze, *Columbus Making His
Report to Queen Isabella*, 1843

The Race for the New World

News of Columbus's journey ran like wildfire through all of Europe—causing both wonder and anxiety. If the Indies could be reached in six weeks, then the nation that controlled these routes would gain a tremendous advantage over its European rivals. It would certainly upend the whole business of bringing goods from the East to the growing markets of Europe, and at a sharply lower cost. Some began to whisper that Spain, which until now had hardly mattered in European politics, would soon have a monopoly on the spice trade—a daunting prospect for her rivals.

Not surprisingly, the Spanish Crown immediately authorized a second journey to the New World to consolidate its possession of these territories and expand them as much as possible. In 1493, Columbus returned with a much larger fleet and reached the Lesser Antilles, exploring what today we know as the Virgin Islands and Puerto Rico. But his patience was running thin. Queen Isabella had made it clear to him that this time, she wanted tangible results. To that end, she had ordered him to treat the natives kindly, so as to integrate them as a peaceful and productive part of the growing Spanish Empire. But once he arrived in the Antilles, the pressure on Columbus to produce material rewards mounted steadily. Weeks went by without any evidence of gold mines or spice plantations. Local tribes had no idea what these Spaniards wanted, or how they were supposed to get it.

Desperate to produce *something* of value, Columbus made a fateful step: he resorted to slavery. It was a tactic that the Portuguese had adopted several decades earlier, when they, too, failed to find anything of material value in their new West African possessions. Soon thereafter, Portuguese bottoms began carrying slaves en masse to Lisbon and Oporto as the most expedient way to turn a profit on their exploits in Africa.

Columbus followed suit. Disobeying Isabella's orders, he captured hundreds of natives from the local Arawak tribe and sold many of them to the Carib tribe as slaves. Exactly how many men, women, and children Columbus would subject to slavery is a matter of debate, but most modern historians agree that he ordered the capture of least fifteen hundred people, not only from the Arawak but also the Carib and Taíno tribes, of which around five hundred natives were shipped for sale to Spain. Of these, some two hundred died during the long voyage. According to Michele de Cuneo, a close friend of Columbus's who recorded the passage, these unfortunates were unceremoniously "cast into the sea."[19] Of the survivors, some were auctioned off in Seville, whereas others were condemned to the Spanish galleys. But even worse was to follow.

In his desperate quest for precious metals, Columbus imposed on the province of Cicao, in Hispaniola, a quota of gold that every person above fourteen years of age was compelled to meet. Since there were hardly any sources of gold on the island, thousands suffered the punishment of having their hands cut off, while others committed suicide.

Only on his third voyage, which sailed in 1498, was Columbus able to get anywhere close to a mainland—in this case, the island of Trinidad off the coast of South America. He then sailed up the Orinoco River and reached today's Tobago and Grenada, still believing that these lands formed part of China.

Meanwhile, stories began to filter back to Spain of the atrocities on Cicao and other instances of cruelty committed by Columbus and his lieutenants. According to a document that came to light only in 2006, his "troops went wild" after Columbus fell ill in 1495, "stealing, killing, raping, and torturing natives, trying to force them to divulge the whereabouts of the imagined treasure-houses of gold."[20] Soon thereafter, the Spanish settlers of the new colony on Hispaniola decided they had had enough as well. They rose in revolt, arguing that the great riches that Columbus had promised them didn't exist. Eventually, some of these settlers made their way back to Spain, where they filed suit in court. In 1500, a court order went out for Columbus's arrest. He was removed from all his positions and brought back to Spain in chains. A more humiliating fall of the man who had changed the face of the earth can hardly be imagined.

This was not only a problem for Columbus but for Ferdinand and Isabella as well. Throughout much of the decade they had loudly trumpeted Columbus's achievements for the glory of their reign. The name "Columbus" was on the lips of every court in Europe. Punishing this man would reflect very poorly on their judgment and the reputation of the Spanish Crown. In the end, Columbus was set free and given one last opportunity to prove that he had indeed found a route to the spice-producing regions of Asia.

This fourth and last journey departed from Cádiz on May 11, 1502, and reached Central America a month later. In December of that year, however, Columbus was overtaken by one of the most ferocious storms he had ever witnessed. "Water never ceased to fall from the sky," he wrote. "I do not say it rained, for it was like another deluge. The men were so worn out that they longed for death to end their dreadful suffering."[21] He had barely recovered from this trial when he reached the Cayman Islands, which he named Las Tortugas ("The Turtles"), only to be caught in another storm that forced him to beach his ships in St. Ann's Bay, Jamaica. Appeals to the Spanish governor of Hispaniola to rescue Columbus and his men went unanswered. At long last, he was able to board a ship and return to Spain, empty-handed, on November 7.

Now facing penury, he strenuously appealed to the Spanish Crown that he receive 10 percent of all profits from the new territories, such as they were, as he believed had been agreed upon at the outset. His request was ignored. Less than two years later, on May 20, 1506, Columbus died at age fifty-four from a severe case of "gout" (or arthritis, in modern medical parlance). But his son Fernando later wrote that the cause of death was the "grief at seeing himself fallen from his high estate, as well as other ills."[22] Indeed, his death would not be officially acknowledged for another ten years.

Modern history has not been kind to Christopher Columbus. Even though schoolchildren continue to be taught today that Columbus discovered America, ending the so-called pre-Columbian Age of Latin American cultures, critics point out that he never set foot in North America, merely on some islands of Central America; that he was the one who launched the Spanish slave trade; that he also initiated the eventual extermination of hundreds of thousands of natives by Spanish conquistadores, both through disease and by the sword; and that to the end of his days, he himself insisted that he had not discovered a new continent but found a new route to the Indies. What's more, as these critics point out, the first Europeans to discover North America were not the Spanish but the Vikings, including the explorer Leif Erikson, who in the eleventh century established a colony known as Vinland on the island of Newfoundland.

But no one can deny Columbus's genuine achievements: his exceptional vision, his determination, and the immense courage of taking three coastal ships into one of the most unpredictable oceans on earth, with little guidance other than ancient maps and an absolute faith in himself. As he had written at the beginning of his journey, his goal was always to "make a new chart of navigation, upon which I shall place the whole sea and lands of the Ocean Sea in their proper positions under their bearings."[23] In that regard he succeeded brilliantly. Indeed, Columbus's achievements would soon inspire many more voyages, as well as the development of maps and charts that would radically change the way Renaissance Europe saw itself and its role in the world.

For that reason, his name is rightfully commemorated in the name of the capital district of the United States, the "District of Columbia," as well as the capital cities of two American states, South Carolina and Ohio. In 1893, when his rehabilitation was at its zenith, Chicago hosted the first of many world fairs, the World Columbian Exposition, which commemorated the four hundredth anniversary of Columbus's first journey. With sprawling palaces and pavilions, built of plaster and wood in the classical style, this sparkling "White City" gave Americans a stunning vision of what their cities could look like if they learned to plan them properly, using the finest that modern Beaux-Arts design and engineering could provide.

The Journeys of Amerigo Vespucci

After Columbus fell out with the Spanish Crown, it was left to Amerigo Vespucci to continue the exploration of the New World. Interestingly, Vespucci was also an Italian. Born in Florence in 1454, he decided not to follow his brothers to the University of Pisa in pursuit of an academic career and instead got a job as a clerk in the Medici Bank. At that time, the head of the Medici family, Lorenzo "Il Magnifico," stood at the helm of Florence during the high mark of the Florentine Renaissance. Vespucci rose through the ranks and, in 1495, when he was forty-one, was sent to Spain to investigate suspicious activities at the Medici branch office in Cádiz. After Vespucci delivered his report, he decided to stay in Spain and became involved with the Italian mercantile family Berardi. When the family's scion, Giannotto Berardi, passed away, Vespucci was charged with serving as the executor of the estate, given his experience as a Medici Bank official.

As it happened, in that same year, the first rumors of Columbus's poor government in Hispaniola reached Spain, whereupon the Spanish Crown decided to break their exclusive contract with the Genoese explorer. In response, Ferdinand and Isabella began to cast about for other explorers who might chart routes to the "West Indies." As part of this endeavor, they had contracted with the Berardi family for the lease of twelve seaworthy ships, complete with provisions. Since Vespucci was the family's executor, he identified himself at the Spanish court and duly fulfilled the original contract by delivering the promised vessels. Vespucci acquitted himself so ably in this task that Ferdinand and Isabella decided to keep him on. Before long, Vespucci was in charge of provisioning one, and possibly two, of Columbus's subsequent voyages.[24] Thus he was in an ideal position to get himself assigned to one of the ships bound for the Atlantic as either navigator or captain.

Strangely, the exact extent of Vespucci's voyages is still shrouded in mystery. The reason is that the two surviving documents about his exploits contradict one another. One, a letter written in Italian, signed by Vespucci and dated September 4, 1504, was reportedly sent from Lisbon to Florence, possibly to the attention of the *gonfaloniere,* or lead magistrate, Piero Soderini—the same gonfaloniere for whom Leonardo da Vinci had just begun painting the vast fresco of the Battle of Anghiari in Florence's city hall.[25] This letter would later be published in Latin under the titles *Quattuor Americi navigationes* ("Four Journeys to America") and *Mundus Novus* ("The New World"), but some modern scholars consider it to be a clever forgery. Further, there is a collection of letters addressed to Lorenzo di Pierfrancesco de' Medici that are generally considered to be authentic.

The reason why the authenticity of these documents is so important is that the first set shows that Vespucci completed *four* voyages, whereas the second set refers only to *two* expeditions. We should also remember that the pace of Spanish and Portuguese explorations increased dramatically around the turn of the fifteenth to the sixteenth century, so the timing of Vespucci's voyages is very significant. In 1497, for example, Vasco da Gama succeeded in sailing around the southern tip of Africa and continuing all the way to Calcutta on the southwestern coast of India. True, the trip took over two years, and da Gama lost two of his four ships along the way. The point was, however, that for the first time in history a maritime route to Asia had been achieved. Several Portuguese explorers would follow in his wake.

The Spanish, however, persisted in their belief that Asia could be reached across the Atlantic. Indeed, most scholars today believe that Vespucci sailed as a navigator in a four-ship convoy that left Spain in May 1499 under the command of Alonso de Ojeda. After reaching the coast of Guyana, Vespucci left the vessel to explore the mainland of South America and eventually reached the mouth of the Amazon River, moving as far as Cape St. Augustine. The disputed letters would suggest that he made an earlier journey in June 1497 under command of Juan de la Cosa, but many historians dismiss that possibility. Whatever the case may be, the second journey of 1499 was particularly important because Vespucci went on to explore the mouth of the Orinoco River before moving on to Haiti. Like Columbus, he was still under the impression that he was traveling through the eastern peninsula of Asia. In fact, he believed he had discovered the legendary city of Cattigara, described by Ptolemy as the principal port of Magnus Sinus—the South China Sea. According to Marinus of Tyre, back in the first century C.E. a Greek explorer named Alexander had reached Cattigara and found it to be populated by "fish eaters." Arguably, he is talking about the Mekong Delta in southern Vietnam.

Upon Vespucci's return to Spain, he breathlessly reported his findings and immediately prepared to lead a second expedition. This new journey was supposed to move past Cattigara and eventually reach Southeast Asia—or so he hoped. The Spanish Crown, however, turned him down. Vespucci then promptly switched his allegiance to Portugal and found a willing ear. The Portuguese, capitalizing on the success of their eastward route, agreed to fund his new westward attempt. Thus on May 13, 1501, Vespucci set sail once more and this time reached the coast of Brazil. From there, he claimed to have traveled down to the Río de la Plata and the coast of Patagonia, in today's Argentina, though some modern historians dispute this.

According to Vespucci's letter to Piero Soderini, published in 1505 as *Mundus Novus*, the explorer was struck by the lifestyle of the natives he encountered in Brazil. "These people are naked," he reportedly wrote, "handsome, brown, well-shaped in body, their heads, necks, arms, private parts, feet of men and women are a little covered in feathers." What's more, he added, "the men also have many precious stones in their faces and breasts. No one has anything, but all things are in common." Furthermore, they engaged in rather unusual sexual relations. "The men have as wives those who please them," he wrote, "be they mothers, sisters, or friends, therein they make no distinction."

But there was one thing that Vespucci found particularly revolting: apparently, these tribes engaged in cannibalism. "They also fight with each other," he wrote, and "they eat each other, even those who are slain, and hang the flesh of them in the smoke." It was this gruesome feature, the reported cannibalism of Brazilian natives, that would make a particular impact on the cartographers of later periods.

The most important consequence of this voyage, however, was that Vespucci began to face the possibility that this landmass was not part of Asia but an entirely new continent. Soon after he returned to Lisbon in July of 1502, he reported these findings in the now famous letter to Lorenzo di Pierfrancesco de' Medici. "Concerning my return from those new regions which we found and explored," Vespucci wrote, "we may rightly call a new world . . . for in those southern parts I have found a continent more densely peopled and abounding in animals than our Europe Asia or Africa, and, in addition, a climate milder and more delightful than in any other region known to us."[26]

FIG. 18. Johann Froschauer, illustration from *Mundus Novus*, depicting cannibalism among the tribes of Brazil, 1505. This is the first known depiction of cannibalism in the New World.

These magical words, *a new world*, struck a chord with humanists across Europe. They perfectly captured the possibilities of what man, released from medieval doctrine and driven only by his intellect and curiosity, could achieve if given the means to do so.

One of these humanists was a German cartographer named Martin Waldseemüller. Born near Freiburg im Breisgau, today in the German state of Baden-Württemberg, Waldseemüller was educated at the University of Freiburg and in 1507 was living in Sankt Didel, in the Duchy of Lorraine. Here, he and his collaborator Matthias Ringmann came up with the idea of translating the great discoveries of Columbus and Vespucci into cartography. Their ultimate goal was to reconcile the maps from ancient sources such as

Ptolemy, which were still in use throughout Europe, with the new data from the Spanish and Portuguese expeditions. The result was a massive atlas, five feet high and seven feet wide, printed in twelve separate panels that were then glued together, under the title *Universalis Cosmographia* ("Map of the World").

As we saw, before Waldseemüller the traditional view of the world held that it consisted of only three continents: Europe, Asia, and Africa. Now that view was disrupted by the addition of a fourth continent, a new world that no one had ever heard of before. How should that continent be called? Waldseemüller decided to credit it to the first explorer who recognized it as a separate landmass, rather than to Columbus. Thus the continent was named "America," after Vespucci's first name, Amerigo. To further underscore this tribute, Waldseemüller depicted both Ptolemy and Vespucci at the top of the atlas.

FIG. 19. Jan Galle, *Vespucci Awakens America*, an engraving from 1615

Ringmann describes how they arrived at their choice for "America" in the accompanying book *Cosmographiae Introductio* ("An Introduction to Geography"), writing that "a fourth part has been discovered by Americus Vesputius as will be heard in the following, and I do not see why anyone should justifiably forbid it to be called *Amerige*, as if 'Americus' Land,' or *America*, from its discoverer Americus, a man of perceptive character; since both Europa and Asia have received their names from women."

For a long time, it was believed that the Waldseemüller world map did not survive; some historians even suggested that the map was simply a myth. That changed in 1901, when a print of the map was discovered in Schloss Wolfegg, a German castle in Upper Swabia, by German cartographer Joseph Fischer. In 2003, this only surviving whole copy was acquired by the Library of Congress for $10 million. Five other copies survive in the form of slices, or gores, used to make an early globe.

It only takes a quick look at this map to see how little data Waldseemüller and Ringmann had to depict this new continent. Though they used latitude and longitude to project the location of the lands, the actual sizes of the northern

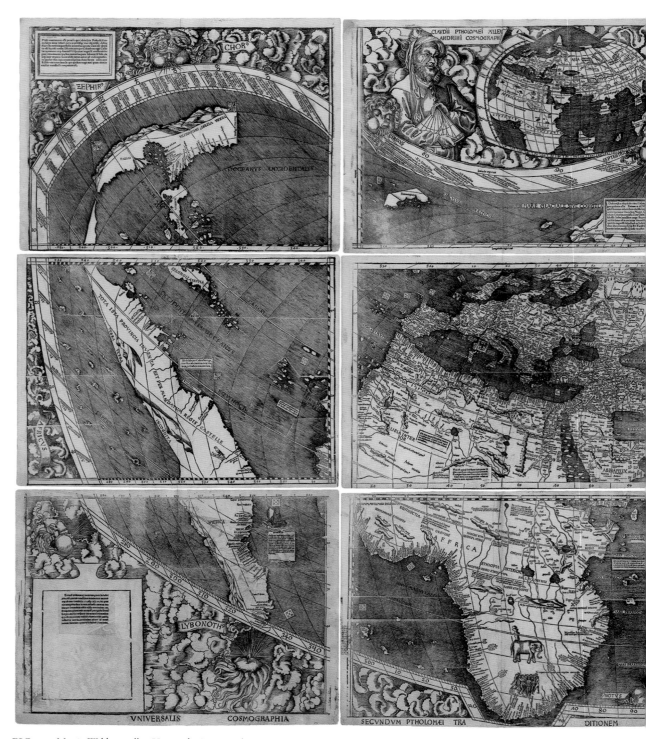

FIG. 20. Martin Waldseemüller, *Universalis Cosmographia*, 1507

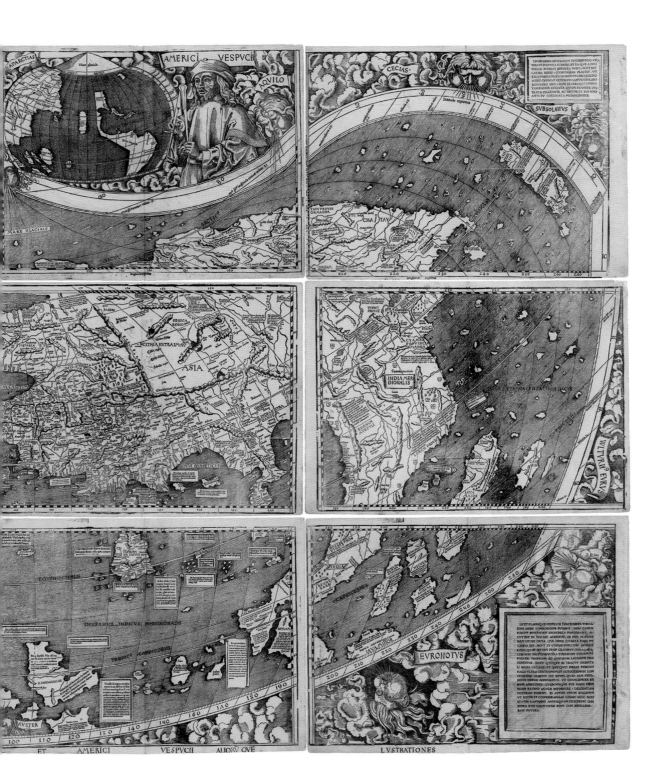

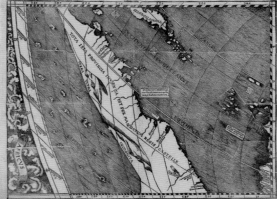

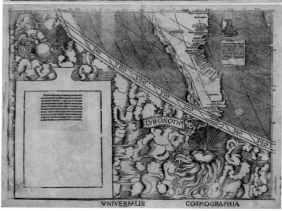

FIG. 21. North and South America as depicted in Waldseemüller's first map, with the name "America" on the bottom plate

and southern parts of America remained largely indistinct. They even showed a break between the two continents, in keeping with the persistent wish that this isthmus could provide a passage to the East. The continent of North America, meanwhile, remained largely terra incognita.

Not everyone was pleased with this projection of the world. The belief in a three-continent world ran strong in Europe, and Columbus himself was adamant that the so-called new world was actually part of Asia. This may explain why a few years later, Waldseemüller decided to publish an "updated" version of his map, in which the new continent was once again joined to Asia, to conform to Columbus's view. It speaks volumes, perhaps, that the name "America" is omitted from this version, arguably because during the intervening years, Vespucci's claims seem to have lost considerable ground. Instead, the annotation of this second version reads that "these are lands (discovered by) the Admiral, i.e. Columbus." As a result, this map became known as the "Admiral's map," and is priced at auction today at $75,000.

At the beginning of the sixteenth century, then, Waldseemüller's work posed a challenge to cartographers. Whom should they believe: Columbus or Vespucci? The issue was vitally important because the race between Spain and Portugal to unconquered worlds now became a conflict between two superpowers, similar to the way the US and the USSR raced to reach the moon in the 1960s. Spain and Portugal were each determined to claim the New World before the other could get at it.

To underscore what was at stake, in 1504—just three years before the publication of the Waldseemüller map—King John III of Portugal even issued a decree that anyone caught with Portuguese maps of areas below the equator would be sentenced to death.[27]

Meanwhile, other countries had joined the race as well, further upping the ante. In 1497, the Italian navigator Giovanni Caboto (known in English texts as John Cabot) received a commission from the English king Henry VII to explore the northern part of the New World. Departing from the city of Bristol, the second largest English seaport at the time, he sailed northward across the Atlantic Ocean and reached the coast of North America—the first European to do so since the eleventh-century exploration of the Vikings. Cabot is believed to have landed in Bonavista Bay on the northeast coast of Newfoundland, but did not go much farther. As a 1565 entry in the chronicle of the city of Bristol (or Bristow in sixteenth-century parlance) proudly proclaims,

FIG. 22. A statue of John Cabot gazing across Bonavista Bay (Courtesy, Evan T. Jones)

> *This year, on St. John the Baptist's Day [June 24, 1497], the land of America was found by the Merchants of Bristow in a shippe of Bristowe, called the* Mathew; *the which said the ship departed from the port of Bristowe, the second day of May, and came home again the 6th of August next following.*[28]

Not to be outdone, the Portuguese King Manuel I then charged an explorer named Joao Fernandes Lavrador to head north as well. In 1498, Lavrador sailed to Greenland and from there to today's Canadian province of Labrador (which was subsequently named after him), though it is not clear whether he actually explored this region in depth. Two Spanish explorers, Gaspar and Miguel Corte Real, followed close in his wake and traveled to Greenland, Labrador, and even Newfoundland, naming these the *Terra Verde* or "Green Land."

The rapid rate of these discoveries was astonishing, certainly by the standards of the early Renaissance, and left much of Europe both excited and bewildered. What did these reports mean? Was there indeed a new continent, and if so, what did it look like? And how would it change the world as the early sixteenth century knew it?

Making Sense of the New Discoveries

That was the question that confronted the Genoese sailor and mapmaker Vesconte Maggiolo. In 1508, he tried to make some sense of this flood of discoveries by developing an atlas that would form the frontispiece of a series of so-called portolan maps—charts designed to assist ships in navigating coastlines to their ports of destination, based on specific compass and distance calculations. On the first page of this atlas, he tried to imagine what the world could look like, based on the discoveries of the last two decades. Maggiolo's is the first Italian map to include the North American coast, including the newly described territories of Labrador and Greenland.

But as in the case of Waldmüller's map, the remainder of that continent seems to float away into thin air. There simply wasn't enough information to imagine what it actually looked like. The same is true for Maggiolo's depiction of the South American continent, where the northeastern coast is fairly developed, but the rest is depicted as an amorphous mass.

A more telling impression of the general confusion of the time can scarcely be imagined—not in the least because Maggiolo hedged his bets and left open the possibility that these two new continents were part of Asia after all. Nor did he use the name "America" for either of the two territories, choosing the vague term *Septem Civitates* ("Seven Communities") instead.

Many years later, in 1527, Maggiolo would correct some of his assumptions with a new map based on the travels of his friend and fellow Italian, Giovanni da Verrazzano, who sailed on behalf of the kingdom of France, a relative newcomer to world exploration. But in the meantime, the next and perhaps most important step was taken in German-speaking lands, by a physician named Lorenz Fries.

Fries, who would later Latinize his name as "Laurentius Phrisius," was born in 1490 in either Mülhausen or Colmar, both in today's Alsace-Lorraine. Though the record is unclear, it is likely that he was educated in Padua or Montpellier and subsequently became a practicing physician. In 1518, he made quite a name for himself with a handbook of medical practice, known as *Spiegel der Arznei* ("Mirror of Medicine") dedicated to a patron named Johann Dingler. The following year he moved to Strassburg and on to Freiburg in today's Switzerland, as his book had made him famous, greatly increasing the

FIG. 23. Vesconte Maggiolo,
Map of the World, from
his collection of portolan
charts, 1508

demand for his services as a physician. Somewhere along the way, Fries became enamored with cartography. After he returned to Strassburg in 1520, he was inscribed in the *Zur Steltz* guild of goldsmiths and printers, which suggests that his medical practice now also involved a keen interest in printing.

Among other works, Fries produced a booklet entitled *Kurze Schirmred der Kunst der Astrologiae* ("Brief Defense of the Art of Astrology"), published in November of 1520.[29] Apparently, what prompted him to write the pamphlet was the hostility that the great reformer Martin Luther bore toward astrology.

Fries took issue with that and wrote a fictional dialog between himself and Luther—a favorite literary format from antiquity—in which he argued that astrology was perfectly acceptable from a Christian point of view and therefore not a pagan science, as Luther had maintained.[30] By way of evidence, Fries not only cited the Gospels but also Muslim astronomers and physicians, including Ibn Sina (Avicenna), Muhammad ibn Zakariya al-Razi (Rhazes), and 'Ali ibn al-'Abbas al-Majusi (Haly Abbas). Unfortunately, only one copy of this work is still extant.[31]

To move from celestial to geographical observations was but a small step, and so Fries decided to tackle the challenge of integrating the various views on the shape of the world—including the ideas of Ptolemy, Marinus, Columbus, Vespucci, and other explorers of the time—into one consolidated series of maps. The result was an atlas of forty-six maps that would serve as the basis for the great flowering of cartography in the seventeenth century. With a physician's eye, trained in clinical diagnoses, Fries used Waldseemüller's map as a foundation, but then added Southeast Asia and South Africa as well. And rather than choosing between Ptolemy's view of the world and that of contemporary explorers, he presented *both*—the ancient Ptolemaic version as well as the modern version, which once more reveals the astonishing authority that Ptolemy still commanded at this stage of European cartography. For his world map, for example,

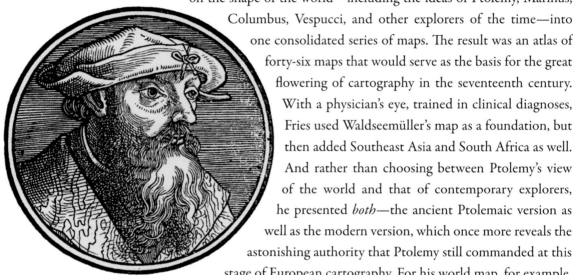

FIG. 24. *Portrait of Lorenz Fries* in an engraving from 1523

Fries developed *three* versions: one of the ancient world without the Americas; one based on the Waldseemüller map without the name "America"; and a third one where America is engraved on the southern continent.

Unlike the Waldseemüller maps, the Fries atlas enjoyed tremendous commercial success. It was printed three times: in 1522, 1525, and 1541. Most importantly, in all of the reprints Fries decided to adopt Waldseemüller's choice of "America" as the name for the New World. Because of the wide distribution and popularity of Fries's work, the name stuck. That is how "America" became the default name for the New World and the name that is still with us today.

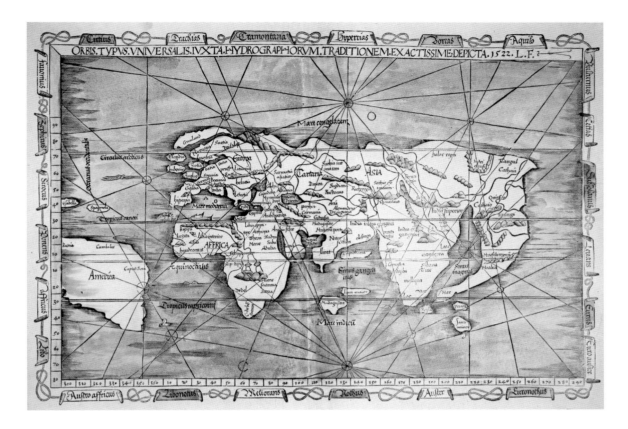

FIG. 25. Lorenz Fries, *Map of the World*, 1522. In this version, the name "America" is prominently featured on the South American continent.

The Discovery of Florida

Meanwhile, the exploration of the New World continued apace. In 1493, a military officer named Juan Ponce de León had accompanied Columbus on his second voyage to the West Indies. Eight years later, he was serving as the military commander in the Spanish colonial government of Hispaniola, the island that today comprises both the Dominican Republic and Haiti. The island's native Taíno tribe, acting in concert with the Carib people, rose in revolt against the harsh Spanish demands for tribute. Rallying his company of troops, Ponce de León ruthlessly crushed the rebellion and burned one of the tribal leaders, the Taíno chieftain Hatuey, at the stake. This must have pleased the Spanish Crown, for in 1508 Ponce de León was authorized to colonize the island of Puerto Rico and rule this new territory as its viceroy. Unfortunately, this brought him in conflict with Diego Colón, Columbus's son, who believed that the right to govern this island was his. Colón duly brought suit in a Spanish court, claiming that the government of Puerto Rico had been deeded to Columbus instead. In 1511, the court ruled in his favor, and Ponce de León suddenly found himself without a job.

King Ferdinand, however, deeply regretted this ruling, and in order to thwart Colón's authority in the region authorized Ponce de León to go northward and explore the lands bordering the Caribbean Sea, including the mythical "islands of Benimy." If he discovered this new territory, the king promised, Ponce de León would be appointed governor for life. With this powerful incentive, Ponce de León launched a three-ship expedition including the *Santiago*, the *San Cristobal*, and the *Santa María de la Consolación*.

On March 27, 1513, Easter Sunday, these ships brought him to the doorstep of North America's southernmost coast. He disembarked and, charmed by the profusion of exotic plants and flowers, called it the "Land of Flowers," or *la Florida*. This was fitting, for Easter season in Spanish is known as *Pascua Florida,* or "Feast of Flowers." From there, he carefully charted Florida's Atlantic coast before sailing north along the Gulf Coast.

Returning to Spain in 1514, Ponce de León was received as a hero and raised to the knighthood by King Ferdinand. Even sweeter was the king's decision to remove Diego Colón and reinstate Ponce de León as the governor of Puerto Rico. The untimely death of King Ferdinand in 1516 upstaged these plans, however, and it was not until 1521 that Ponce de León returned to Florida. He had high hopes of establishing a Spanish colony there—the first Spanish colony on American soil—but faced unexpected resistance from the native Calusa people. This resulted in several clashes, during which Ponce de León was seriously wounded. He was taken to Cuba, where he succumbed to his wounds. Today, his remains are buried in the Cathedral of San Juan Bautista in Puerto Rico's capital of San Juan.

And so, Florida became the first American territory to be given a name on a map that endures to this day. In fact, for lack of any other data about this strange new land, the name "Florida" soon became pars pro toto for much of the southern region of the North American continent.

As such, it appears on a map drawn by the Spanish royal cartographer Geronimo Chiaves, many years later republished by Abraham Ortelius in his *Theatrum Orbis Terrarum.* At that time, Florida was integrated in the rapidly growing Spanish Empire as a territory that included not only modern Florida

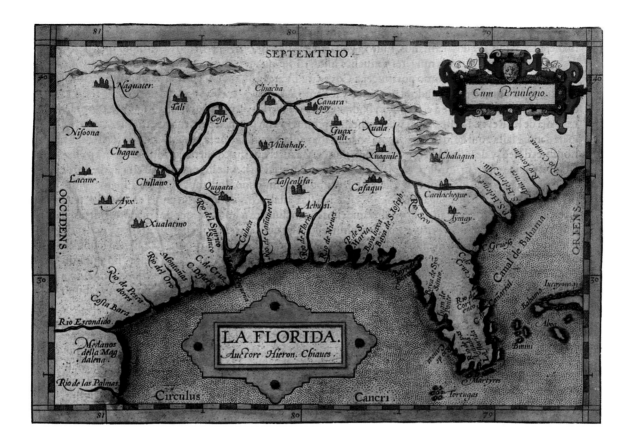

Text on map: SEPTEMTRIO · — Naguater · Tali · Cosſe · Chiacha · Canaragay · Guaxulti · Xuala · Niſoona · Chague · Vtibabaly · Xuaquile · Chalaqua · Rio de Canaas · Lacane · Chillano · Quigata · Taſſealiſa · Caſaqui · Cacilacheque · Ayx · Achuſi · Aymay · S. Helena Su · Rio del Spirito Santo · Xualatino · Culua · Rio de Cuſſacheru · Rio de Flores · Rio de Nieus · P. de S. Maria · Baſia hoea · Bayu de S. Joſeph · Rio Seco · Rio de Peſcadores · Rio del Oro · Montanna · C. de Cruz · C. Deſarto · Cruz · C. Grueſo · Canal de Bahama · Coſta Bara · Baya de S.os Sunes · Rio Cordico · Bahama · Iunyoyo, p. · Rio Escondido · Medanos della Magdalena · Martyres · Bimini · Abaco · Rio de las Palmas · Tortugas · Circulus · Cancri · OCCIDENS · ORIENS · Cum Priuilegio ·

LA FLORIDA.
Auctore Hieron. Chiaues.

but also portions of today's South Carolina, Louisiana, Mississippi, Alabama, and Georgia.

Buoyed by these discoveries, Spain relentlessly pursued the ongoing exploration of the new continents. In 1513, Vasco Núñez de Balboa crossed the Isthmus of Panama and reached the Pacific Ocean. There, he claimed all of the Pacific Coast for the Spanish Crown, a move that in the future would produce the Spanish colonization of *Las Californias*. Just eleven years later, an Italian explorer we encountered earlier, Giovanni da Verrazzano, secured funding from the French king François I to explore the Atlantic coast of North America—the first European to do so. He is believed to have traveled along the Eastern Seaboard from what is now Long Island down to the Carolinas. Shortly thereafter, a Portuguese navigator named Estêvão Gomes—ironically sailing on behalf of the Spanish king Charles I—found the Maine coast, explored today's New York Harbor, and logged the location of the Hudson River.

FIG. 26. Map of "Florida" showing much of the southern region of the American continent, originally drawn by the Spanish royal cartographer Geronimo Chiaves and published by Ortelius in 1584

All of these discoveries would be featured in a 1529 map by the Portuguese cartographer Diogo Ribeiro. Ribeiro is a unique case in the history of cartography, for he was both an accomplished mapmaker and an experienced sailor who had led several expeditions to India by rounding the Cape of Good Hope. Some believe that Ribeiro also sailed with Pedro Afonso de Aguiar, who had served as captain in expeditions for Vasco da Gama in 1502 and Lopo Soares in 1504. The experience gave Ribeiro a unique sense of the scale and depth of the territories he had visited, which is reflected in his 1529 map—a landmark in cartography for its accuracy in charting the principal dimensions of the coasts of South America as well as the Gulf and Eastern Seaboard of North America.

Another key factor in the success of this map was that in 1519, together with other cartographers and explorers, Ribeiro had defected from Portugal and gone to work for the Spanish court of Charles V, the Holy Roman Emperor. Ribeiro's world travels had given him a keen sense of international politics, and he accurately judged that the zenith of Portuguese exploration had been passed. From this point forward, Spain would lead the exploration of the new world. The move also allowed him to study all of the charts that Spanish explorers had developed to date.

The Spanish king knew a good thing when he saw it, and soon recognized the Portuguese's exceptional talent by naming him royal cosmographer and "master in the art of creating maps, astrolabes, and other instruments." As we saw previously, the Spanish did like to keep their maps close to their chest and considered them state secrets. In 1527, Ribeiro produced his first major map of the world, the *Padrón Real*, which included charts of the North and South American coastlines, as a secret master map to be used by all ships sailing under the Spanish flag. Proprietary charts such as these had been issued since 1503 by the Spanish *Casa de Contratación*, in order to create a central pool of all the knowledge brought back by Spanish vessels, but Ribeiro's map was a major leap forward.

The principal outlines of this map, published in 1529, then played an important role in resolving a diplomatic crisis. Back in the early 1490s, Pope Alexander VI had been deeply concerned that the competing ambitions of Portugal and Spain in global exploration might bring these two major Catholic powers into conflict. In an effort to separate their spheres of influence, the pope drew an arbitrary dividing line, granting all new territory west of the Azores to Spain. Portugal strenuously objected. Subsequent negotiations produced the Treaty of Tordesillas of 1494, by which the two explorer nations carved up the world among themselves. Portugal gained control over Africa, Asia, and the eastern part of South America (analogous to today's Brazil), while Spain received all lands to the west of that line—much of which was still to be explored.

Spain wasted no time in seizing the land apportioned to it. As we saw, in 1513 Juan Ponce de León claimed a territory that he named Florida. Six years later, conquistador Hernán Cortés reached the Yucatán Peninsula and made contact with the Maya civilization. Soon thereafter, rumors reached Spain that precious metals could be found aplenty among the Aztec and Maya civilizations. This spurred a new wave of explorations with the full support of the

Spanish king Charles V. In 1530, Francisco Pizarro landed in Peru with a force of two hundred men and succeeded in defeating the far greater Inca forces. One by one, the indigenous civilizations of Central and South America were suppressed and replaced by colonial administrations. But inevitably, Spanish and Portuguese colonizers in South America came into conflict, and the Vatican was once again called upon to arbitrate in the matter. The pope did so, using Ribeiro's 1529 map to set clear boundaries between the two powers.

Twenty years later, the German cartographer and biblical scholar Sebastian Münster made the next attempt to create an accurate vision of the world based on the explorations of the time. The result was his atlas *Cosmographia,* the earliest known description of the world in the German language.

In this iteration, South America is termed *Die Nüw Welt*, or "The New World," while the territory of Brazil features the now obligatory scene of cannibalism. Much of the southern region of North America is called *Terra Florida*, "the Land of Florida." Canada is designated as *Francisca*, while Japan is named *Zipongi,* based on Marco Polo's use of the name "Cipangu," Chinese for "Japan." Cuba, formerly known as *Isabella*, is already designated as "Cuba." At the bottom of the map is the picture of a ship to mark the 1522 attempt to circumnavigate the globe, begun by the Portuguese explorer Ferdinand Magellan and later completed by Juan Sebastián Elcano.

Cosmographia became one of the most successful maps of the sixteenth century. It was translated in five languages and enjoyed twenty-four editions over a one-hundred-year span. Its appeal was boosted by the fact that it featured woodcuts by the renowned artist Hans Holbein, later court artist to King Henry VIII.

It was at this point that the French decided to join the rush to the New World. In 1534, Jacques Cartier set his sights on the Gulf of Saint Lawrence and claimed much of this region for François I, thus establishing the French hold on much of Canada. He was followed in 1608 by Samuel de Champlain, who founded Quebec City—the first permanent French settlement in North America, now grandiosely known as *Nouvelle France.* He then moved deep into the interior via the Ottawa River to Lake Simcoe, often finding himself in battle with the Iroquois native Indians. As a result, the Iroquois became the sworn enemies of France, with grave consequences for the future, as we will see.

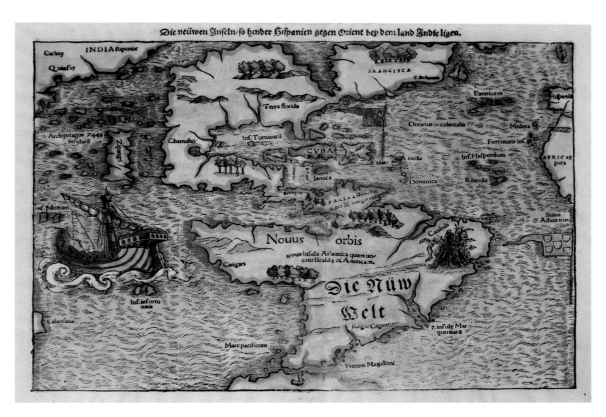

FIG. 28. The 1550 map of North and South America by
Sebastian Münster

THE FIRST EUROPEAN
SETTLEMENTS

SHE WAS A FRAIL YOUNG BRUNETTE WITH A NARROW FACE AND pouty lips, hardly the Spanish black-haired, dark-eyed beauty who would inspire the likes of Velázquez and Zurbarán in the centuries to come. But behind Isabella's soft, green-blue eyes was a keen, razor-sharp intellect. It was her wits that had enabled her to outflank her rivals and become the heiress to the throne of Castile, the largest kingdom in Spain. Of course, as a crown princess she immediately became the target of several marriage suits. Among the gentlemen in play were Alfonso V, the king of Portugal; the Duc de Berry, Prince Charles of France; the Duke of Gloucester or, if this were more amenable, his brother, the English king Edward IV; and, last but not least, Ferdinand, king of the northern territory of Aragon. Isabella surprised everyone by choosing Ferdinand. It was true, they were second cousins, but she prevailed on Pope Pius II to issue a papal dispensation, which he was more than happy to do. The fact that Pius II had actually died five years earlier did not seem to bother anyone.[32]

Others were not so sanguine. There were very powerful factions in Portugal and Castile that were dead set against the marriage, for it would involve the union of Aragon and Castile, thus creating a vast new realm on the Spanish peninsula. But Ferdinand—who with his heavy-lidded eyes, prominent nose, and permanent five-o'clock shadow was no great beauty himself—was determined to have his bride. In 1469, with tensions high, he secretly crossed into Castilian territory, disguised as a servant, and embraced Isabella in a quiet ceremony at the Palacio de los Vivero in Valladolid. As soon as news of the marriage spread, the opposing factions in Castile and Portugal were shocked. Their shock turned to open revolt when Isabella's half-brother King Henry IV died suddenly in 1474, making her Queen of Castile. The result was a vicious

FIG. 29. Isabella I of Castile,
ca. 1490, in a portrait by an
anonymous artist

war of succession that was not settled until five years later, in 1479.

This brutal experience did not fail to shape Isabella's character. It forged an iron will that would become legendary in the years to come. It was she who strongly supported the expedition proposed by Christopher Columbus. She foresaw the immense advantage that Spain would gain over her rivals if the newly unified kingdom could reap the promised bounty in gold and silver, or the vastly improved sea routes to the spice lands of Asia.

Thus it was Isabella, not Ferdinand, who in 1503 ordered the establishment of the *Casa de Contratación de las Indias* ("House of Trade with the Indies") in the port city of Seville. The purpose of this new Crown agency was to have complete control over anything related to Spain's overseas colonies, including their shipping, funding, cartography, governance, and trade. Unlike the Dutch and English governments, which would leave it up to private enterprise to develop their overseas colonies, Isabella considered Spain's overseas enterprises a state matter, to be developed, charted, and exploited to the greatest extent possible. That meant that any portolan charts, maps, or other cartographic data acquired by Spanish conquistadores were considered state secrets, to be protected and guarded as such.

In this, Isabella was perhaps the first European ruler to recognize that trade, not European territory, was going to become the decisive factor in the coming rivalry between nations. "That hee that commaunds the sea, commaunds the trade," Sir Walter Raleigh once said, "and hee that is Lord of the Trade of the world is lord of the wealth of the worlde."[33] Isabella would have agreed.

In the decades to come, the wisdom of Isabella's vision was borne out in ways that few could have imagined. In a short period of time, the unified kingdom of Spain was catapulted into the role of the most powerful empire on earth, largely based on its holdings in the Americas.

FIG. 30. Diego Gutiérrez, entitled *Americae sive quartae orbis partis nova* ("A New Depiction of America or the Fourth Part of the World"), 1562

In fact, in 1562 the Spanish House of Trade proudly declared its claim over much, if not all, of the Western Hemisphere, in the form of a map commissioned from the Spanish royal cartographer Diego Gutiérrez. Three feet square, it shows us what was known about the Americas at that time. Apart from the vivid depictions of sea monsters and naval battles, that knowledge was mostly limited to the coastal areas, while the interior contained largely imaginary geographical features as well as the obligatory depiction of cannibals. The map also reveals that North America remained largely terra incognita, even though it was the first map to apply the name "California" and to correctly identify it as a peninsula rather than as an island off the coast, as later maps would have it. Technically, however, this map—of which only two copies have survived[34]—was beyond the powers of Spanish engravers, particularly in the depiction of oceanic weaves. In response, the *Casa de Contratación* enlisted the services of the renowned Flemish artist Hieronymus Cock, and thus the map was printed and issued in Antwerp, which formed part of the Spanish Netherlands at the time.

While Columbus himself never found the vast gold and silver ores he dreamed of, Spanish conquistadores did. According to Spanish records, a staggering forty-five thousand tons of pure silver were found and harvested from the mines of Potosí in the Andes, and those of Zacatecas and Guanajuato in Mexico. At its peak in the seventeenth century, Potosí was one of the largest and most affluent cities in Latin America, with a population of two hundred thousand and no fewer than eighty-six churches. Month after month, ships sailed to Spain with their bottoms filled with precious metals. Spain's European rivals could only watch in envy.

Of course, they didn't sit and watch for long. Eventually, the crowned heads of Europe decided that it was only fair to take some of this stupendous wealth for themselves. First the French and then the English governments began to authorize privateers to prey on the slow-moving bullion ships and take what they could. In 1523, for example, much of the Aztec gold that had been captured by Hernán Cortés in the early 1520s was intercepted by French pirates on the high seas of the Atlantic and swiftly brought to France.

Emboldened, French pirates expanded their operations to the Spanish islands of the Caribbean, where they pillaged and looted to their heart's

FIG. 31. John Ogilby, *The Town of Potosí*, 1671. Potosí, in today's Bolivia, was founded by the Spanish in 1546 as a mining town in the viceroyalty of Peru and soon became its principal source of silver.

content—even going as far as to burn Havana, Spain's principal port, to the ground. Not to be outdone, the English buccaneer Francis Drake, a protégé of Raleigh's, raided Spanish shipping along the coast of modern-day Peru and Mexico—much to the delight of Queen Elizabeth I of England, who found herself in a perennial state of war with the Spanish anyway.

Outraged, the Spanish Crown responded by building a new class of battleship. Galleons bristled with guns on multiple decks and used three sets of towering masts to propel themselves across the heaving seas. These behemoths now sailed in convoys to safely shepherd the bullion ships to ports in Spain. Of course, this also vastly increased the expense of transport, which led to heavy taxes on the spoils.

The introduction of armed convoys compelled Spain's rivals to resort to another strategy: smuggling. This allowed them to circumvent the import and export duties imposed by Spain on its new territories and offer goods below the official rate. As a result, the bounty from South America was more equally distributed across both northern and southern Europe than we might have thought. In fact, this influx of gold and silver created an entirely new, global

FIG. 32. A modern replica of
a Spanish galleon, the *Galeón*
Andalucía, in Quebec City
(Source: Cephas)

economy based on hard currency. Silver and gold coins such as the real, the crown, and the guilder had face values that matched their actual silver and gold content. But all this wealth came at a terrible cost in the lives of indigenous workers, who were forced to work in unsafe tunnels or shafts burrowed deep into the mines.

When English pirate attacks continued unabated, the Spanish tried another gambit: putting a bounty on Sir Francis Drake's head. Today, that premium would have been worth the equivalent of £4 million (or $5,355,844)—an astounding amount, which shows just how much the English buccaneer was costing the Spanish Crown. In response, Queen Elizabeth and Drake put their minds together and hatched a daring plan: for Drake to sail around the southern tip of the Latin American continent, previously charted by Magellan, and surprise the Spanish treasure ships where they least expected him—off the Pacific coast. It was an audacious if not foolhardy plan, for even Magellan's lieutenant had said that "nevermore will any man undertake to make such a voyage" through these treacherous shoals at the bottom of the world.[35]

Indeed, the expedition got off to a bad start. After running into a storm on November 15, 1577, the ships were forced to return to Plymouth. One month later, Drake tried again, this time with five ships under his command, and successfully captured a Portuguese ship, the *Mary*, near the Cape Verde Islands. But the loss of many crew members during the Atlantic crossing forced him to scuttle two ships, and by the time he limped into the bay of San Julián in today's Argentina, the mood of his crew bordered on mutiny. Rather than continuing the voyage, Drake decided to winter in San Julian and wait for more clement weather. When, at long last, the weather improved, he carefully made his way through the treacherous waters of the Strait of Magellan. Alas, as soon as he reached the Pacific coast of South America, a violent storm flayed his ships once more. One vessel, the *Marigold*, was lost, while a second ship, the *Elizabeth*, was so badly damaged that its captain, John Wynter, decided to sail back to England.

That left only Drake and his flagship, the *Golden Hind*. Undaunted, Drake decided to carry out his orders and wreak havoc on the Spanish ships. In the pearly light of dawn, he sailed close to the Spanish anchorages along the coast and unleashed his eighteen cannons. Bright spears of flame spit out, lashing the unsuspecting vessels with round shots that tore through the wooden hulls and showered sailors with lethal splinters. For the Spanish, the shock of seeing an English warship in these waters was overwhelming. No one had ever imagined that English pirates could travel so far to prey upon Spanish ships. Worse, as he ravaged his victims, Drake seized not only valuable booty but also every Spanish chart and map he could lay his hands on, thus providing England with priceless maritime intelligence—even more so since the Spanish considered any charts of their New World territories state secrets.

Equipped with these maps, Drake was able to attack Spanish ports on the Pacific with ever greater accuracy and stealth. He even surprised the great Chilean port of Valparaíso, capturing Spanish loot worth 37,000 ducats (the equivalent of almost $10 million today).

Soon thereafter, Drake learned that a Spanish treasure ship, the *Nuestra Señora de la Concepción,* had just slipped its moorings and was on its way to Manila in full sail, in a desperate attempt to escape from Drake's rapacious exploits. Drake immediately ordered his crew in full pursuit, knowing that

FIG. 33. Drake and his crew
resting in California, in a 1590
print by Theodor de Bry

his target was weighed down with twenty-six tons of silver and eighty pounds
of gold. Before long, the doomed ship appeared on the horizon, and Drake's
delighted crew prepared to seize her. Grappling hooks were thrown, rope lines
were swung, and heavily armed English sailors dropped down on the Spanish
crew. They were subdued with hardly a shot being fired. As they boarded the
ship, Drake and his lieutenants were astonished to find not only the promised
mounds of gold and silver but also thirteen chests full of jewels and royal plates.
It was one of the largest hauls ever made by a privateer. However, not a single
Spanish crewman was hurt. Drake even gave every seaman forty pesos as com-
pensation for the inconvenience.

Now loaded with loot, it was time for Drake to begin the journey home.
That was easier said than done, for by now the southern passages were heavily
defended by Spanish warships. The only option, then, was to try to do what
Magellan and others had attempted before him: to try to circumnavigate
the globe and return to England via the western route through Asian waters.
Having rested his crew in California (or "Nova Albion"), Drake left the Pacific
Coast on July 23, 1579 and sailed relatively undisturbed for sixty-eight days
before reaching the Moluccans in today's Indonesia. A century-long goal had

finally been met: Drake had found a western route to the Spice Islands. From there, he set sail around the Cape of Good Hope on the southern tip of Africa on June 18, 1580, and finally reached the welcome shores of Plymouth three months later, on September 26.

Drake's booty of gold, silver, and jewels was so large that it exceeded all of the English Crown's tax revenue of that year. Of even greater value was the immense cartographic intelligence, laboriously collected by Spanish sailors and explorers, and now in English hands. It was a pivotal moment in the history of world exploration. From this point on, England would become a sea power to be reckoned with, set on developing an empire of its own.

The Spanish Conquest of the Americas

Of course, in the greater scheme of things, Drake's raids amounted to little more than jabs at Spain's growing grip on South America, where Spanish conquistadores were hard at work to expand the territories under their sway. In North America, conquerors such as Francisco Vázquez de Coronado, Álvar Núñez Cabeza de Vaca, and Hernando de Soto pushed into the territory of today's New Mexico, Arizona, and California, which were added to the original lands of "Spanish Florida." From there, de Soto led a campaign up north, into present-day Georgia and the Carolinas, where he ran into strong resistance from North American Indians. A string of clashes ensued, which culminated in the Battle of Mabila. Though largely forgotten today, this was one of the biggest battles between Indians and European colonists on American soil. It claimed the lives of over 2,500 Indians with 170 killed or wounded on the Spanish side.

Historians still debate the extent of the Indian population in North America before the arrival of the conquistadores. What we do know is that both North and South America were probably the last continents to be occupied by people, since the oldest discovered human remains are less than fifteen thousand years old.[36] The predominant theory is that during the last ice age, so-called land bridges appeared between Europe, the Americas, and even parts of Asia (such as Australia) that allowed large migrations to occur. Since climate change had decimated animal herds, many of these migrations were probably prompted by the search for new hunting grounds. As part of this mass

FIG. 34. An Indian mother
and her child, and an Indian
warrior, as depicted in colored
prints from 1585

movement, nomadic peoples crossed from Siberia into the Americas in search
of herds of caribou, bison, and other animals. Cooling temperatures also forced
these humans to husband fire as a source of warmth, and possibly as a means to
cook their food, increasing the protein content of their diets and the growth
of their brains. That in turn allowed them to come up with better tactics in the
hunt for large animals.

Eventually the climate began to warm, the ice receded, and the oceans
stabilized, reaching their present form around ten thousand years ago. This
is when Paleo-Indians known as the Athabascan people settled in Alaska and
northern Canada before slowly moving southward along the Rocky Mountains.
Here, they eventually split into the Navajo and Apache tribes.

These Paleo-Indians were primarily hunter-gatherers, unlike ancient
peoples elsewhere who had moved from a destructive to a productive lifestyle:
from hunting and gathering to domesticating animals and crops. There was
little incentive for these people to do so, because the American valleys were
stocked with vast herds of bison, caribou, deer, and moose that had yet to learn

that human beings posed a lethal threat. For a long time, this provided the Indian tribes with a rich diet that prompted an explosive population growth, and inevitably the decimation of animal herds. One by one, the wild horse, the mammoth, the giant bison, the mastodon, and even the camel became extinct on the American continent, only to survive and flourish in parts of Asia after their migration east across the few remaining land bridges. The horse in particular would not reappear in America until the arrival of the Spanish conquistadores. The dwindling wild herds forced many tribes to split and go in search of new resources elsewhere. They learned to fish in rivers and to gather edible foodstuffs such as nuts, berries, and seeds. Thus, different tribal cultures began to develop, each with its own rituals, religion, and language. Some historians believe that at the time of Columbus's journey to the New World, there were at least 375 different languages in use across the North American continent.

In Central and South America, on the other hand, the domestication of both animals and crops had begun thousands of years earlier, thus fostering the rise of several impressive agricultural cultures along the main rivers. The most prominent of these so-called Mesoamerican cultures was the Olmec civilization, which emerged in the tropical valleys of today's south-central Mexico. The Olmecs used their growing prosperity to develop large cities, often grouped around impressive pyramids. The largest of these is the Great Pyramid of La Venta, Tabasco, which today still soars to a height of 112 feet.

The Olmec civilization flourished from 1500 to 400 B.C.E., at which point it quite suddenly went into decline. But by then, a number of other early cultures were emerging throughout the Americas. One of these was the Chavín de Huántar culture in the Andes mountains, known for its finely woven textiles, as well as the Adena people in the Ohio River valley and the Cochise culture of today's New Mexico and Arizona. The Inuits and Aleuts founded a number of settlements in the Arctic, while in California, Pinto Indians built villages made of reeds and covered with earth. In the lower Mississippi, people built a mysterious group of earthen ridges and mounds in a spot that modern archaeologists refer to as Poverty Point. Around 1300 C.E., the city of Cahokia, located near today's East St. Louis in Illinois, became the largest urban concentration in North America, with a population of over twenty thousand. In other words, North America before the arrival of Europeans was not the untamed land that we often believe it to be; it, too, had a history of many diverse cultures and traditions.

Elsewhere in America rose the most impressive pre-Columbian culture of all, known as the Maya civilization. At one point, the Mayas controlled a territory equal to Guatemala, Belize, southeastern Mexico, and the western parts of El Salvador and Honduras. Here, they built the largest and most impressive pyramids of Latin America while also introducing a calendar based on lunar and solar cycles, as well as the most sophisticated writing system on the continent to date, using over five hundred glyphs.

Unfortunately, some three hundred years later, after the arrival of Europeans, these and other cultures had all but vanished. Many native Indians perished not by the sword but as a result of diseases introduced by Europeans. In New England, nearly 90 percent of American Indians succumbed to an outbreak of hepatitis between 1606 and 1620. Smallpox is believed to have been the cause of the death of half the population of Peru, which would explain why Pizarro was able to defeat the Inca armies with a force of only 168 men. The Catholic priests who followed in his wake ordered most of the Maya texts destroyed, since they were tokens of a pagan culture. Thus, thousands of Maya codices were lost, with the exception of three precious books that today are held by museums in Madrid, Dresden, and Paris.

And so, by the dawn of the seventeenth century, virtually all of the native civilizations of North and South America were either destroyed or in sharp decline as a result of the colonization efforts of Spanish, Portuguese, French, Dutch, and English settlers. Which raises the questions: What came in their stead? What were these early colonists trying to achieve? What was their motive in building settlements in these foreign lands?

Initially, as we saw, the principal driving force for expeditions to the New World was the quest for gold and any other precious metals. That quest was successful in some parts of South America, but not in the North. Therefore, the early settlers in North America struck about for goods that could justify the great expense of building and maintaining these early colonies and settled on fur. In Europe, and particularly in the colder climates of the North, fur from ermines, martens, mink, foxes, and beavers was a precious commodity, usually reserved for the elite.

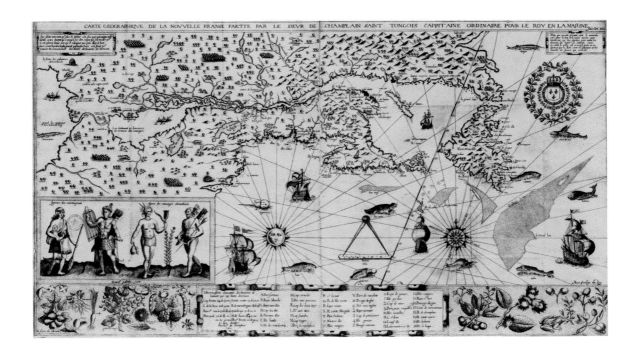

The French Exploration of the St. Lawrence River

It was the search for fur that led the French to concentrate their colonizing activity along the St. Lawrence River, where the local Montagnais and Algonquian tribes were ready to trade. Much of that effort was led by a colorful character named Samuel de Champlain. Born into a family of sailors and navigators, Champlain imbibed the love of the sea with his mother's milk. He served in the French army during France's religious wars of 1562 to 1598 and soon showed an aptitude for drawing maps.

Champlain had an uncle who served as a navigator on the French brig *Saint-Julien,* and one day he invited young Champlain to sail to the West Indies. The voyage was an eye-opener, and filled Champlain with a lifelong fascination with the New World. Upon his return to France, he wrote a detailed report on the trade with French colonists and got himself appointed as a royal geographer at the court of King Henri IV. When a few years later his uncle died, leaving much of his estate to his nephew, Champlain suddenly found he was a rich man. This gave him considerable freedom in plotting his movements, which is why, over the remainder of his life, Champlain would make more than twenty-two trips across the Atlantic.

FIG. 35. A map of *Nouvelle France, or* "New France," drawn by Samuel de Champlain in 1612

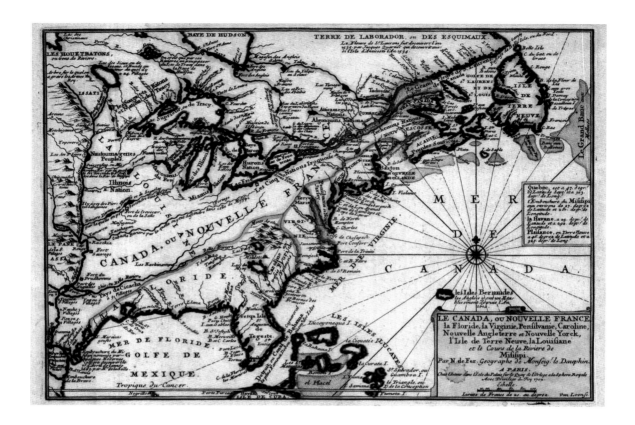

FIG. 36. A 1702 map of the eastern part of North America by Nicolas de Fer, showing French possessions including *La Louisiane* and *Nouvelle France* outlined in yellow, and English and Spanish territories delineated in green

In 1603, he sailed to North America to see the new French possessions for himself—particularly the territory along the St. Lawrence that had been claimed in 1534 by Jacques Cartier. From that point on, he traveled up and down the region to look for sites where the French could build a permanent settlement. Eventually, in 1608, Champlain settled on an area near an abandoned settlement of Iroquoian Indians that he named *Pointe du Quebec*. That small habitat would eventually grow to become one of the oldest continuously inhabited cities in North America, known as Quebec City. For the remainder of his life, Champlain devoted himself to developing this settlement, which sixty years later had grown to a town of 550 people. As we will see, it would play a major role in the wars of the seventeenth and eighteenth centuries, culminating in the American Revolutionary War.

Champlain was a keen observer of human nature and realized the importance of peaceful relations with surrounding Indian tribes long before many of his fellow Frenchmen did. Most colonists considered Indians to be children at best or savages at worst; for them, they were natives with whom one could trade only by the blade of a sword or the barrel of a gun. Champlain, by contrast, negotiated an alliance with the Montagnais, the Algonquian, and the Wendat (or Huron) nations to ensure the steady supply of fur to French traders. This, in turn, gave the colonists unimpeded access to water, fishing, and hunting grounds, as well as cultivation fields. But there was a flip side to this alliance. Many Indian nations had long lived in enmity with one another, and Champlain was forced to choose sides. Thus, in return for peace with the Montagnais and other tribes, he was forced to declare war on a group of Iroquois Indians later known as the Five Nations. As the historian Alan Taylor put it, "the French embraced the northern alliance and made southern enemies."[37]

The Iroquois became the sworn enemies of France, with fateful consequences for the future.

With Quebec as their base, the French colonists of *Nouvelle France,* "New France," continued to expand their territory. As the map by Nicolas de Fer shows, by the end of the seventeenth century, New France comprised not only French Canada (including Quebec, Montreal, and Trois-Rivières) but also Newfoundland; Hudson's Bay; parts of Maine and Illinois, including the Great Lakes area; and today's Louisiana. On paper, *Nouvelle France* was a sprawling territory that cut a swath across North America from Newfoundland to the Gulf of Mexico, there to encroach on—and eventually threaten—the budding English colonies along the Eastern Seaboard. Were it not for France's ill-fated launch of the Seven Years' War in 1756, and the devastating terms of the peace settlement known as the Treaty of Paris of 1763, it is likely that most of us would be speaking French today rather than English.

The English Colonies

Unlike the absolutist monarchies of France and Spain, sixteenth-century Elizabethan England had neither the resources nor the political will to engage in costly expeditions to the New World. With the constant threat of a Spanish invasion, England had to conserve what military and naval assets it had to protect its tenuous existence as an island nation, surrounded by hostile territory.

In addition, England was wholly absorbed in a colonizing effort much closer to home: the conquest of Ireland.

Therefore, Queen Elizabeth had little choice but to outsource overseas exploration to brash seafarers who were ready to explore the New World on their own in return for a split of the proceeds with the English Crown. Several adventurers responded to her call, including a group of men later known as the West Country Men. This gang included such august names as Sir Walter Raleigh, Sir John Hawkins, Sir Richard Grenville, and Sir Francis Drake. Their principal goal was not to build settlements or to develop trade with American natives but to get rich quickly by preying on Spanish vessels.

But this changed after Sir Francis Drake's stunning circumnavigation of the globe. Queen Elizabeth recognized that with these new routes, England could not allow itself to be left behind. And so, just four years later in 1584, she granted Raleigh a seven-year patent to explore and colonize any "remote, heathen and barbarous lands, countries and territories, not actually possessed of any Christian Prince or inhabited by Christian People."[38] Here, for the first time, the English Crown explicitly declared its intent to not only explore but also *settle* the new territories to be found. And if Raleigh was successful, the queen promised him a fifth of all the gold, silver, and other treasures that might be found there.

At first, Raleigh undertook several attempts to establish a colony of English settlers on Roanoke Island, in today's North Carolina. The location was poorly chosen: there were few arable lands in the vicinity, making the colonists entirely dependent on resupply from the home country. Worse, the local Indians, most notably the Algonquians, refused to provide the colonists with maize after their own stocks ran low. A group of English settlers led by a veteran of the Irish War, Ralph Lane, retaliated by killing the chieftain. Thus ended any chance of a reconciliation. Unfortunately, these events took place just as England faced the threat of invasion by the Spanish Armada. This forced the English Crown to keep most of its ships in port. When at long last, a relief ship arrived off the sandbars of Roanoke Island, the colony had vanished.

In response to these setbacks, the new English king James I authorized a group of investors in 1606 to form the Virginia Company. This was to be a private enterprise with a charter to govern and exploit the new territory to

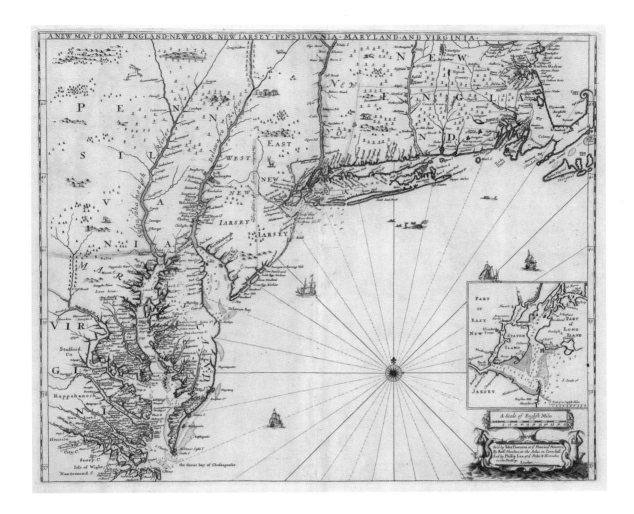

FIG. 37. One of the earliest maps of English colonies in North America, centered on the Chesapeake Bay. The map was published by John Thornton in 1685.

the fullest extent possible on behalf of the Crown. With colony fever now running high in London's financial circles, the company quickly organized a new expedition to explore the James River and if possible to establish a new colony. Thus, Jamestown was established as the first permanent English town in the Americas, located some sixty miles upriver from the bay and just two and a half miles southwest of Williamsburg. Before long, Jamestown would begin to attract large numbers of men and women who wanted to escape England in the hope of a better life.

In 1607 a second settlement was established on Chesapeake Bay, an estuary filled with large stocks of fish and fowl. Even better, it was located at the nexus of several rivers that ran deep inland, including the Potomac,

FIG. 38. John Smith's map of New England, based on his 1614 voyage along the coast, published in 1624

the York, the Rappahannock, and the James. Furthermore, the area had fertile lands and valleys where the local Indians cultivated maize, squash, and beans.

However, these Native Americans were very different from the Indians up north along the St. Lawrence River in one important respect. They were unified. At their head stood a *mamanatowick*, or "paramount leader," known as Wahunsenacawh. The English called him "the Powhatan," or "the chief." Wahunsenacawh watched the growing English presence with deep apprehension. Though the settlers had goods that the chieftain wanted—such as axes, blankets, and shovels that they traded in exchange for Indian corn—tensions between the Natives and colonists remained and even produced several minor clashes. This did not deter the colonists from building and fortifying their settlement, which they proudly named Virginia, in honor of Queen Elizabeth, the "Virgin Queen."

The desire to establish colonies overseas was prompted by major social changes in England. At the beginning of the seventeenth century, new laws allowed the English aristocracy to appropriate large tracts of land, displacing thousands of farmers and peasants who had tilled the soil of these plots for generations. As a result, countless impoverished men, women, and children had flocked to London where they lived in the most abject squalor, often mere footsteps from the patrician homes of the wealthy. Thus, the opportunity to leave England for a new future in the New World could not have come at a better time. It is estimated that between 1607 and 1620 the Virginia Company would carry around ten thousand would-be colonists to the shores of the Chesapeake Bay and Jamestown. Unfortunately, only 20 percent of these hopeful men and women were still alive in 1622.[39] Though no one knew this at the time of its founding, Jamestown bordered on a large swamp that in summer became a breeding ground for mosquitoes, while also preventing the circulation of fresh groundwater. Most Jamestown colonists therefore died from dysentery, malaria, or typhoid fever. Analysis of ancient cypress trees in both North Carolina and Virginia shows that these regions also suffered from a devastating drought between 1606 and 1612.

Something had to be done, and the man to do it was John Smith, an English explorer and future admiral who had taken over as leader of the Virginia colony. Smith realized that the future of the settlement entirely depended on its ability to secure its food supply from clean, well-watered fields and rivers.

This prompted him to systematically reconnoiter the surrounding territories, together with a handful of colonists and militia. The search for food was even more urgent because the relations between the English and their native neighbors had sunk to a new low. Several hungry colonists had defected to Indian villages in the hope of finding food there. Those who were smart enough to bring gifts, particularly firearms, were allowed to stay, but those who didn't were promptly killed. This brought tensions between the English and the local Indian tribes to a boil.

FIG. 39. Map of "New
Virginia" with the "Powhatan"
at top left and Pocahontas, with
bow, at far right

Even though it was bound to be dangerous, Smith insisted on proceeding with his expedition along the Chickahominy River. It didn't take long for the local Indians to discover his intentions, and they set up an ambush. While his escort was killed, Smith himself was captured, bound, and brought to the Indian chieftain, Wahunsenacawh. The Powhatan did not hesitate to summarily condemn him to death. But just as he raised his club with the intent of crushing Smith's skull, the chieftain's daughter Pocahontas threw herself across Smith's body to protect him from the blow. "At the minute of my execution, she hazarded the beating out of her own brains to save mine," Smith wrote later, "and not only that, but so prevailed with her father, that I was safely conducted to Jamestown."

Modern historians have cast doubt on the episode, but that did not prevent the story from spreading like wildfire throughout Europe. A young Indian woman had saved the life of an English colonist, just as the two parties were about to go to war! The fact that Pocahontas was a lovely young woman did not go unnoticed either, and soon, publishers rushed out engravings that depicted this remarkable event. It also prompted the creation of a map from 1640 by the Blaeu family, whom we shall meet shortly, which depicts the Chesapeake Bay region based on Smith's exploits.

In the meantime, clashes between the colonists and their Indian neighbors continued, and in 1613 Pocahontas herself was captured by Jamestown settlers. While in captivity, the seventeen-year-old girl was persuaded to convert to Christianity, and in 1614 she even married a local tobacco planter, John Rolfe. One year later, she bore him a son, Thomas Rolfe. The Virginia Company, always ready to promote its cause at court, instantly recognized the public relations value of the story and ordered that Pocahontas, now known as Rebecca Rolfe, be shipped to England with her husband and child. Here, they did the rounds, making presentations while raising funds for the Virginia Company. The Londoners were charmed and utterly delighted. Pocahontas herself, dressed in the latest fashion, created a sensation as a Pygmalion-like example of how a "savage" could be turned into a fair young lady. What better evidence of England's holy obligation to settle the New World and raise loyal and faithful Christians?

Unfortunately, the fairy tale did not have a happy end. Three years later, just as the family was preparing to return to Virginia, Pocahontas fell ill and died. She was buried in St. George's Church in Gravesend, Kent.

The struggles of these early settlements did not deter English colonists and explorers from establishing other settlements in North America, including Popham (in today's Maine, 1607); Bermuda (first settled in 1609); Plymouth (settled in 1620); and various locations in Newfoundland. Most of these were abandoned just a few years after their founding, but one that endured was the colony of Plymouth, located on a spot that had previously been surveyed by John Smith. The motive for Plymouth's foundation, however, was different from that of all other English settlements. Its colonists had come to America not to seek gold or to trade in fur but to escape religious persecution.

The English Colonies as a Religious Refuge

Religious tensions in England originated with King Henry VIII's frantic attempts to divorce his Spanish wife, Queen Catherine, and marry his English paramour Anne Boleyn instead. When the pope refused to give him an annulment, he saw no alternative but to break with Rome and create his own church, the Anglican Church, or Church of England. From that point on, the country was riven by tensions between traditional Catholics and the new Protestants: between those who remained loyal to the pope and those who embraced the Anglican Church. The English Reformation continued apace under Henry VIII's successor, King Edward VI, until the young king's untimely death led to the accession of Mary Tudor. Under her rule, the pendulum swung back to Roman Catholicism, which led to a vicious persecution of all things Protestant throughout the nation.

The next monarch, Queen Elizabeth I, tried to heal the divisions by adopting an Anglican liturgy that she hoped would be acceptable to believers on both sides of the divide. But during the subsequent interregnum of Oliver Cromwell, Lord Protector of England between 1646 and 1660, a new movement made its appearance: that of the Puritans. Similar to the Scottish Presbyterians, the Puritans wanted to rid the Anglican Church of any lingering Catholic elements, such as the office of the bishop, and to refocus the faith on Protestant piety and simplicity. The restoration of the English monarchy in 1660, however, put an abrupt end to their influence. Suddenly, there were thousands of English Puritans who desperately wanted to flee for fear of another bloody persecution, such as the one that had taken place during the reign of Mary Tudor.

They fastened their hope on the new English settlements that had been planted on American soil.

Already, a Puritan colony had been established as early as 1618 in Virginia, followed by a settlement in Salem, Massachusetts, in 1620. An offshoot of the Puritans—the so-called Pilgrims led by William Brewster—decided to establish a colony in Plymouth that same year. In their wake, thousands of Puritans left Europe to settle in New England. Thus, the foundation was laid for a New World community that would prize political and religious freedom above all else.

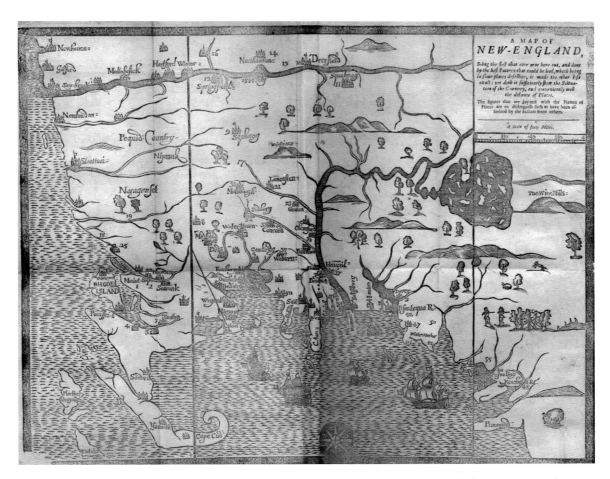

FIG. 40. A 1677 map of New England, including Plymouth, by William Hubbard. Based on a 1665 survey by William Reed, this is the first map to be drawn, engraved, and printed in North America. Although its geographic features are largely indistinct, its principal purpose was to identify the boundaries of the colony of Massachusetts.

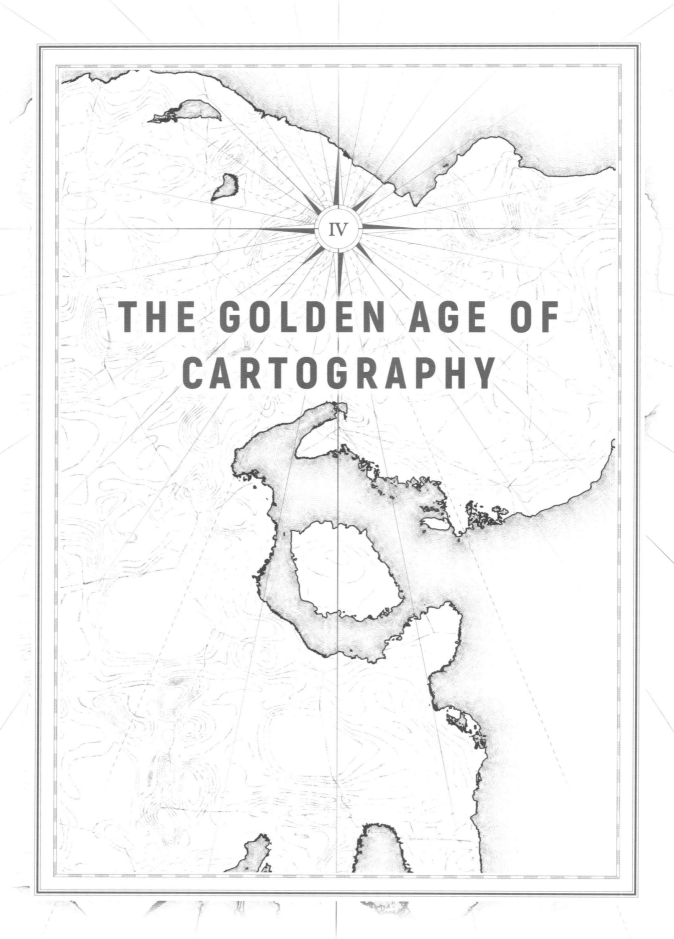

THE GOLDEN AGE OF
CARTOGRAPHY

IV

W E ARE VERY FORTUNATE THAT THE RAPID GROWTH OF European colonies in the New World coincided with a unique moment in art history. During this era, a variety of new and largely unrelated technologies conspired to produce an entirely new level of mapmaking, one that gives us a privileged window on the gestation of colonial America. For eighty long years, the seven provinces of Holland waged a bitter war to free themselves of the Habsburg yoke of the Spanish king Philip II. Long before that conflict would result in the Peace of Münster of 1648, the Dutch government had decided to become a leading player in the growing global economy of maritime trade, ultimately beating Spain at her own game. Their secret weapon for doing so was a revolutionary long-distance ship known as the "fluyt," first designed by Dutch shipwrights in 1581. This was an agile, three-masted vessel in which, shockingly, most armament was thrown overboard in favor of creating the maximum amount of cargo space. This resulted in its characteristic pear-shaped profile, with the hull bulking out to the sides. More importantly, without the ubiquitous rows of cannon, these eighty-foot ships became much easier to equip, maintain, and operate. The fluyt required a far smaller crew than large armed ships like galleons—no more than thirty-five sailors—while costing about half as much to build. Within decades, Amsterdam had replaced Lisbon as the leading shipyard of the seventeenth century.

Of course, the brazen lack of armament was a clear sign of the kind of strategy the Dutch were plotting. Their goal was not to prey on Spanish ships, as the French and English were doing, but to chart entirely new routes and territories for themselves. In 1596, a four-ship expedition led by Cornelis de Houtman dropped anchor on the shores of Java, thus beginning a nearly four-century

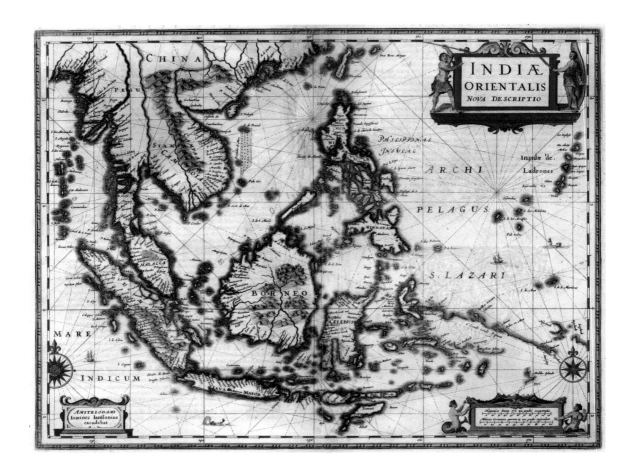

FIG. 41. *Indiae Orientalis Nova Descriptio*, "A New Description of East India," was published by Jan Jansson around 1630, based on the growing knowledge of the region reported by Dutch ships after their return from Southeast Asia. The map includes the first depiction of the rim of Australia in the southeast corner.

occupation of the island group known today as Indonesia. Five years later, Willem Janszoon, captain of the vessel *Duyfken* ("Little Dove"), discovered a large landmass that became known as *Terra Australis Incognita* ("Unknown Land in the South"), today simply known as Australia. Two years after that, another Dutch explorer named Jan Huygen published a book detailing the principal sea routes to the East Indies, which in one fell swoop eliminated Portugal's competitive edge. To fully exploit their gains, in 1602 Dutch traders formed the *Vereenigde Oost-Indische Compagnie* (VOC), the first multinational corporation in history. For the next two hundred years, the VOC would dominate European trade with Asia, dispatching 4,785 ships that carried 2.5 million tons of cargo, virtually monopolizing the trade in spices.

Along the way, Dutch mariners gathered a treasure trove of data about uncharted routes throughout Southeast Asia, which were collected by the

VOC as part of a secret collection, the *Zeefakel Atlas* ("Sea Torch Atlas"). Cartographers were sworn to secrecy not to divulge any of this sensitive data to anyone outside the company. But, of course, such a prohibition ran entirely against human nature when Holland was rapidly becoming the new European center of cartography. Indeed, somehow news of the *Duyfken* discovery of Australia was leaked, and Australia was included in Jan Jansson's map of the East Indies, published in 1630.

The most prominent of these map publishers were two families, those of Willem Blaeu and Jodocus Hondius, who drew much of their inspiration from maps developed by leading sixteenth-century Flemish cartographers such as Gerardus Mercator and Abraham Ortelius. But the flood of reconnaissance reports and maritime observations from long-distance ships was not the only reason why seventeenth-century maps suddenly reveal a major improvement in the detail and accuracy of their charts. Another key factor was the development of a new technology of image reproduction: copper engraving.

Through much of the sixteenth century, the mechanical printing of illustrations, including maps, involved the use of woodcuts, carved by leading artists such as the German painter Albrecht Dürer. However, woodcuts imposed severe limitations on the level of detail that the master carver could achieve, simply because of the inherent fragility of the medium of wood. Indeed, while Dürer achieved an unparalleled quality of detail in his woodcuts, most other artists could not match this virtuosity, which is why many sixteenth-century illustrations—including the maps that we saw up to this point—are relatively unsophisticated.

This changed with the invention of an entirely different form of mechanical reproduction, the engraving and reproduction of a copper plate. Rather than requiring the artist to carve into a wooden block, this new medium allowed the artist to draw on the metal surface with a fine sharp instrument called a "burin." Once the design was finished, the engraver would rub ink into the incisions and then use a press to reproduce the plate on a paper sheet. In this manner, an artist or a cartographer could produce an image with much greater precision and detail. Techniques such as hatching and cross-hatching, for example, which are extremely difficult to do in woodcuts, allow the engraver to suggest shading by creating highly concentrated areas of thin lines, which the human eye interprets as a single tone.

By the sixteenth century, the city of Antwerp in Flanders was becoming one of the leading centers in the production of illustrated books, in part because of its prominent role as a major center of European trade and the location of one of Europe's largest ports. Another factor was that its neighbor to the north, the seven provinces of Holland, had decided to join the Reformist movement of Calvin, while the territories under Spanish sway (including Flanders) remained resolutely Catholic. Known as *De Hervormde Kerk*, or "The Reformed Church," Dutch Calvinism did not tolerate any religious art in its churches, considering it a form of idolatry. During a phase known as the *Beeldenstorm*, mobs had stormed local churches to smash sculptures, deface paintings, and even destroy stained-glass windows. The inevitable result was a creative brain drain from these territories, as large numbers of painters, sculptors, weavers, glaziers, engravers, and cartographers fled to the south and settled in and around Antwerp.

Close to Antwerp was the town of Rupelmonde, where in 1512 one of the most influential cartographers was born. Surprisingly, Gerard Mercator was not a mariner, explorer, or even traveler himself. But he did nurture a near-insatiable curiosity about the rapidly expanding world of his time. Enrolled at the University of Leuven, he met the intelligentsia of his day, including the renowned anatomical physician Andreas Vesalius and the theologian George Cassander. While at university, he also fell under the spell of Gemma Frisius, a Dutch mathematician and cartographer who had begun to create three-dimensional globes based on the latest reports of overseas discoveries. While his first globe, made with the help of the engraver Gaspar van der Heyden, was made in wood, in 1535 Frisius set himself to create a new globe with the gores, the individual slices of the curved surface, made in copper so as to allow for greater detail. Mercator was enlisted in this ambitious enterprise, and together they produced the globe that today is in the collection of the Austrian National Library.

The experience of producing this stunning globe set Mercator on the path of his career. A voracious reader, he began to accumulate a vast library of over

FIG. 42. Terrestrial globe of Gemma Frisius and Gerard Mercator, 1536

a thousand books and maps, with which he tried to stay fully au courant with the latest discoveries in overseas territories. What he couldn't find in books he learned from travelers, merchants, and mariners whom he met along the docks of Antwerp harbor, and with whom he maintained a steady correspondence in six languages. Meanwhile, the vast demand for more Frisius-Mercator globes gave him a stable income with which he was able to purchase a home and marry a young local woman named Barbara Schellekens. She would bear him six children.

In 1538, Mercator produced his first attempt to create a map of the world, known as the *Orbis Imago* ("Image of the World"). Rejecting the conventional map formats of the time, Mercator struggled to accurately convey the spherical shape of the earth and thus arrived at a solution of using two heart shapes in an arrangement known as a "double cordiform projection." This was the first map to adopt Waldseemüller's claim of naming the Western Hemisphere "America," after Amerigo Vespucci, and to explicitly differentiate North and South America as two separate continents.

Unfortunately, this map had unforeseen consequences. In the growing tension between the northern and southern Netherlands, between strict Calvinism and Roman Catholicism, the Inquisition swooped down on Flanders to eradicate anyone suspected of Protestant sympathies. After the city of Leuven was briefly occupied by the Lutheran duke Wilhelm of Cleves (brother of Anne of Cleves, who was briefly married to the English King Henry VIII), the Inquisition was particularly intent on eradicating any Lutheran sentiments. This inspired some of Mercator's rivals to get rid of the young cartographer by denouncing him. They claimed, without any evidence, that the *Orbis Imago* contained Lutheran symbols.

Nothing more needed to be said. A warrant was issued for Mercator's arrest. The hapless cartographer got wind of the warrant and escaped by fleeing to his native town of Rupelmonde.

FIG. 43. A 1574 portrait of Gerard Mercator by Frans Hogenberg

The inquisitor tracked him down, however, and Mercator was hauled back and thrown in prison for seven months. There, he would have been tortured on the rack, standard procedure for many other victims of the Inquisition, were it not for some of his influential friends and clients. They intervened on his behalf, and in 1543 Mercator was released, vowing never again to utter another word about religious matters. Two years later, he was formally rehabilitated when he received the royal seal of approval from the Spanish emperor Charles V.

Mercator now focused all of his energies on a map that would combine all of the knowledge that modern explorers had accumulated to date.

This became his famous *Nova et Aucta Orbis Terrae Descriptio ad Usum Navigantium Emendate Accommodata* ("New and More Complete Representation of the Terrestrial Globe, properly adapted for use in Navigation"), printed in 1569. This magnificent map raised the bar for cartography on a number of levels. One is Mercator's use of numerous legends and citations to underscore the scientific basis for his illustrations. The 1569 world map, for example, includes a five-thousand-word narrative, organized in fifteen separate "legends." Second, Mercator used not only previous maps but also portolan charts prepared by Spanish and Portuguese sailors. Many earlier cartographers had ignored such charts, since their primary purpose was to help sailors plot a particular route across the sea, rather than to delineate specific geographical features of the landmass. But Mercator combined the two, thus producing a map that was of equal value to mariners as to explorers. As Mercator himself wrote, "It is from an equitable conciliation of all these documents that the dimensions and situations of the land are given here as accurately as possible."[40]

But the third and most important innovation of this map was its use of the so-called "Mercator projection," whereby the constant bearings of sailing courses (known as "rhumb lines") intersect with straight lines on the map for accurate charting. Mercator himself described this novel way of representing the earth as follows: "to spread on a plane the surface of the sphere in such a way that the positions of places shall correspond on all sides with each other, both in so far as true direction and distance are concerned and as correct longitudes and latitudes." This is why this map looks so "modern"; the Mercator projection is still being used today, including at NASA and National Geographic.

FIG. 45. *Europae descriptio,* "A Representation of Europe," drawn by Mercator in 1554 and published in 1595 by his son Rumold as part of his *Atlas*. Mercator reportedly worked on this map for twelve years.

It took eighteen separate sheets, printed from copper plates, to produce this immense map, resulting in a surface print of 79 by 49 inches (202 by 124 cm). Each sheet spans a longitude of 60 degrees. Records of the time suggest that several hundred copies were made, but only a few have survived; a copy once held in the city library of Breslau (today's Wrocław in Poland)was destroyed in World War II.

FIG. 46. *(Next page)* Gerard Mercator, *Nova et Aucta Orbis Terrae Descriptio ad Usum Navigantium Emendate Accommodata,* printed in 1569

Not surprisingly, Mercator's great advance had a major influence on the Dutch seventeenth-century school of cartography. His son Rumold continued to publish Mercator's maps and atlases, particularly since his father's 1554 map of Europe had become a major commercial success. According to one sixteenth-century source, it "attracted more praise from scholars everywhere than any similar geographical work which has ever been brought out."

Mercator's most loyal follower was another Flemish cartographer named Abraham Ortelius. Born in 1527 in Antwerp, Ortelius is recognized as the author of the first modern atlas, *Theatrum Orbis Terrarum,* or "Theater of

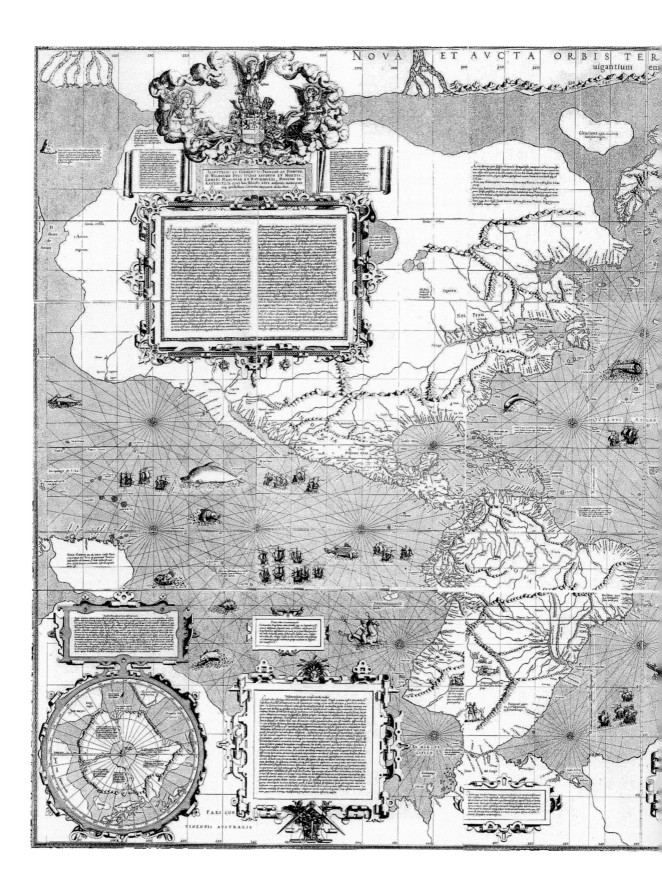

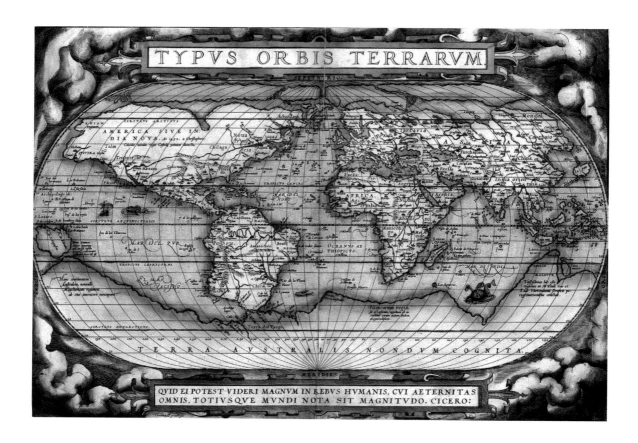

FIG. 47. Abraham Ortelius, *Typus Orbis Terrarum*, 1570

the World." Published in 1571, it established all that was known at the time about the Americas, even allowing for the fact that much of North America was left to the imagination and the shape of South America was largely faulty. Its popularity is attested by the fact that it was reissued between 1570 and 1612 in Latin, Dutch, French, German, Italian, Spanish, and English, even as new information about the Americas became available. Many scholars therefore consider this publication the beginning of the Golden Age of Dutch cartography.

Unfortunately, as in the case of his predecessor Mercator, Ortelius's family fell under suspicion for its rumored Reformist sympathies, and some members had to flee to London to avoid persecution. Ortelius remained, however, and in 1575 was appointed the official cartographer to Philip II, king of Spain, thus removing any suspicion of heretical activity. That also allowed Ortelius to travel widely, as Mercator never did. He is known to have visited Germany,

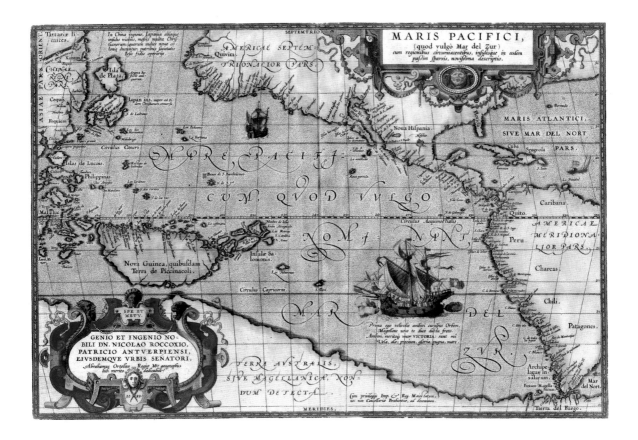

France, Italy, England, and Ireland, thus enhancing his scientific knowledge with personal observations.

As information about South America and the Pacific Ocean flooded into Antwerp and other ports from returning mariners, Ortelius rectified some of the errors in his depiction of South America in a follow-up map from 1589. This was entitled *Descriptio Maris Pacifici,* "Description of the Pacific Ocean," the first dedicated map of the Pacific ever produced. On this map, New Guinea is huge, while almost the entire bottom of the map is occupied by a landmass of truly gigantic proportions: *Terra Australis.* Ortelius, however, hedged his bets by declaring in his annotation that much of this continent was *nondum detecta,* "not yet explored."

Equally intriguing is the attention given to the island group of the Moluccas, which soon would become the focal point of Dutch exploration of the area. The map also reveals a unique quality of Ortelius's work: his use of pictorial flourishes, such as a cartouche with legends, sixteenth-century

FIG. 48. Abraham Ortelius, *Descriptio Maris Pacifici,* 1589. This map shows parts of North and South America as well as a vast coastline of the territory known as *Terra Australis,* Australia.

scrollwork ornaments, and calligraphy—elements that were often enhanced with hand-drawn coloring. And finally, Ortelius also created a new mystery that would haunt mapmakers for decades: the curious land of Frislant.

Frislant, or "Friesland," is today a northern province of the Netherlands. But in one of his maps of the North Atlantic, Ortelius placed a territory called Frislanda west of Greenland. What motivated him to include this legendary land is still an enigma, but most historians believe he got it from a sixteenth-century work entitled *De I Commentarii del Viaggio*, or "Travel Diaries," by the Venetians Nicolo and Antonio Zeno. As the book claimed, these two brothers once sailed across the North Atlantic—in the fourteenth century, at least a century before Columbus! The work was published in 1558 by a descendant, Nicolo Zeno, who argued that it was therefore the Zeno brothers, and not Columbus, who deserved credit for discovering the New World. To make his case, the book provided a stunningly detailed description of the North American coastline from Nova Scotia to Virginia, with lots of riveting detail about how the local natives hunted, what food they ate, what farming techniques they used, and what clothes they wore. How did the Zenos come by this information?

FIG. 49. *Frislant insula,* the "island of Frisland," in a Mercator map from 1623

Other than Frislanda, the Zeno map also included several other mysterious lands, including Icaria, Estotiland, and a place called Drogio. The truth is, no one knew exactly where "Frislanda"—or any other of these islands—was located, but many sailors, including captains who had sailed the North Atlantic route, swore that it existed. It was a marvelous place, they said, with beautiful buildings, canals, and people dressed with the most exquisite sense of fashion—a suspiciously close description of Venice. Moreover, the people were all seven to eight feet tall and cooked the most wonderful cuisine![41]

Because the Zeno family was known as a leading aristocratic family that once held the franchise for shipping Crusader armies from Venice to the Holy Land, the book had considerable credibility. Alas, modern scholarship has unmasked the Zeno work as a sixteenth-century hoax. That does not

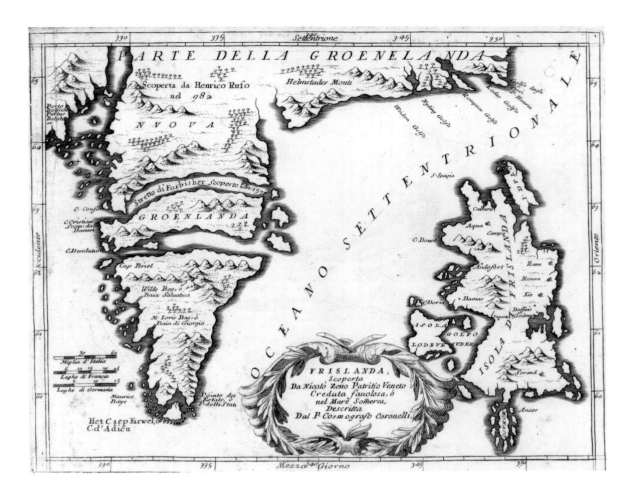

diminish the fact that because of the immense influence of Ortelius's maps, this phantom land continued to be featured on many maps of the period, like some latter-day Atlantis. That was also true for the wonderful prints produced by the three leaders of Dutch cartography: Johannes De Laet, Willem Blaeu, and Jodocus Hondius.

FIG. 50. Map of "Frislanda" and "Groenlanda," Greenland, based on the travel diaries published by Nicolo Zeno, in a Venetian map from 1690

The Rise of Dutch Maritime Power

The immense influence of maps by De Laet, Blaeu, and Hondius in the seventeenth century can hardly be overstated. The newly independent Dutch Seven Provinces had wasted no time in charting new sea routes to the Spice Islands and other destinations in Southeast Asia. The republic and its mercantile corporation, the VOC, had concluded that of all of its rivals, the weakest was Portugal. Though it had once been Spain's most important rival, in 1580 its last king died without heirs and Portugal was forced into a dynastic union with Spain. This essentially broke Portugal as a major naval power and rendered its possessions in Asia, Africa, and South America highly vulnerable to attack.

The Dutch, who as a result of their war with Spain had amassed a formidable navy, did not hesitate. They began to pounce on Portuguese colonies throughout the world. As we saw, they first captured Portuguese outposts in the East Indies as well as Ceylon (today's Sri Lanka), thus replacing the Portuguese as Europe's primary purveyors of spices and silk. Next, a Dutch flotilla occupied the Cape of Good Hope, at the southern tip of Africa, to protect the eastern route to Asia at its most vulnerable choke point. Here, they built a settlement that in future years would be known as Capetown.

They then set their sights on Portugal's other principal commodity from overseas colonies: sugar. Sugar, which in the seventeenth century was still considered a luxury product, was primarily cultivated in nearly three thousand plantations on the north coast of Portuguese Brazil, as well as Demerara (now Guyana) and the island of Surinam.

In fact, the sudden need for sugar mills had produced a veritable technological revolution in Europe in the design of axles, levers, gears, and other components of sugar-refining machinery. Unfortunately, sugar production was also very labor-intensive, requiring a vast and concentrated workforce. That inevitably made sugar plantations also very unhealthy places, and scores of native and imported laborers, including Native Americans, died as a result of smallpox, malaria, and yellow fever. In response, the Portuguese made a fateful decision: they decided to import slaves from their West African territories en masse. Thus, at the beginning of the seventeenth century the Portuguese led the world in the slave trade.

The Dutch assault on the Portuguese monopoly in sugar was first concentrated on the port of Recife, the center of Portuguese sugar cultivation in Brazil and today the capital of the Brazilian state of Pernambuco. The Dutch burned the nearby village of Olinda to the ground and developed Recife into one of the most formidable fortifications on the continent, renaming it Mauricia, or Mauritsstad. The new city included not only a host of new churches but also the first synagogue ever built in the Americas. From here, Dutch mariners rolled up most of Portugal's possessions on the Brazilian north coast while also occupying the islands of Curaçao, St. Maarten, and St. Eustatius, which remain Dutch Crown territories to this day. The huge cost of this campaign was funded in no small measure by their 1628 surprise seizure of a Spanish convoy that was carrying two hundred thousand pounds of silver from the Caribbean to Spain, where it was desperately needed to fill the badly depleted coffers of the Spanish Crown. The capture of so vast a fortune shocked Spain and pushed the Spanish monarchy close to bankruptcy, while making the Dutch West India Company (the western equivalent of the VOC) fabulously rich.

Not surprisingly, this news inspired Henricus Hondius, son of Jodocus Hondius, to produce a detailed map of Dutch Brazil in the mid-1630s. Most of the detail and descriptions in this map are concentrated along the coast, as the Dutch had little interest in venturing deep inland. As a result, the geographical features of the interior are largely speculative. The Hondius map is a great example of the way Dutch cartographers were able to capitalize on new developments overseas and rush out illustrations to an eager market. At the same time, it illustrates the shift of seventeenth-century cartography from Flemish Antwerp to Amsterdam, capital of Holland.

The Cartography of De Laet

The first Flemish cartographer to move north was Johannes De Laet. Born in Antwerp in 1581, De Laet was the son of a successful merchant of cloth, a main product of Flanders that was sold all over Europe. But the War of Independence fought by the Low Countries against their overlord, the Spanish Empire, had put a deep crimp in that business. When, in 1584, Spanish troops succeeded in occupying Antwerp, De Laet's family joined thousands of Flemish citizens fleeing to the North, for many were Protestant and feared the heavy hand of the Spanish Inquisition. The family settled in Amsterdam, and young Johannes was dispatched to the University of Leiden to study theology and philosophy.[42] This once again underscores the fact that in the seventeenth and eighteenth centuries, cartography was not yet a profession but rather

FIG. 51. *Accuratissima*
Brasiliae Tabula, "A Detailed
Map of Brazil," by Henricus
Hondius, early 1630s

a scholarly pursuit by highly educated and versatile men whose principal occupation lay elsewhere. That was certainly true of Johannes, for in 1603 he followed in his father's footsteps as a merchant and moved to London to seek his fortune. While there, he married the comely daughter of another Dutch expatriate, Jacobmijntje van Loor. Arguably, in London is where De Laet would have remained were it not that in 1607 Jacobmijntje died suddenly. Grief-stricken, De Laet returned to Holland and found a new occupation in land reclamation.

As Holland gained in prosperity, the nation recognized it needed more land to cultivate and feed its growing population, and one way to do that was to reclaim land from Holland's inner sea, the Zuider Zee.[43] The highly specialized technology of coaxing land from the sea brought De Laet in touch with a relatively new startup, the VWC, or the Dutch West India Company, modeled after the successful operation of the VOC. While the latter focused on Asia, the VWC was set up to supervise all trade with the Western Hemisphere and particularly the growing Dutch presence in North America. De Laet joined the VWC as one of its founding directors, and soon reaped its rich rewards. Married once more, to a young woman from Leiden, his growing wealth and stature gave him leisure to pursue other interests, including the development of an impressive library filled with books, manuscripts, globes, and art from prominent Dutch seventeenth-century painters. When the governor of newly conquered Dutch Brazil, Johan Maurits, commissioned a book entitled *Historia Naturalis Brasiliae*, or "Natural History of Brazil" to solidify the Dutch claim on the former Portuguese possessions, De Laet made sure it was published in Amsterdam in 1648. But De Laet was also deeply smitten with the growth of Dutch settlements in North America and had for some time nurtured the idea of creating a work that would likewise anchor the legitimacy of *Nova Belgica*, or "New Netherland," as these settlements were rather grandiosely referred to at the time. The result was an impressive compendium, bound in vellum, of which at least one copy is held in the United States as part of the Asbury Collection.

Proudly dedicated to the *Staten Generaal*, the parliament of the Dutch Republic, the book's stated intent was to secure the necessary funding for the provision of shipping, goods, and colonists to sustain these settlements through the difficult period of their initial growth.

To illustrate this appeal, De Laet included thirteen maps of the Americas, drafted based on on-site reports, charts, and soundings delivered by Dutch captains to the VWC upon their return home. Because of their astounding accuracy, these maps became so-called foundation maps, meaning that generations of cartographers, including Janszoon, Hondius, and Blaeu as well as French and English engravers, would use the De Laet maps as the basis for their own cartography, long after De Laet himself had died in 1649. A case in point is De Laet's highly detailed map of the East Coast of North America, from the Carolinas to Nova Scotia. This map is the first to name Manhattan, New Amsterdam, the Hudson River (or the "North River"), the Delaware River (or the "South River"), and Massachusetts.

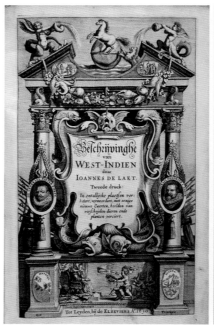

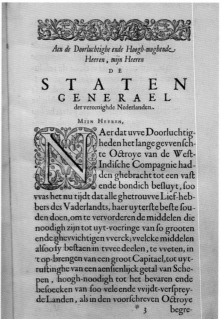

FIG. 52. Johannes De Laet, *Description of the West Indies*, 1630. The book, which contains thirteen maps of the Western Hemisphere based on the carts of the VWC, would form the basis for much of the seventeenth-century cartography of the Americas.

The House of Hondius

De Laet's close contemporary and fellow southerner Jodocus Hondius (the Latinized version of his Flemish name, Joost de Hondt) was born in 1563 in Wakken, Flanders, and grew up in Ghent, where he studied to become an engraver and instrument maker. In 1584, as the Spanish army was poised to occupy Flanders, he fled to London. Here, Hondius became fascinated with the wild exploits of Sir Francis Drake, as did much of the English population at the time. In 1589, he produced a rather crude map of New Albion, the territory claimed by Drake on the West Coast of North America, largely on the basis of accounts by eyewitnesses who had sailed on the voyage. Hondius was so impressed with his English hero that he even produced several portraits of him, which are now in the collection of the National Portrait Gallery in London.

Four years later, in 1594, Hondius decided to move to Amsterdam, as did many other artists, engravers, and instrument makers, following in De Laet's footsteps. The heated passions of the *Beeldenstorm* had passed, and while Calvinism was still the official state religion, Amsterdam was beginning to make

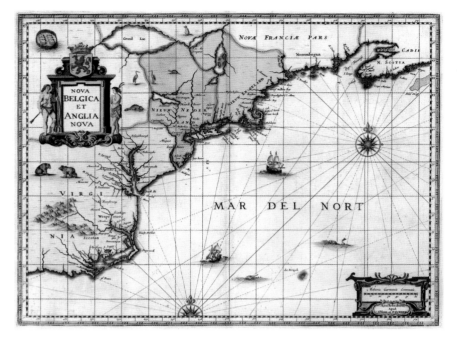

FIG. 53. Johannes De Laet, *Nova Belgica et Anglia Nova* ("New Netherland and New England"), 1630. This map became a foundation map for most seventeenth-century depictions of the Eastern Seaboard.

a name for itself as a center of religious tolerance and intellectual freedom. This in itself was rather remarkable, because elsewhere in Europe, political systems were exactly the opposite. France, Spain, Sweden, the German states, and Russia were steadily moving toward a highly concentrated form of absolutism in which the king ruled supreme, and tolerance of any dissent was hard to find. Even England, a bastion of parliamentary democracy, could not rid itself of the perennial tensions between Protestantism and Catholicism.

Holland, by contrast, was ruled by merchants and aristocrats who had only one thing on their minds: trade. In that sense, welcoming French Protestants, Spanish Jews, or English dissidents was good business. And so, in the decades to come, Amsterdam would become an intellectual powerhouse, giving rise to the publication of works by John Locke, Spinoza, Descartes, and scores of other philosophers of the Enlightenment.

For a population of just 1.5 million (as compared to five million English and twenty million French), that also meant that the wealth pouring into Holland vastly increased per capita income, boosting a middle class of traders, merchants, notaries, teachers, artisans, and writers. Hondius's choice for Amsterdam was therefore a wise one, not only because it was the nucleus of

FIG. 54. Jodocus Hondius in a
1619 engraving by his daughter,
Colette Hondius

Dutch maritime exploits but also because it offered an affluent market of buyers right on his doorstep.

To launch his new enterprise, Hondius purchased the original copper plates of Mercator's renowned atlas from Mercator's grandson and republished the work with thirty-six all-new maps, some of which he produced himself. Remarkably, in an age that gave little thought to copyright or authorship, Hondius went out of his way to recognize Mercator as the original author, while identifying himself as merely the publisher. One significant map from this series is the 1606 illustration of *Septentrio America*, "Septentrional America," as North America was known in the seventeenth century. This was one of the most accurate depictions of the Americas at the time, notwithstanding the exaggerated breadth of the North American continent.

The coastlines of South America are particularly detailed and identified with place-names, which shows once more that Hondius took care to document his maps with the latest information. Another unique element is the profusion of illustrative detail, such as the scene on the bottom left that shows a group of indigenous men and women preparing what appears to be an intoxicating drink. To the right, we see another group of natives traveling in a canoe, in striking contrast to a man-of-war proudly flying the flag of the Seven Provinces.

An even more influential map was Hondius's attempt to capture the situation in English Virginia and the Carolinas, which as we saw were going through a difficult period of colonization. Given that so much of this region was in flux, Hondius based his work on two authoritative sources, John White's map of Virginia and Jacques Le Moyne's map of Spanish Florida, both dating to the late sixteenth century.

Many of the details, such as the names and locations of prominent mountains, lakes, and rivers, were derived from Le Moyne's original. Some of Hondius's changes, such as the depiction of the River May, were erroneous and would confound explorers for the next 150 years. Nevertheless, the Hondius

FIG. 55. Jodocus Hondius,
Septentrio America, 1606

map served as the leading reference for the region for much of the seventeenth century. After Jodocus died in 1612 at age forty-eight, the business was continued by his widow, his sons Henricus and Jodocus Jr., as well as a son-in-law, Jan Jansson, whose map of the East Indies we previously saw. With the paterfamilias no longer around, the family decided to just rerelease the original 1606 atlas with steady updates, which ultimately led to fifty editions around Europe, translated in all of the main European languages. These atlases are referred to as the Mercator/Hondius/Jansson series, giving due credit to all of the principal contributors.

FIG. 56. Jodocus Hondius, "A New Description of the American Provinces of Virginia and Florida," 1623

The House of Blaeu

One of Hondius's main rivals in Amsterdam was the House of Blaeu ("Blue" in Dutch), including father Willem and sons Cornelis and Johannes. Unlike previous cartographers, Blaeu was a born and bred Dutchman, the son of a herring salesman who grew up in Alkmaar. There, he found himself attracted to mathematics and astronomy. He even studied with the renowned Danish astronomer Tycho Brahe, one of the last "naked-eye" astronomers who is credited with the identification of *stellae novae*, "new stars"—or what today we call "supernovas." Like Ortelius, he specialized in the design of instruments and globes and eventually set up his own printing shop. He soon attracted a broad clientele of renowned poets, authors, and philosophers, including Grotius, Vondel, Vossius, and Descartes, which brought him to the attention of the VOC, the Dutch East India Company. In 1633, he was appointed VOC's official cartographer, which gave him access to the treasure trove of maps, charts, and portolan maps that the VOC had accumulated over the past decades—a major advantage over his rivals.

One of these rivals was Jan Jansson, who as it happened had set up his print shop right next door to the Blaeu store! Needless to say, while this was very convenient for customers, it also intensified the competition between the two leading cartographers of the mid-seventeenth century. One possibly apocryphal story tells us that Willem Janszoon was so worried about the possible confusion between his name and that of his rival, Jan Jansson (a different spelling of the same patronym, "son of Jan"), that he decided to assume the nickname of his grandfather, *Blauwe Willem*, or "Blue William." From that moment on, he was known as Willem Janszoon Blaeu.

In 1635, the same year that Jan Jansson published a detailed map of South America, Blaeu came out with a major collection of maps under the title *Atlas Novus*, "New Atlas." In an effort to seek a competitive advantage, Blaeu had quietly acquired the copperplates of dozens of maps by Hondius from Hondius's widow (and his rival's mother-in-law!), just as Hondius himself had once purchased the original Mercator plates from Mercator's widow. This explains why the evolution of Dutch seventeenth-century cartography is remarkably consistent in the growth of its quality and detail, since it always drew from what preceding generations had produced while augmenting that knowledge with a steady stream of new intelligence.

FIG. 57. Portrait of Willem Janszoon Blaeu by Thomas de Keyser, early seventeenth century

In that sense, Blaeu's 1636 map of the Americas, *Americae Nova Tabula,* offered a number of improvements over previous editions. For one, Blaeu chose not to depict California as an island, a common misconception at the time. With a fine eye for ornamental detail, he also continued the trend of embellishing maps with close-up images of the various indigenous peoples who lived in these territories. In this case, that led to ten miniature depictions of Native Americans in various poses and occupations, real or imagined. Furthermore, along the top he added nine views of the most prominent cities and ports in the Americas at that time, which gives us an unprecedented impression of Havana, Cartagena, Mexico, Rio de Janeiro, and Olinda as they appeared in the 1630s. Meanwhile, the Atlantic and Pacific oceans are decorated with frigates, cargo ships, and sea monsters, to enhance the sense of drama and adventure of these long sea voyages. As a result, Blaeu's maps perfectly capture the new role

FIG. 58. *Americae Nova Tabula*, "New Map of America," originally published by Willem Blaeu in 1636

of these maps in the milieu of affluent seventeenth-century burghers: not as documents of maritime science but as conversation pieces, as curiosities that could be endlessly pored over and discussed during the long winter months.

Not coincidentally, these beautiful maps also became status symbols, to be prominently displayed on the wall of the main sitting room, there to advertise the owner's sophistication and erudition. This explains why Blaeu's maps would become a key attribute in the art of Johannes Vermeer, one of the leading artists of the Dutch seventeenth century. Vermeer's intimate observations of domestic life in the homes of the well-to-do invariably feature a Blaeu map, not only to anchor his fondness for geometric composition but also to remind his audience of the source of the Dutch bourgeoisie's newfound wealth.

After Willem Blaeu died in 1638, his flourishing business was taken over by his son Johannes (sometimes erroneously referred to as "Joan" in the literature), with his other son, Cornelis, in a supporting role. Johannes also succeeded his father as the lead cartographer of the VOC and eventually published an opus magnus of his own: the *Atlas Major*. But then, in 1672, tragedy struck. A fire broke out and destroyed much of the shop's stock of maps, books, atlases, and copper plates. Devastated by this loss, Johannes died less than a year later.

FIG. 59. Johannes Vermeer, *The Art of Painting*, 1666–1668. The background depicts a map of the Seven Provinces of Holland, published by Willem Blaeu and Balthasar Floriszoon van Berckenrode in 1621.

The Birth of New Amsterdam

While much of Dutch exploration in the first decades of the seventeenth century was focused on the Moluccans and the former Portuguese possessions in Africa and Brazil, something else was stirring on the East Coast of North America. In 1609, the VOC had retained an English explorer named Henry Hudson to see if he could plot a so-called Northwest Passage to the East, using an Arctic route from Norway through the Canadian Arctic archipelago. This was a counterpoint to attempts to find the Northeast Passage to the Indies, along the Arctic coast of Russia, which Hudson had previously attempted to chart for English traders.

Hudson accepted the Northwest challenge and in the process stumbled on a huge saltwater lake surrounded by today's Quebec, Ontario, Manitoba, and Nunavut. Today, it is known as Hudson Bay. Of even greater consequence was the mariner's exploration of a 315-mile river that ran from the Adirondack Mountains along the spine of today's New York State, ending near an island that the local Lenape Indians called Manna-hata. Back in Holland, the strategic value of this river, which likewise would soon bear the explorer's name, was instantly recognized. Here, at last, was an excellent way to connect with the Iroquois Indians—the same Indians against whom the French of Quebec had entered into an alliance with local tribes. The Dutch West India Company wasted no time in exploiting this opportunity, and just five years after Hudson's landmark voyage, a permanent Dutch settlement was built on the Upper Hudson River. It was called Fort Nassau, in honor of the royal house of Orange-Nassau, whose members served as quasi-republican stadtholders of the Dutch Seven Provinces.

Fort Nassau (later called Fort Orange) was managed as a corporate overseas office. The parsimonious Dutch limited its population to just fifty people—half soldiers, half traders—since its objective was not to colonize but to make money. This they did through the trade in furs with local Indians, just as the French were doing up north in Quebec. Of course, the lack of military defenses also made this post extremely vulnerable; all it would take for the French or English to put a stop to this lucrative trade was to sail up the Hudson and bombard the tiny outpost to smithereens. Thus the idea was born to fortify the mouth of the Hudson and protect the access way up north—for example, by building a fort on this island called Manna-hata. Negotiations with the local Lenape Indians were quickly finalized, and thus the property rights to the island were purchased for the sum of sixty guilders, or about $5,900 in today's currency.[44] Construction of a settlement was begun in 1625. Today, that year is recognized as the birthdate of New York City.

Of course, England, Holland's chief competitor at this time, was alarmed by the string of Dutch successes and refused to acknowledge the Dutch claim on Manhattan. In 1600, the English had established an East India Company of their own, which shortly thereafter established a foothold in India. A hundred years later, England was in virtual control of the entire Indian subcontinent. At the same time, English companies had been busy expanding their presence on

America's East Coast. In 1629, non-separatist Puritans had established a large colony of four hundred settlers in Massachusetts Bay, which ten years later had grown to a town of twenty thousand. Other Puritan colonies followed in New Haven and Saybrook.

Furthermore, Puritans were not the only religious minority that sought safe haven in North America. In 1632 Lord Baltimore, the former secretary of state to the English king Charles I, petitioned the king for permission to establish a large settlement north of the Potomac River for English Catholics, another persecuted group. The king agreed, provided this new colony was named after his much-beloved consort, Henrietta Maria of France, who was likewise a Catholic. Thus, the colony named "Maryland" was born.

As a result, the scope of English territory in the mid-seventeenth century America was considerably larger than it had been at the dawn of the century, and any attempts by a foreign power to encroach on that territory were to be repulsed at all costs. It didn't help that England and Holland, who by now were recognized as the reigning maritime powers of the world, were soon enmeshed in a series of wars throughout much of the second half of the seventeenth century. The Dutch burghers of Manhattan realized that they needed to bulk up, and fast, if they were to resist the inevitable pressure that England was expected to bring to bear. Thus, in the years to follow, a steady flow of Belgian, French, German, Scandinavian, and even English immigrants made their way to Manhattan, now dubbed "New Amsterdam," as well as surrounding territories. This gave the new colony a uniquely international flavor that, in a way, has persisted to this day. By 1674, New Netherland (or *Nova Belgica* as it is called on the maps of the era) had a population of between seven and eight thousand inhabitants, spread across parts of today's New York, New Jersey, Delaware, and Connecticut.

Mapmakers followed this tense overseas rivalry with keen interest, of course.

Both British and Dutch settlements were documented and updated on maps by Johannes De Laet and Hessel Gerritszoon, including a series of maps of the coastline of *Nova Anglia, Novum Belgium et Virginia,* produced between 1630 and 1633. One of these, later reprinted by Nicholas Visscher, shows perspective views of New Amsterdam, the area now known as Manhattan, as it appeared at that time. It even shows the wall that later became known as Wall Street.

The outcome of this great international competition was never really in doubt. The four Anglo-Dutch Wars fought between 1652 and 1684 drained the treasury of both combatants, but England, with its rapidly growing imperial base, was in a far better position to hold out than the tiny Dutch republic. Even though the Dutch admiral Michiel de Ruyter scored a stunning coup in 1667, when he led a flotilla up the Thames Estuary and destroyed the pride of the English fleet, by the end of the century Dutch maritime might was a shadow of its former self. In 1664, the English succeeded in taking possession of New Amsterdam and promptly renamed it "New Yorck," after the English Duke of York who would soon ascend the throne as King James II. The conquest was actually a rather gentlemanly affair, with documents of transfer specifying the rights of New Amsterdam's citizens under the new regime, including full religious tolerance. The transfer was officially recognized in 1674 by the Treaty of Westminster, which ended the Third Anglo-Dutch War.

Not all of the Dutch history in Manhattan was erased, however. Even though Robert Holmes's map of Manhattan, printed to document the 1664 acquisition, shows New York Harbor filled with triumphant English warships, it did include some notable Dutch features, such as the house of the Dutch governor on "Whitehall" street, a "Battery" of cannon, and a barricade known as "Wall Street," both of which had been installed in 1643 to ward off any potential attacks by Native Americans. All these names are still in use today; the battery would become Battery Park, and of course, Wall Street is today a center of world finance. Scores of original Dutch citizens chose to stay in New York, including the last Dutch governor, Peter Stuyvesant, as did many of the local millers and shopkeepers.

Nevertheless, from this time forward, the history of the American colonies would primarily be written by the English. In time, the English colonies would become of tremendous importance to the motherland—so much so, in fact, that in 1776 England was prepared to expend all of its treasure, and the cream of its forces, to maintain its presence in America.

But first, the English settlers would have to contend with their other rivals on the continent: most notably, the French and the Spanish colonies.

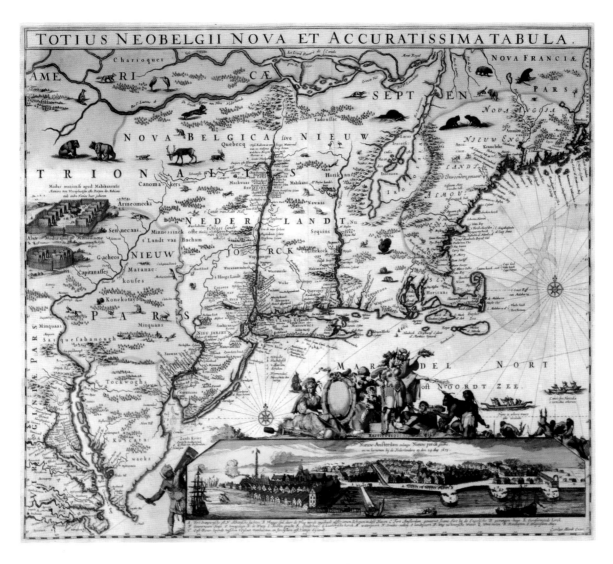

FIG. 60. Nicholas Visscher's map of *Nova Belgica*, or "New Netherland," shows an inset view of *New Amsterdam*. The map visibly shows the region's vulnerability to attack.

THE
EIGHTEENTH-CENTURY
COLONIZATION OF
AMERICA

"I THANK GOD THAT MY LOT IS TO BE AN AMERICAN FARMER instead of a Russian boor or a Hungarian peasant," wrote a colonist in Virginia in 1768; "could the English farmer have some of those privileges we possess, they would be the first of their class in the world."[45]

The writer, French-born J. Hector St. John de Crèvecoeur, was not wrong. Once the far-flung settlements in the English-speaking colonies sunk roots and became permanent villages or towns, a wave of immigrants from all over Europe set their sights on English North America. German farmers settled in the fields of Pennsylvania, Maryland, and New York, eventually making up of over 10 percent of all European colonists by the mid-eighteenth century. Large numbers of Scotch-Irish, though less numerous than Germans, preferred to settle in urban areas and would later excel in politics, including two signers of the Declaration of Independence. And after Louis XIV's renunciation of the Edict of Nantes, which deprived French citizens of the right to choose their religion, tens of thousands of French Huguenots crossed the Atlantic to settle in and around the coastal cities, including such prominent families as the Reveres, the Bowdoins, and the Faneuils in Boston and the De Lanceys and Jays in New York.[46]

But it was the European farmer who would create the basic economic foundation of the new colonies. "Every year I kill from 1,500 to 2,000 weight of pork, 1,200 of beef, half a dozen of good wethers in harvest," de Crèvecoeur wrote with pride, "and of fowls my wife has always a great stock." To de Crèvecoeur and thousands of other farmers in the eighteenth century, life in this arcadia was an opportunity for humankind to start afresh—free from politics, the stultifying strictures of European society, and the political ambitions of its urban elite. "I ceased to ramble in imagination through the wide world," he explained, "my excursions have not exceeded the bounds of my farm, and all my principal pleasures are now centered within its scanty limits."

By the same token, de Crèvecoeur felt that the experience of being a settler-farmer had taught him what really matters in the world: a return to the essential human virtues of love, work, and family. "When I contemplate my wife by my fireside while she either spins, knits, darns or suckles our child," he wrote, "I cannot describe the various emotions of love, of gratitude, of conscious pride, which thrill in my heart."[47]

For many of us, the eighteenth century is the era of the Baroque and composers like Johann Sebastian Bach and Georg Friedrich Handel. It is also a period marked by a new wave of architecture called "classicism," prompted by the discovery of amazing Roman structures and frescoes under the ashes of Pompeii. In painting, it was the era of a new form of art, Rococo, which displaced Holland and Italy as the European centers of artistic endeavor and made France the new nexus of painting and fashion.

But it was also the era of the Counter-Reformation. As the flood of wealth from the Americas continued to pour into Spanish coffers, it galvanized a campaign to combat the Protestant Reformation of Luther, Calvin, and other reformers. This led to a hardening of the stance between the Protestant North and the Catholic South, a conflict that directly affected the French emigration to the five colonial regions of *Nouvelle France*, "New France."

French Colonization in North America

For a long time, the French Crown did not consider the colonization of North America a matter of high priority. Through much of the early seventeenth century, French attempts to build permanent settlements had ended in failure. The settlement of Île-Saint-Croix on the Bay of Fundy in today's New Brunswick, founded in 1604, was abandoned in 1607, then reestablished in 1610, only to be destroyed in 1613. Quebec, France's most prominent colony, suffered greatly from disease as well as its unforgiving climate, so that by 1630 its population numbered slightly more than one hundred hardy colonists, in stark contrast to the prosperous English colonies farther south. In 1627 Cardinal Richelieu, who

FIG. 61. *The Arrival of the French Girls at Quebec* by Charles William Jefferys

ruled France in all but name, decided to place French colonization in America on a sound footing by authorizing a New France Corporation, in imitation of the Dutch and British West India Companies. But he made the fateful error of forbidding any non-Catholics to move there. As a result, thousands of highly educated French fled to the English colonies instead.[48] Worse, Richelieu also subjected farmers in French overseas territory to a semifeudal system, similar to the way French farmers were kept as mere serfs at home, thus depriving them of freehold land titles. Instead, the French habitants were compelled to lease their farm at a cost of 10 percent of the annual crop.[49]

All this explains why in 1650, when the colonization of English lands was in full swing, the grandiosely named territory of "New France" had fewer than seven hundred colonists, which left it vulnerable to increasingly bold incursions by hostile Iroquois tribes. When in 1666 the new king, Louis XIV, ordered a census of his French colonies, the population had barely risen to over three thousand, two-thirds of whom were men.

Louis XIV, the *Roi Soleil*, or "Sun King," decided to act. He recognized that French Canada could become a strategic asset in the growing contest between the European superpowers. But—and this was a big "but"—these settlements had to demonstrate their long-term viability and produce goods that could justify the costs of maintaining them.

In contrast to his predecessor, Louis XIV was a highly intelligent and perceptive man. He realized that what the colonists needed foremost was womenfolk, so that the male settlers could marry and begin families of their own. In response, the French Crown launched an ambitious program known as *Les filles du roi,* "The King's Daughters," which promised every woman between the age of fifteen and thirty free passage to New France, as well as a grant of either goods or money to serve as her dowry. French records show that around eight hundred young women, all commoners from Paris, Normandy, or central-west France, answered the call. Within two years, most of them were married. As a result, by 1672, the population of New France had doubled, to sixty-seven hundred.[50] What's more, the ready access to a rich diet of meat, fish, and clean water enabled these women to bear, on average, around 30 percent more children than those who remained in France.

Another strategy in the effort to populate New France was to make these new regions attractive not only financially but also visually. The only medium that could do so was the printed map, usually colored by hand, which could be produced and distributed cheaply and in great numbers. This, Louis knew, was particularly important, since most Dutch or English maps either ignored New France entirely or left it deliberately ill-defined. The king therefore authorized the establishment of a Royal Cartography Department with the French cartographer Nicolas Sanson in charge. The choice of Sanson was not surprising. Even Cardinal Richelieu (as well as his mentee, Louis XIII) had been impressed by Sanson's early maps; several accounts suggest that the mapmaker was retained as a tutor of geography for both Louis XIII and Louis XIV. The royal appointment was bittersweet, however, because in 1648 Sanson had lost his son Nicolas in the fighting of the Fronde—Louis XIV's bloody campaign to decapitate the power of the nobility and establish himself as an absolutist monarch.

Two years later, in 1650, Sanson produced the first map of North America for his royal patron. For the first time it charted the Great Lakes, and it also listed the names of Lake Ontario and Lake Superior, while in the south it identified Santa Fe as well as the lands of the Apache, Navajo, and Taos Indians.

FIG. 62. Portrait of Nicolas Sanson by Konrad Westermayr, ca. 1802

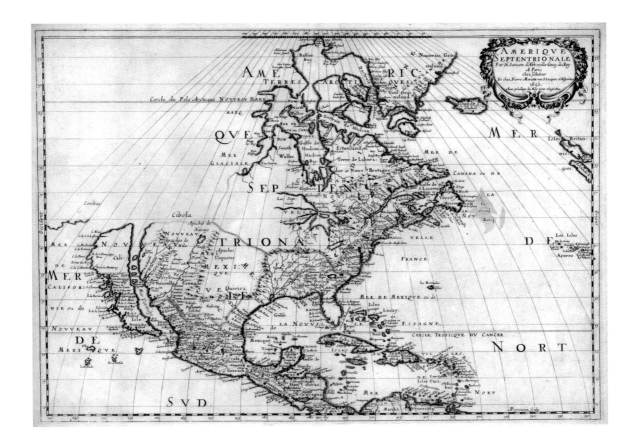

Sanson also produced an authoritative set of maps of South America that would guide explorers for many decades to come. Among others, he charted the lands of today's Chile, Paraguay, Uruguay, Argentina, Venezuela, and Colombia, including the mystical location of El Dorado—the legendary city of gold that continued to fascinate explorers.

In the meantime, French explorers and their militias were working hard to extend the reach of New France across the continent. In 1682, René-Robert Cavelier traveled down the Ohio River and the Mississippi River valleys as far south as the Gulf of Mexico, claiming both for *la Nouvelle France.* This prompted several mapmakers to publish depictions showing the North American continent all but consumed by triumphant French power, including a map by Claude Bernou that illustrated the conquest of the Mississippi River valley.

Of course, much of this was pure propaganda, for the reality was starkly different. In today's Texas, Cavelier had indeed tried to establish a settlement, named

FIG. 63. Nicholas Sanson, *l'Amérique Septentrionale* ("North America"), published in 1650 as part of an atlas entitled *Cartes générales de toutes les parties du monde.* In this map, California is still depicted as an island.

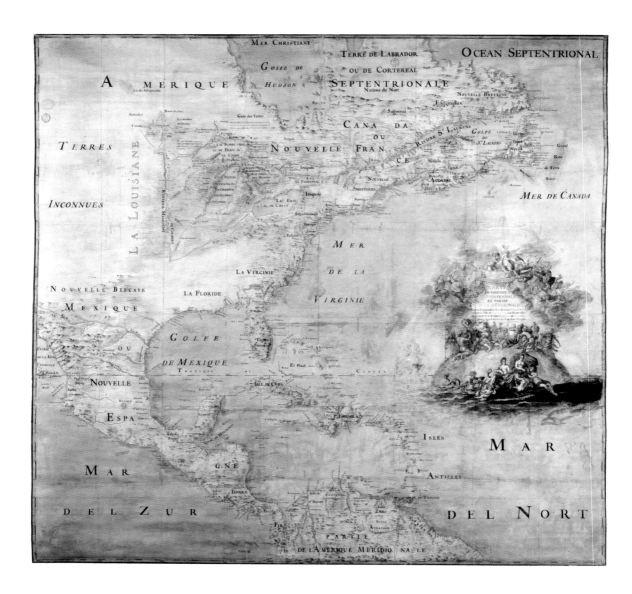

FIG. 64. Claude Bernou, *Carte de l'Amérique Septentrionale*, 1682

Fort-Saint-Louis, but by 1688 the colonists had disappeared, succumbed to either disease or persistent Indian attacks. Attempts to create settlements in the territory named "Louisiana," named after King Louis XIV, were more successful but came at a great cost. Between 1717 and 1730, for example, the French *Compagnie d'Occident*, or "Company of the West," shipped fifty-four hundred colonists from Europe and six thousand African slaves from Senegal and Benin, destined for sugar and tobacco plantations. Many of these European colonists were French conscripts, vagabonds, or criminals, since few free citizens were attracted to the swampy fields and humid subtropical climate of Louisiana. The harsh conditions inevitably took a heavy toll, in the form of malaria and dysentery. Many of the colonists fled to Spanish Florida where conditions were rumored to be better. Inevitably, in 1731 the *Compagnie d'Occident* went bankrupt with a loss of over 20 million livres, and France ceased most shipping to Louisiana. By that time the territory had become an unbearable drain on the French treasury. Alan Taylor has estimated that Louisiana cost the French around 800,000 livres annually, roughly the equivalent of $10 million in today's currency.[51]

Investment in the French territories was dealt a further blow by a curious pyramid scheme that shook the French financial system to its core. Such financial schemes were nothing new in the eighteenth century. In Holland, for example, investors had created a huge speculative bubble in the trade of exotic tulip species, a phenomenon known as Tulip Mania. When the bubble burst in February of 1637, much of the bourse collapsed.

Something similar, but with graver consequences, unfolded in 1716 when the Duke of Orléans, the regent for the youthful King Louis XV, placed a British economist named John Law in charge of a new bank, the *Banque Générale Privée*. Law passionately believed that currency should be issued in the form of promissory notes, backed by trade obligations. Thus was born the idea of paper currency, of bills, to replace coins (such as the gold Louis) then in circulation. The problem was that Law secured his notes with France's trade monopoly in Louisiana, including the trade nexus of the Mississippi Delta. And as we saw, all of the commercial activity in this region was supervised by the *Compagnie d'Occident*, which was nearing bankruptcy.

The motive for Law's risky scheme was simple: France was all but bankrupt as well. Its treasury had been depleted by Louis XIV's zest for building and war-making. Thus, Law was under pressure to promote the Louisiana venture as an economic success of unprecedented proportions, thereby boosting the value of its stock and paper notes.

But the scheme began to unravel when, in 1719, rumors began to circulate on the Paris bourse that mineral deposits, including gold, had been found in Louisiana. Given the mad scramble for El Dorado in centuries past, this claim sounded credible, and investors rushed to buy stock in the *Compagnie d'Occident*, thus inflating the value of Law's notes. In 1720, the bubble burst when

FIG. 65. Map of *La Louisiane* by Christoph Weigel of 1719, used to promote sales of notes issued by the *Banque Générale Privée*, as shown by the vignette of speculators (bottom right)

the value of the notes was revealed to exceed the value of actual coinage in France's treasury by far—or the value of Mississippi trade, for that matter. The Company of the West collapsed, investors suffered heavy losses, and Law fled to Venice, where he spent his remaining years gambling away his fortune. Small wonder, then, that eighty years later, Napoléon Bonaparte was all too happy to sell Louisiana to the government of the new United States in what become known as the Louisiana Purchase.

As part of its "stock offering," Law had commissioned a map of *La Louisiane* from the German cartographer Christoph Weigel the Elder.

This signaled that at long last German cartography was making a comeback, having long ceded the business to Dutch mapmakers. Indeed, Weigel was followed by several other prominent cartographers, including Johann Baptiste Homann and Heinrich Scherer.

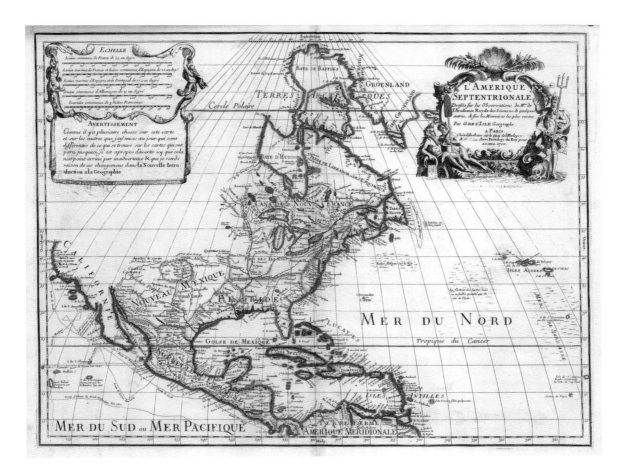

In the meantime, Sanson had been succeeded as royal cartographer by Guillaume De L'Isle. He, too, set himself to produce the first truly accurate map of the Mississippi River valley, Texas, and the region of Ohio, which the French had claimed before the British could properly colonize the area. His 1700 depiction of *l'Amérique Septentrionale*, "North America," is important for several reasons. It depicts the continent of North America from Baffin Bay down to the Spanish Main, westward to Cape Mendocino, and eastward to the Azores and the Sargasso Sea. Most scholars consider this a foundational map of America, even though much of the West was still ill-defined. The map also shows California as a peninsular state, thus firmly ending the myth of California as an island.

Then came the Treaty of Utrecht of 1715, which brought an end to the War of the Spanish Succession. As we will see, it also put a sudden brake on French

FIG. 66. Guillaume De L'Isle, *l'Amérique Septentrionale* ("North America"), produced in 1700 and published by Covens and Mortier in 1708

expansion in North America. The sun was slowly setting on France's possessions in this continent. Perhaps in response, De L'Isle shifted his focus and produced a series of detailed maps of the Middle East, which was beginning to attract the eye of French speculators.

The Spanish Territories in North America

Where were the Spanish while all this was going on? Were they still a major force in North America, or was the attention of the Spanish Crown now resolutely focused on its possessions in the southern part of the hemisphere? The answer is that although some seventeenth-century maps still show Spanish Florida extending into Georgia, Alabama, Mississippi, and South Carolina, in reality Spain controlled only the immediate ground around its missions and fortified settlements. The focus of the Spanish Crown remained on South America, rather than the north. Growing pressure from English and French colonists sapped Spanish control even further, so that by the mid-eighteenth century, Spanish Florida had been reduced to its principal centers of St. Augustine, Pensacola, and St. Marks in present-day Florida. To the Spanish Crown, it mattered not. No gold was ever found in "Spanish Florida," in contrast to its territories in Mexico, Bolivia, and Peru. Nor did the Spanish make any concerted effort to develop plantations, beyond the modest attempts by its missions, since there was not sufficient local labor that could be indentured.

The idea of mission towns, or *reducciones*, was originally conceived by Francisco de Toledo, viceroy of Peru, as "concentration areas" to better govern the local population. But in time, many of these missions became havens for natives desperate to escape the slave hunters. The development of such missions was the brainchild of the Jesuits, or the Society of Jesus, founded in 1539 by Spanish theologian Ignatius of Loyola. The Jesuits saw themselves as elite soldiers on the front lines of the Counter-Reformation. They recognized that education was the key to raising new generations beholden to Catholic doctrine, or to attract pagan souls to Christianity through religious instruction. As a result, by the mid-seventeenth century, Jesuits ran more than five hundred schools and universities across Europe as well as the newly colonized Spanish territories overseas.

FIG. 67. John Ogilby, *View of St. Augustine*, 1671. This was the most important Spanish settlement in North America and served as the base of Spanish operations, though Ogilby's depiction is mostly imaginary.

These Spanish missions were built not only in Spanish Florida and the territories in Central and South America but also on the west coast of "New Spain," in the region the Spanish referred to as *Las Californias*. Here, the Jesuit Eusebio Kino built the first Spanish mission, known as Misión San Bruno, in 1683, but this settlement failed soon thereafter. A more successful attempt was made in Loreto in present-day Mexico, where the Jesuit Juan María de Salvatierra built a settlement in 1697, commonly regarded as the first permanent European settlement in California. In the decades to come, the Jesuits (as well as the Franciscans and the Dominicans) would build a total of twenty-one missions up and down the California peninsula and in Baja California, connected by the six-hundred-mile *Camino Real*, or "Royal Road."

From the beginning, it was clear that these frontier settlements had to be entirely self-sustaining, drawing their sustenance from the cultivation of local crops such as maize, as well as the domestication of native (and some imported) livestock. Largely through the determined efforts of the padres and their military escorts, several of the Jesuit missions became veritable townships with churches, schools, libraries, and even local industries. Unfortunately, the Spanish clergy and their retainers also introduced a host of European diseases

FIG. 68. The Mission of San Juan Capistrano in today's Orange County, California, built by Spanish Franciscans, is one of the loveliest missions from the eighteenth century.

that decimated the indigenous peoples. For example, it has been estimated that in the century after the foundation of the first Spanish missions, the Native American population of Baja California declined from sixty thousand to twenty-one thousand; by 1800, their number had dwindled to fifty-nine hundred.[52]

From 1700 onward, another threat emerged in the eastern part of New Spain in the form of attacks by English and Scottish raiders from Carolina, often assisted by their Native American allies. In 1704, for example, a force of colonists and Indian tribes led by James Moore went on a rampage throughout the Apalachee province, destroying most of its Spanish missions and enslaving the Indian population.

Finally, in 1763, Spain gave in to the pressure and traded Florida to England in exchange for Cuba and the Philippines, which the English navy had seized during the Seven Years' War. Strangely enough, Spain then changed its mind, and in 1783, after the American Revolutionary War, took back control of Florida. But forty years later, after American forces occupied the Florida panhandle, the Adams-Onís Treaty of 1819 returned Florida to the United States. In the meantime, however, Pope Clement XIV had ceded to intense Portuguese and Spanish pressure to disband the Society of Jesus, precisely because their missions were safe havens for Native Americans in

FIG. 69. Jean Covens and Cornelius Mortier, *Coastal Area of Brazil with Depiction of a Sugar Mill,* 1740, based on a 1662 Blaeu map. The conditions in Brazil's sugar plantations were not as idyllic as the print suggests.

danger of being enslaved. This led to the wholesale suppression of Jesuit activity in Latin America—an event that inspired the 1986 motion picture *The Mission*.

Indeed, outside of North America, Spain and Portugal ruled virtually unchallenged by any of the other European powers. In the Spanish territories, the replacement of the Habsburg dynasty by the House of Bourbon led to a series of reforms during the eighteenth century, designed to improve the efficiency of the viceroyalty governing New Spain. The goal of these policies was to improve the local economy and to reduce the influence of the Catholic Church; indeed, the suppression of the Jesuits had been part of that strategy. Portugal, too, was once more in control of its territory in Brazil, after the Dutch had withdrawn from the coastal areas in 1654.

But the appalling conditions at the sugar plantations, where thousands of slaves were kept in the most abject conditions, prompted several slave rebellions. One of these, led by a slave from the Congo named Zumbi, succeeded in 1605 in establishing a free state in the hinterland of Pernambuco, called Quilombo dos Palmares. At its height this state had a population of thirty

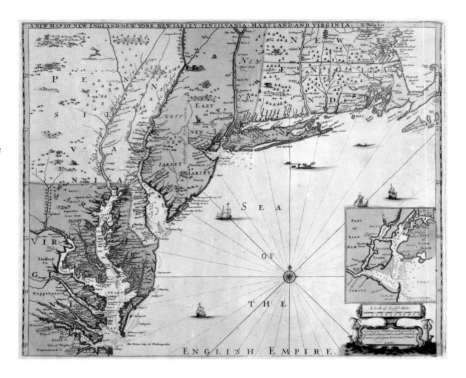

FIG. 70. Robert Morden et al., *Map of the English Empire in North America*, 1685. This is perhaps the finest map of England's American colonies at the close of the seventeenth century, from the Hudson to the Chesapeake Bay.

thousand, notwithstanding repeated attempts by Portuguese forces to conquer them. Only in 1695 did the Portuguese succeed in overrunning the enclave.

Then, in the early eighteenth century, Portuguese explorers discovered gold in the southeastern part of the country, soon to be called the *Minas Gerais* ("General Mines"). Of course, this prompted a frenzied gold rush. It also switched the emphasis of Brazil's economy from sugar cultivation to gold mining. Most of the mine operations, however, still relied on slave labor.

The Growth of the English Colonies

By the beginning of the eighteenth century, the English colonies of North America were shifting from living as isolated communities to becoming a true melting pot of a whole host of Europeans: English Quakers and Puritans who settled in New England; Swedes and Finns who built their farms along the Delaware River; English and French Catholics who settled in Maryland; Germans who colonized the mid-Atlantic regions; and Ulster Scots who headed for the Appalachian Mountains. Eventually, all these territories would become known as "the thirteen colonies"—a remarkable achievement, certainly given the mostly fruitless efforts of the French, the Spanish, and the Dutch to accomplish something similar on North American soil. Other than two brief revolts—Leisler's Rebellion in New York and Bacon's Rebellion in Virginia, both in the last quarter of the seventeenth century—the relations between these highly diverse European communities were surprisingly peaceful, certainly considering that back on the European continent, many of their home countries were at war for one reason or another.

Eventually, these colonies coalesced into four main territories, including New England (comprising today's Massachusetts, Connecticut, New Hampshire, and Rhode Island); the Middle Colonies (present-day New York, New Jersey, Pennsylvania, and Delaware); the Chesapeake Bay Colonies (including Virginia and Maryland); and the Southern Colonies (including the Carolinas and Georgia), which after 1763 also included Florida.

As these communities grew, the English Crown realized that their supervision could no longer be entrusted to the various commercial companies that had fostered colonization to begin with. In 1625, the government set up the Board of Trade, tasked with addressing any issues or problems that affected the colonials in America.

As the name "Board of Trade" suggests, the primary purpose of the English colonies was to foster trade between themselves and the home country. Since no one had found any meaningful sources of gold and silver, as in the Spanish and Portuguese territories down south, it was clear that the whole point of American colonization was to encourage an ever-growing mercantile exchange between American colonists and English merchants back home. This was done by deploying an elaborate system of trade regulations, barriers, and subsidies guaranteed to maximize profits for the English Crown (in the form of trade duties) and to discourage trade with anyone else. What it also meant, however, was that the colonies became a captive market for English industry and that every attempt was made to dissuade the Americans from doing business with any of England's rivals.

The idea that the English government could tax its overseas colonies—as well as the products that flowed back from those colonies—would later become a major source of contention. But from the English perspective, it

was eminently justifiable. After all, Great Britain (the new name adopted by
England in 1707, after the unification of England and Scotland) had expended
vast treasure in building and populating the colonies to begin with. What's
more, Britain continued to maintain the world's largest fleet of mercantile and
naval ships, both to protect the colonies from their enemies and to ensure safe
passage of their goods to the London markets. And for the time being, at least,
American colonists shared that view.

Thus the English territories of the New World grew and eventually developed distinct cultures. In many ways, these were no less sophisticated than the
ones in the Old World. America's first university, Harvard, was founded in
Massachusetts in 1636. In 1693, the College of William and Mary was founded
in Virginia. In the years to come it would educate future presidents such as
Jefferson, Monroe, and Tyler. Virginia was also the birthplace of four of the five
first US presidents—Washington, Jefferson, Madison, and Monroe—which
explains why Virginia was long considered the preeminent social and cultural
heart of the colonies, in contrast to the mercantile cities in the north. St. John's
College was established in Maryland in 1696, followed by Yale University in
Connecticut in 1701.

Nevertheless, over time these four regions also developed distinct social systems that reflected the unique bases of their economies. The South, for example, retained much of the class stratification that had ruled society in Great Britain. At the top was a landed gentry of about 5 percent of the population. This upper class owned vast plantations and used them as leverage to control much of the political, social, and religious scene, including the power to appoint local Anglican ministers. Below this elite came a large middle class of farmers, or yeomen, consisting of about 40 percent to 60 percent of the population, who owned modest parcels of land and cultivated the soil at primarily subsistence levels. The bottom third, however, did not own any property and worked as either tenant farmers or laborers, hovering at the edge of poverty.[53] The balance between these three principal groups varied by territory, particularly in areas where arable land was scarce or where the population experienced fairly high levels of new immigration.

The Middle Colonies, by contrast, were far more egalitarian, arguably because of the mix of different nationalities, which produced a large and vibrant middle class of hardworking families: toolmakers, tanners, butchers, brickmakers, carpenters, clockmakers, and fishermen. "The people of this province," declared the *Pennsylvania Journal* in 1756, "are chiefly industrious Farmers, Artificers or Men in Trade; they enjoy in Freedom, and the least among them thinks he has a right to civility from the greatest."[54]

This remarkably egalitarian approach is vividly reflected in the design of Philadelphia, the "City of Brotherly Love," as shown in the map by its architect, Thomas Holme, of 1683. Holme created a grid pattern whereby everyone, including those with the smallest parcels, still had space for a garden and a small orchard, as well as access to one of the city's two rivers, the Delaware and the Schuylkill. This plan reflected the ideals of the city's founder, William Penn, to create a "Holy Experiment" based on democracy, economic opportunity, and religious freedom.[55]

The New England colonies, by contrast, were much more homogenous, having sprung from a variety of English religious groups, including several Puritan sects. For them, colonization had a specific purpose: to create a society based on religious values, including a concern for social justice, probity, civility, and charitable works. This fostered the idea of a "Redeemer Nation," a "City

FIG. 72. Thomas Holme,
*A Portraiture of the City of
Philadelphia*, 1683

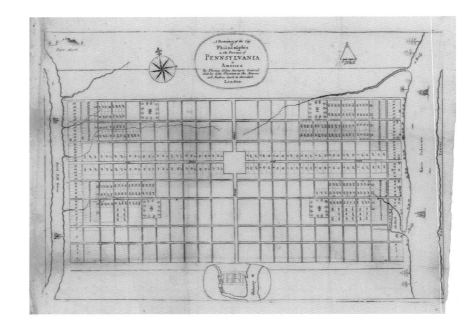

on a Hill" that could become a beacon of freedom, justice, and comity for all the world to follow. It also spurred these colonists to the greatest possible self-reliance, planting broad-spectrum crops at subsistence levels to support themselves and their families, rather than the cash crop plantations of the South that produced staples such as tobacco.

As a result, the standards of living in New England were on average higher than anywhere else in the American colonies, which in turn made the region the preeminent mercantile center of trade, finance, and shipbuilding. It also explains why New England retained closer bonds with the mother country than any other colony.[56] Not surprisingly, perhaps, by the middle of the eighteenth century the White population of the northern provinces was almost double that of the South, at 1,247,000 versus 727,000, respectively. At this time, the population of Black slaves in the South nearly equaled that of Whites, at roughly 700,000.

Even so, some of the more insular communities of New England retained deep-seated prejudices capable of producing horrors such as witchcraft trials. In Salem Village, for example, where "men still wore buckskin breeches" and "the sword and the rapier were still worn at the side," education was generally spurned in favor of religious sermons.[57]

As late as 1692, many of Salem's citizens could neither read nor write, and Puritan obedience was enforced with a strong belief in demons and other supernatural phenomena. At the same time, women continued to be viewed with suspicion as seductive carriers of sin. In Salem and other villages, such as Ipswich and Andover, this created an oppressed atmosphere where reports of witches could find fertile soil, particularly because Salem Town was convulsed by conflicts over grazing rights, property lines, and other issues. It became quite convenient to denounce a rival with an accusation of witchcraft if no plausible accusation could be found. Indeed, some historians believe that the first Salem arrests of women for witchcraft were prompted by a family feud. In total, around two hundred people in colonial Massachusetts—including girls as young as twelve—would find themselves accused or arrested on grounds of witchcraft between 1692 and 1693. Of these, fourteen women and five men would be hanged, while five others died in jail, making the Salem trials the deadliest witch hunt in colonial North America.

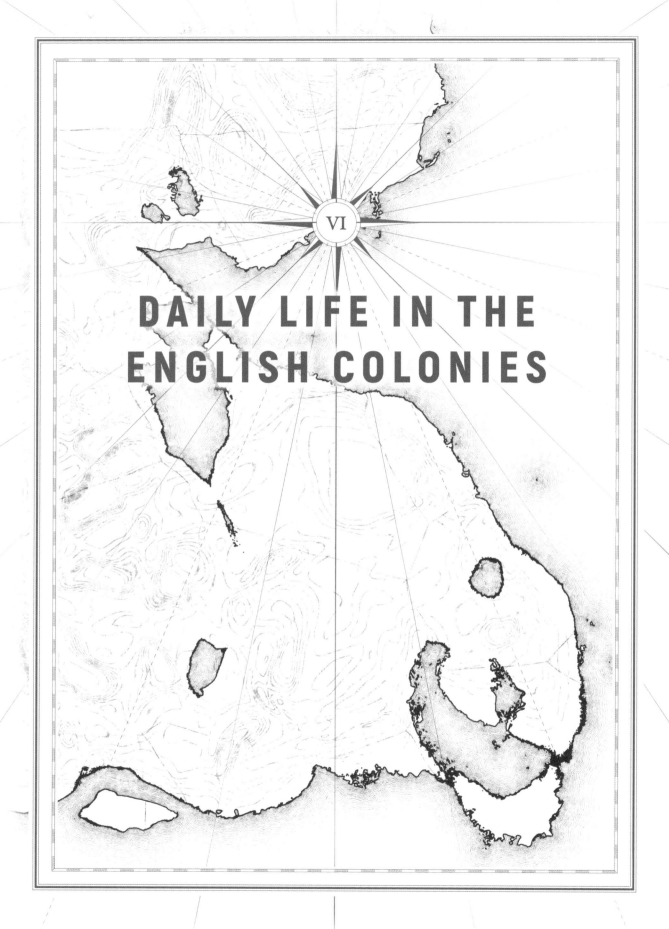

DAILY LIFE IN THE ENGLISH COLONIES

From the very beginning, what set the people of the English colonies apart from their peers back in Europe was a degree of self-governance that many Europeans could only dream of. Almost every colony would create some form of legislative assembly that served as a check on the English governors and administrators appointed by the Crown. In practice, most of these chief executives were keen to cooperate with the local assemblies and do their bidding. After all, London was very far away, and the local legislatures often had the power of the purse, which gave them the right to decide on the salaries of the executive. From there, power trickled down to the community at large in ways that varied from colony to colony. New England communities held town meetings to poll their inhabitants on current issues and policy decisions. Others used a system of elected municipal boards, or of county commissions. Not everyone had the right of suffrage, but in most colonies the ownership of some property, no matter how small, qualified a White man to vote.[58] This made local elections a highly spirited affair, where candidates were known to liberally dispense beer, pieces of beef, and other treats in their quest for votes. George Washington, for example, spent around £140 to procure rum punch, beer, wine, and brandy as part of his campaigns for the legislature.

Another unique aspect of life in the colonies was that young men and women were encouraged to marry, and marry early. Particularly in the seventeenth and early eighteenth century, there was safety in numbers, since the colonists were often outnumbered by the Native American nations that surrounded them. Those who remained bachelors well into adulthood were frowned upon and even considered unpatriotic. The problem, of course, was that in the early days, there were not nearly enough women for the overwhelmingly male

FIG. 74. Henry Mosler, *Just Moved*, 1870. During the nineteenth century, domestic scenes of young couples who had recently immigrated to America became a popular motif.

population of colonists. As in the case of France, which tried to woo women of marriageable age to *Nouvelle France* by any means necessary, this prompted many communities to reach out to England and recruit young women for the cause. The Virginia Company, for example, shipped more than 140 girls to its colonies over a period of just three years.[59]

Other companies extended an offer to any English girl to pay for her passage to the New World if she was willing to work as a servant in one of the more affluent homes. For the elite, female attendants were likewise in short supply, but as one author wrote, this stratagem often backfired when the young lady in question was quickly "courted into a Copulative Matrimony."[60] On the whole, however, the fact that young males quickly embraced the bonds of marriage served as a great social stabilizer in these incipient communities. Benjamin

Franklin, who in 1746 wrote a pamphlet on the matter entitled *Reflections on Courtship and Marriage,* estimated that there were twice as many marriages, proportionally speaking, in the American colonies than in Europe and that on average these produced twice as many children. Indeed, one observer marveled that "Whenever one meets a woman, she is either pregnant, or carries a child in her arms, or leads one by the hand." This great fecundity, no doubt nurtured by the availability of a richer and varied diet than the one available to most women in Europe, was the reason why, by the early eighteenth century, the imbalance between the sexes was largely corrected. "Almost everybody is married," wrote our French-American author, the farmer de Crèvecoeur in the 1780s, "for they get wives very young and the pleasure of returning to their families overrules every other desire."

This also fostered the genesis of what in later years we would call the "American Dream," the idea that any man or woman in America, regardless of rank, class, religion, or education, could have a fair chance of building a productive and happy life, provided one was prepared to work hard and rely on oneself. De Crèvecoeur believed that the wholesomeness of these early

FIG. 75. John Wollaston, *Portrait of a Young Man and Woman*, 1749. Simple portraits of affluent young couples such as this one could be found in manor houses throughout the English colonies.

Americans and their unbridled optimism were the result of their physical environment. "We are nothing but what we derive from the air we breathe, the climate we inhabit, the government we obey, the system of religion we profess," he wrote in his *Letters from an American Farmer*, which created a sensation when it was published in London in 1782, in the wake of the Revolutionary War. "The goodness and flavor of the fruit proceeds from the peculiar soil and exposition in which they grow."[61]

Nautical Improvements

As the American colonies evolved from villages into towns, and agricultural output produced an ever greater surplus, the Atlantic Ocean changed from a barrier to a bridge and became a great highway of international trade. In the 1670s, there were on average around five hundred transatlantic crossings per year. Sixty years later, this number had tripled to fifteen hundred crossings, an astounding achievement in an age before the development of the steam turbine.[62]

This increase was due to a number of improvements. While the principal design of the seventeenth-century galleon remained largely unchanged, construction methods were constantly being improved based on the reports of captains who had sailed their long-distance ships on either the eastern or western route. Ships were now built in ways that are not dissimilar from the design of today's metal-hulled vessels: as a series of frames made of curved timber, which were attached to a long keel made of elm. Elm was more plentiful than oak, required less seasoning, and lasted better under water. The strength of the frames, a necessity in the storm-swept Atlantic waters, was dramatically improved by increasing their width and by allowing their sections to overlap, thus producing "compound frames." The entire structure was further reinforced with V-shaped timber sections known as "breasthooks" or "crutches" in the bow and stern. The hull was then fitted with seasoned or kiln-dried oak, while transverse deck beams held both sides of the hull firmly together.[63]

The decks were finished with pine and subsequently caulked with a mixture of putty and white lead. The seasoning of oak took time, three years on average, which became a problem during the Seven Years' War when England's

FIG. 76. Eighteenth-century diagram of a British battleship, showing the position of the foremast, mainmast, and mizzenmast

frenzied shipbuilding used up its supply of seasoned oak. As a result, the Royal Navy was forced to build ships with "green" unseasoned oak, which left them vulnerable to dry rot. That, in turn, severely shortened their life spans, just as England stumbled into another war, this time with its American colonists.

The principal element of any ship, however, was the mast. Masts—whether the foremast; the mainmast, with its lower, topsail, topgallant, and royal sections; or the aftmost mizzenmast—had to be incredibly strong, since they served as the sole propellant of the vessel. These soaring spars, often as tall as forty yards, were made of several sections of strong timber such as conifer or white pine and for a full-fledged ship of the line could weigh as much as eighteen tons. The construction of a compound mast alone took two months, involving a dozen experienced shipwrights.[64]

Navigational aids improved as well. As we saw, Columbus largely eschewed dead reckoning in favor of his compass and the passing of time as measured

FIG. 77. Andreas Cellarius, *Celestial Chart with Signs of the Zodiac*, 1660. The map shows the constellations of the Southwestern Hemisphere superimposed over a southwestern orientation of the earth, centered on the ecliptic pole down to 20 degrees in the Northern Hemisphere.

by a sandglass, which a servant or mate was tasked to change whenever it ran out. But in the seventeenth century, the art of dead reckoning became more sophisticated as celestial observations improved and cartographers began creating maps of the sky, rather than the surface of the earth. This was based on the discovery that, whereas the ecliptic course of the sun and the planets is constantly changing, the positions of the stars in the firmament appear fixed because of their extreme distance from earth. This prompted seventeenth-century cartographers such as Andreas Cellarius to produce stunningly beautiful maps by depicting the positions of the stars in their signs of the zodiac.

In the early age of exploration, celestial positions could be determined with relatively crude devices such as a cross-staff or an astrolabe. The eighteenth century, however, produced two revolutionary navigational aids in the form of Hadley's quadrant, essentially a variation of Newton's reflecting quadrant with the addition of a small sighting telescope, and an even better device known as the "sextant." While the quadrant enabled a navigator to estimate the distance of a star relative to the instrument, the sextant made it possible to accurately measure the angle between an astronomical object and the horizon, known as the "altitude." In this manner, a navigator could calculate a position line on a nautical chart based on his knowledge of the position of the celestial object in the night sky.

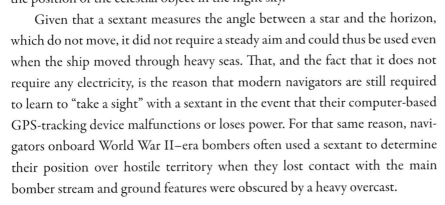

FIG. 78. The eighteenth-century sextant revolutionized navigation during the long Atlantic crossing (Courtesy, U.S. National Oceanic and Atmospheric Administration)

Given that a sextant measures the angle between a star and the horizon, which do not move, it did not require a steady aim and could thus be used even when the ship moved through heavy seas. That, and the fact that it does not require any electricity, is the reason that modern navigators are still required to learn to "take a sight" with a sextant in the event that their computer-based GPS-tracking device malfunctions or loses power. For that same reason, navigators onboard World War II–era bombers often used a sextant to determine their position over hostile territory when they lost contact with the main bomber stream and ground features were obscured by a heavy overcast.

Trade with the Motherland

At the same time, trade between the colonies and England underwent a rapid change, not only in terms of volume but also in the type of product that was shipped. Although popular films and novels have created the impression that the most important American crop in pre-Revolutionary times was cotton, that was not the case. The most important commodity imported from North America and the West Indies was sugar. Between 1699 and 1701, imports of sugar worth £630,000, or just over $127 million in today's currency, were shipped from England's West Indies plantations to New England, and from there to the home country. As the century progressed, sugar imports grew by leaps and bounds as this luxury product became a staple of affluent British homes. Just twenty years

FIG. 79. Anon., *Ships in the*
Thames Estuary, 1708. Shipping
to America tripled in the
eighteenth century.

later, in 1721, imports had grown to £928,000, while by mid-century the trade was worth £1,302,000, or $264 million today. Two decades later, on the eve of the American Revolution, that figure doubled once more.

And yet, sugar accounted for only half of Britain's imports from its possessions in the New World. Other top commodities between 1752 and 1754 included tobacco (£560,000), rice (£167,000), dyestuffs (£97,000), and timber (£90,000). The import of cotton was worth only £56,000, up from £23,000 just fifty years earlier. All told, just before the outbreak of war, Great Britain imported over £5 million worth of produce, most of it consisting of raw or semi-processed goods, which today would have been worth nearly a billion dollars (US).[65]

The sharp increase in export also led to an improvement in roads between the major cities and agricultural areas. A first road map, the *Vademecum for America,* was printed in 1732, the same year that a New Jersey stagecoach service from Burlington to Perth Amboy was inaugurated. A trip between New York City and Boston took four days, while the journey from Philadelphia to Baltimore would keep a traveler road-bound for five days.[66] While these roads were still made of packed dirt, and bridges were few and far in between, they nevertheless greatly improved land transport between the colonies.

The better roads also improved the spread of news, something that would become of vital importance as the Revolutionary War unfolded. The first colonial newspaper, the *Boston-News Letter,* was founded in 1704. Some thirty-five years later, there were no fewer than thirteen newspapers across the four main regions, published in places such as Charles Towne, South Carolina; Williamsburg, Virginia; Philadelphia; and New York. The dispatch of mail improved as well. Through much of the seventeenth century, mail was delivered on an ad hoc basis by friends, relatives, or in the case of official notices by royal courier. In 1691, the colonies agreed to establish the first interprovincial postal service. Sixty years later, after Benjamin Franklin took over as deputy postmaster, the time it took for a letter from Philadelphia to reach its correspondent in Boston was reduced from three weeks to just six days.[67]

The question that has preoccupied historians ever since is: where did this voracious English appetite for American export products come from, and how could the colonies meet that staggering increase while still using the tools and technology of the preindustrial era? The answer, as Jacob Price has argued, is that when European farmers settled in the American colonies, they found that they could produce far more efficiently than at home. Greater access to land and water played an important role, as did the more temperate climate, compared to the seasonal cycles of Britain and Northern Europe. Another factor was that Britain deliberately fostered the growth of certain staples in America that could not be cultivated at home, such as sugar, tobacco, and rice, while trying hard to prohibit a surplus of goods that could compete with the home market, such as cereals.[68] Finally, from the early eighteenth century onward, British farmers developed a number of innovations that boosted yields both at home and in the colonies. These included the seed drill, which

FIG. 80. A mahogany secretary and bookcase, Boston, 1750. The secretary-bookcase combination was particularly popular in colonial America because of its high storage capacity on a small footprint.

planted seeds with consistent spacing and depth; the use of crop rotation; and techniques to improve livestock yields through selective breeding. These improvements boosted wheat yields by about one quarter between 1700 and 1800.[69]

Naturally, all of these imported goods were still subject to English taxation at home; the feeling of familial bonds between the colonies and the Crown only went so far. With each new rise in American imports, the English treasury enjoyed a windfall—quite apart from the general salutary effect of the goods on the British economy as a whole. There was, of course, a flip side to that equation, because it made the Crown increasingly dependent on the economic output of its colonies—with dire consequences for the future.

The Art of Colonial America

In the meantime, the sharp rise in exports represented a boon for the American colonists and prompted a steady and commensurate rise in the quality of life. Particularly in the cities, artisans, carpenters, weavers, and furniture makers found a ready market for elegantly crafted tables, chairs, desks, cabinets, and chests. Most of these emulated the fashions of Britain while at the same time fostering the sense that the colonies were slowly developing a culture and style that were wholly their own. Not surprisingly, the main center of furniture production was Philadelphia, which by mid-century had evolved as the center of American cultural and intellectual life. It was followed by Boston and Newport, both seaports in New England, as subsidiary production centers, given their proximity to new shipments from Great Britain. And while some of these cabinets, tables, and chairs may not always have had quite the same refinement as their models in Britain, some distinct American features were already apparent.

One was a concern for elegance of form, rather than ornament, using native species such as walnut, pine, and maple. This focus on economy and simplicity, rather than ostentatious decoration, was an important departure from the prevailing English Baroque. The butterfly table, with its hinged leaves, was a uniquely American invention, particularly prized by middle-class homes where space was at a premium. Equally popular were the slant-front secretary and the high chest of drawers or bookcase, which both offered plenty of storage space on a small footprint.

Near the end of the first half of the eighteenth century, the cabriole leg arrived from Britain, thus introducing the American variant of the Queen Anne style, named after Britain's Queen Anne (1702–1714). Its sensuous curving line soon replaced the robust supports of the High Baroque and dominated much of American cabinetry, in imitation of the changing tastes in Britain. With it came new forms, such as the tea table (and an attendant new taste for tea), the wingback chair with upholstered seats, and the card table, since card playing was now taking Europe by storm.

In architecture, American designers remained faithful to the New England style of wood-frame homes for the middle class and stately mansions for the upper elite, until the Georgian style swept through the colonies from about 1705 onward. This style—named after the four monarchs who ruled Britain under the regnal name of George between 1714 and 1830—marks a rejection of the drama of the Baroque in favor of a return to an orderly, symmetrical arrangement of form, based on Greco-Roman classicism. This movement was fueled by the exciting discoveries of Pompeii and Herculaneum in the early eighteenth century, which infused designers with a new enthusiasm for an almost archaeological imitation of the classical vernacular, sometimes known as Palladian after the Renaissance architect Andrea Palladio. In America, however, this never led to excess and instead inspired a more restrained use of classical models. Thomas Jefferson's home at Monticello, built between 1770 and 1784, is often cited as the best example of the fusion of Palladian and Georgian motives on American soil. This and other similar stately homes were executed in brick and painted wood, rather than the much more expensive marble preferred in Europe.

Artists, too, were beginning to prosper in the vibrant cities on the Atlantic seaboard, where they found a clientele eager for portraits. One of these was John Singleton Copley, the son of recent English arrivals who in 1736 had set up a tobacco shop in Boston. Copley soon distinguished himself as an excellent draftsman and, according to witnesses, became entirely self-taught as

FIG. 81. Thomas Jefferson's Monticello (1770–1784, enlarged between 1796 and 1806) was inspired by designs by the Italian Renaissance architect Andrea Palladio.

a painter. Although in a letter to a fellow American artist, Benjamin West, he complained that "In this Country, as You rightly observe, there are no examples of Art, except what is to [be] met with in a few prints indifferently executed," he obviously developed his talent by working from British portraits that high-born English landowners had brought from Britain. The influence of British portraits by Joshua Reynolds, for example, is quite obvious.[70]

Like many other artists of his time, Copley undertook a "grand tour" of Europe in 1774 in order to absorb the art styles of the continent. But after studying in Rome and other cities, he changed his plans upon the outbreak of the Revolutionary War. Rather than sailing back to Boston, he urged his wife, Susanna, to pack up their children—John, Mary, Betsy, and baby Susanna—and together with her father, Richard Clarke, take the first available ship to London.

Clarke was only too happy to comply, because as a Tory merchant he had lost much of his investment during the Boston Tea Party, when American colonists dumped all of the British tea in Boston overboard. Relieved to have his family back, Copley then painted a large portrait to celebrate their safe deliverance from war-torn America. Ironically, Copley still placed this affectionate scene amid the idyllic hills and streams of New England.

A younger artist of this era was Gilbert Stuart, who was born in Saunderstown, in the colony of Rhode Island, in 1755. Like Copley, he originally came from humble origins: he was the son of a Scottish immigrant who made his living in the local snuff industry. His father's marriage to the daughter of a local landowning family enabled him to move to Newport, where Gilbert Stuart met the Scottish artist Cosmo Alexander. Alexander took the young artist under his wing and in 1771 persuaded him to finish his studies in Edinburgh. Two years later, Stuart returned to Newport, only to find himself in the midst of a brewing revolution. Like Copley, he fled to England, where he developed a reputation as a successful portraitist.

But the lure of his homeland proved too strong, and after peace was concluded between Great Britain and the United States, he decided to move

FIG. 82. John Singleton Copley, *The Copley Family*, 1777. The artist is shown on top, looking at the beholder.

back in 1783. With a studio in Germantown, Philadelphia, Stuart became
the most influential American artist of his time, painting portraits of George
Washington, John Adams, John Quincy Adams, and Thomas Jefferson, as well
as, remarkably, Louis XVI, King of France, and Washington's nemesis, King
George III. John Adams later said that sitting for Stuart was a pleasure, quite
in contrast to his experience with other painters. With those, he wrote, having
one's picture done was a "penance." But Stuart was different, "for he lets me do
just what I please, and keeps me constantly amused by his conversation."[71]

Among others, Stuart painted the famous (and unfinished) portrait of
George Washington, known as *The Athenaeum*. Today depicted on the US
one-dollar bill, the portrait became so popular that Stuart and his daughters,
who were also artists, produced 130 copies that they sold for a hundred dollars
each—an astronomical figure at the time.[72]

Slavery in the Americas

Any discussion of America's early history must address the pivotal role that slavery played in the growth of colonial prosperity. Slavery had been a feature of European society since Greco-Roman times, when slaves provided the essential energy source for a whole host of activities: agriculture, construction, maritime propulsion, and domestic service. Without slaves, Roman society would have collapsed, which is why slave revolts—such as the one led by Spartacus in 73–71 B.C.E.—were considered a major threat to the state. Slaves were usually indigenous people from lands conquered or occupied by Rome who were sold as war booty. Many were therefore Europeans themselves and belonged to any number of Germanic, Slavic, or other tribes. Another source of slaves was a class of impoverished families who were unable to pay their debts and sold their children in lieu of payment. It has been estimated that by the first century, between 30 and 40 percent of the Roman population consisted of slaves.[73]

After the fall of the Roman Empire, slavery was gradually expunged in Europe because of opposition by the Church. It was replaced by serfdom: the concept of having a large number of peasants laboring in servitude on fields owned by feudal nobility. But outside of Europe, the Roman practice of slavery—of owning a human being as personal property—continued, particularly in the Islamic Empire. Many European traders took advantage of that market demand until Christian doctrine, such as the Edict of the Council of Koblenz of 922, forbade the sale of Christian slaves to non-Christian lands. Some European city-states, such as Venice, circumvented that law by shipping slaves from non-Christian areas such as the Balkans and selling them at markets in Muslim Spain, North Africa, and the Middle East.[74] Similarly, affluent Christian households purchased Muslim slaves as domestic servants, particularly in the wake of the Crusades.

All these precedents allowed the fifteenth-century European mind to convince itself that slavery was not a moral wrong, provided the enslaved were not of Christian origin. For the Spanish conquistadores in South America, this impression was reinforced by the fact that slavery was widely practiced in the pre-Columbian societies that now fell under their sway. The Mayas, the Incas, the Tehuelche of Patagonia, the Caribs, the Tupinambá of Brazil, and even the indigenous peoples of the Pacific Northwest all maintained an active and

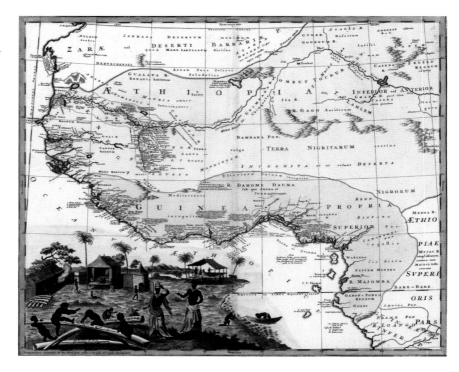

FIG. 84. Johann Baptiste
Homann and heirs, *Map of West
Africa*, 1743

prosperous slave trade. Most of their slaves were prisoners of war who had been
captured in regional conflicts or—as in the case of Rome—children who had
been sold by their parents to settle a debt. Consequently, the often-argued idea
that it was the Europeans who introduced slavery into the Americas is not correct. This does not, in any way, diminish the abject cruelty and immorality of
the practice, but it does underscore the fact that slavery was a persistent feature
of life in much of the known world at the time (including China) rather than
something that European colonists invented and brought to America.

Having said that, there is no question that the Atlantic slave trade to the
Western Hemisphere was unprecedented in its scope, scale, and profitabil-
ity, not to mention the intense violence and disregard for human life with
which it was practiced. As we saw, it was the Portuguese who first enslaved
large numbers of indigenous people from the West African territories they
controlled and brought them to their Caribbean and Brazilian plantations
as forced labor in the harvest and processing of sugarcane. The first ship to
do so was the *Santa Maria de Bogoña*, which arrived in Hispaniola in 1525. A
century later, the prevailing winds of the Atlantic had channeled much of the

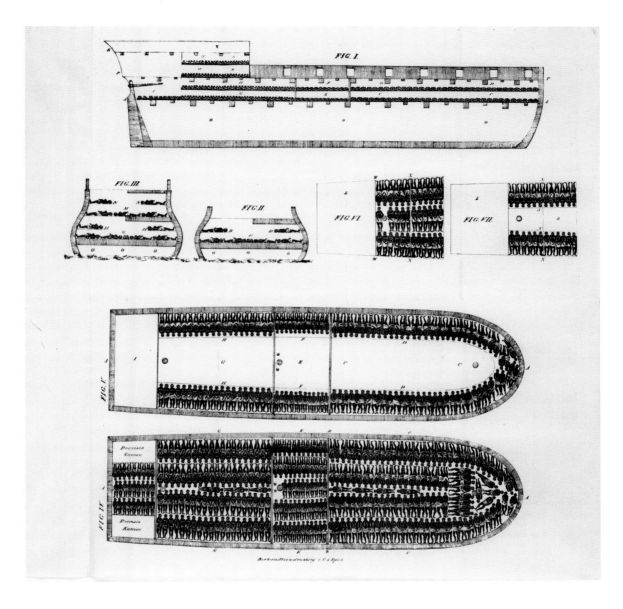

slave trade into two main routes: a northern one to the Caribbean and North America, and a southern route to Brazil. By 1672, all of the main maritime powers—Spain, Portugal, France, Holland, and England—were reaping vast profits from the shipment and sale of African slave labor for plantations and mines throughout the Americas. Many ships operated on a triangular route that brought goods from Europe to Africa; slaves from Africa to the Americas; and raw commodities from the Americas back to Europe. The 1745 print by

FIG. 85. Thomas Clarkson, *Diagram of a Four-Deck Slave Ship*, 1822

the German cartographer Johann Baptiste Homann, which includes an idyllic scene of African village life in "Guinea," cannot conceal the fact that the slave trade from West Africa was reaching its peak when this beautiful map was made. Indeed, the coast of Guinea was known as the Slave Coast, with ports such as Ouidah, Lagos, Agoué, Jakin, and Porto-Novo where English, Dutch, Spanish, and Portuguese ships departed with their human cargo.

The "Middle Passage" across the Atlantic often carried as many as five hundred slaves per vessel, shackled and packed together in truly horrific conditions for a voyage that sometimes lasted ten weeks or more.[75] Estimates differ, but many historians believe that between 1.2 and 2 million Africans perished during the sea voyage to the New World, while great numbers would die soon after their arrival as a result of disease or malnutrition.[76]

The reason why the slave trade was so profitable, and why so many Africans were shipped across the Atlantic, is that the harsh conditions on plantations, mines, and other centers of forced labor diminished a slave's life expectancy. While statistics vary, some historians have pegged the average age of death for Black male slaves born in American colonies at 21.9, compared to 42.2 years for a White freeman. Nor was slavery limited to areas that we would typically associate with labor-intensive cultivation, such as the southern colonies of North America. It was Massachusetts, not Virginia, that in 1641 was the first colony to write slavery into law. While it prohibited the sale of slaves in its commonwealth, it explicitly authorized the keeping of slaves if they were purchased elsewhere or acquired as captives of war. In the eyes of the law, these were not "Englishmen" but "strangers," such as Native Americans or Africans, and therefore outside the protection of the British Crown. As a study by Richard S. Dunn has shown, African slaves then began to replace English servants in the Chesapeake Bay area, which explains why the roughly 1.5 million slaves imported to the British colonies between 1600 and 1780 were more evenly distributed across the four main territories than we often assume.[77] This number is even more astounding when we remember that only 17 percent of all slaves taken from Africa wound up in the English colonies of North America. The greatest number by far were forced to work in Portuguese Brazil or New Spain, including the Caribbean, where they suffered unspeakable horrors.

Even though in 1735 the Trustees of Georgia were the first to enact a law prohibiting slavery in their new colony (though this ban was lifted in 1751), enslavement continued to be practiced in the other twelve English colonies well into the nineteenth century. Only in the 1810s, during a period known as the Second Great Awakening, did various preachers raise their voices to say that America was to be a "Benevolent Empire" of impeccable moral, social, and spiritual standards. This meant, among other ideas, that it needed to abolish the "sin" of slavery. As the century wore on, the issue of slavery drove a wedge between the North and the South, particularly when the Underground Railroad spirited some one hundred thousand slaves from southern plantations to safety in northern territories.

The importation of slaves was gradually outlawed, so that in 1808 only South Carolina still allowed the practice, but most plantation owners circumvented that restriction by smuggling slaves through Florida (which did not become a US territory until 1821) or the Gulf Coast regions. At the same time, slaves were encouraged to reproduce and thus sustain the slave population from within, particularly when cotton replaced tobacco as the main cash crop of the South.

FIG. 86. Henry P. Moore, *African-American Slaves at Work on James Hopkinson's Plantation*, ca. 1862 (Courtesy, The New York Historical Society)

Keen observers such as the French writer Alexis de Tocqueville, author of the 1835 book *Democracy in America*, expressed dismay at the continued use of slaves in America, particularly when the practice had been abolished in England and other European nations. He warned of dire consequences to the future stability of the United States unless slavery was entirely erased from its shores. Not until the American Civil War, and President Lincoln's Emancipation Proclamation of 1862, did America finally turn a page on this dark stain in its founding history. Indeed, some historians have argued that the reason why racial tensions persist in our modern times is that slavery was allowed to fester in our nation's history for so long.

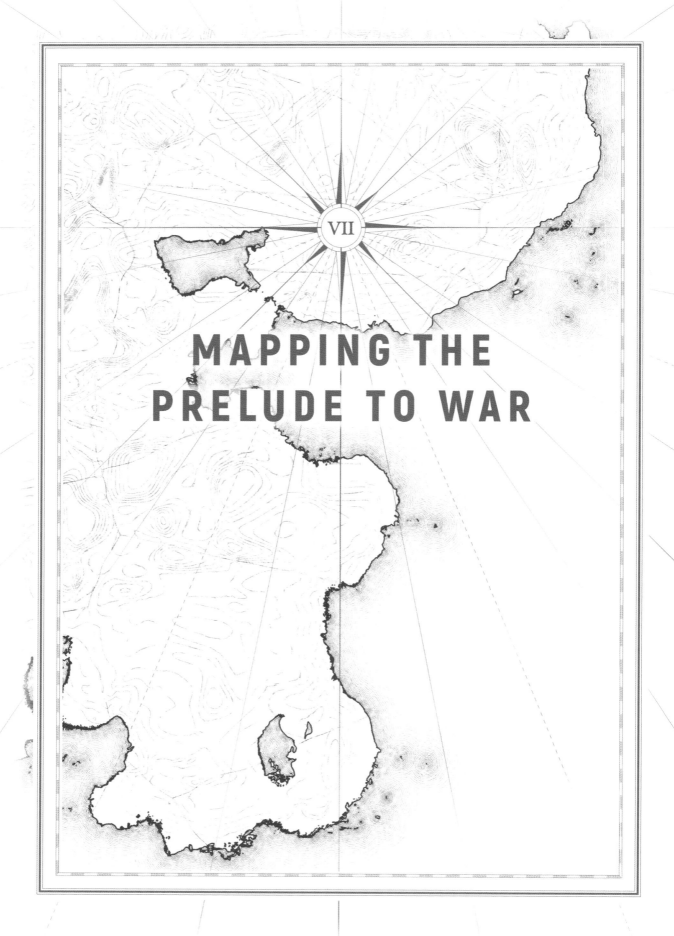

MAPPING THE PRELUDE TO WAR

As the eighteenth century wore on, mapmakers, survey-ors, and cartographers of the English colonies in America took on a new role. Up to this point, creating maps of the American continent had been an art as much as a science, designed to appeal to a broad public on both sides of the Atlantic Ocean. For European buyers especially, a map of America was a glimpse of a faraway and exotic land, populated by Indians and fearsome animals amid a wild and exuberant landscape that had yet to be tamed by human hands.

But this changed as the conditions on the ground shifted, and life for the colonists became more perilous. The reason is that for much of the seventeenth century, the American colonies had been shielded from the great conflicts that scourged Europe. True, there were clashes between French, Dutch, English, and Spanish colonists, but most of these contests had to do with local boundaries or trade rather than the big political matters that vexed the European powers some three thousand miles away. But as the American colonies matured into a powerful entity in their own right, they were bound to be sucked into a string of conflicts that roiled Europe throughout this period.

The major powers of the European continent had always been at odds. But in the eighteenth century, these contests coalesced into a series of intensely violent wars that ravaged much of the land and killed or uprooted thousands of Europeans. Since Portugal and Holland had by now largely faded from the scene, it was France, England, Spain, and an emerging Prussia that were testing the limits of their spheres of influence, not only politically but also commercially.

The first conflict that spilled over into the colonies was a rather bizarre series of events known collectively as the War of the Austrian Succession. As

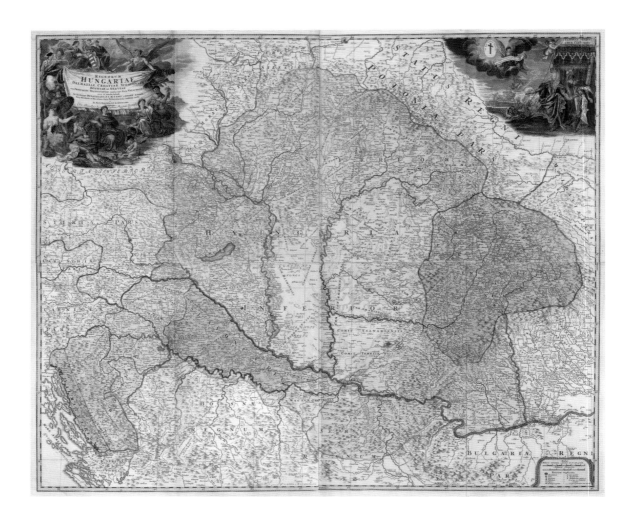

FIG. 87. Johann B. Homann,
Map of Habsburg Hungary,
Croatia, Bosnia, Serbia and
other territories, 1720

the name suggests, the European powers took issue with the idea that King Charles VI of the Habsburg Empire—a motley collection of today's Hungary, Austria, Serbia, and other lands—should be succeeded in 1740 by his daughter, Maria Theresa. The Habsburg Dynasty had traditionally carried the honorary title of Holy Roman Emperor, a position that, in the eyes of her rivals, could never be filled by a woman.

In truth, the real casus belli was rather more mundane, in that France and Prussia shared a common interest in containing the Habsburg domain before it became too powerful. As shown in Johann Homann's beautifully illustrated map, the Habsburg domain had by 1720 also swallowed Slavonia, Transylvania, the southern Netherlands, Milan, and Naples and was on its way to becoming the dominant power in Central Europe. Therefore, as soon as war was declared, Prussia promptly decided to invade Silesia and succeeded in capturing much of that region before it was dealt a bloody nose by Maria Theresa's determined defense. In response, Prussia's King Frederick II turned to France and persuaded King Louis XV to join the conflict, in the hope of forcing Maria Theresa into a two-front war. Things went downhill from there, and soon forces from a range of European principalities were locked in battle without anyone really knowing what they were fighting for.

In 1743, King George II of Britain decided to enter the fray and see what spoils he could get for himself. Before long, the English and French armies met at the cataclysmic Battle of Dettingen, which ended in a heavy defeat for the French. Of course, this called for revenge, and so the French generals came up with a rather daring gambit: to invade Great Britain and restore a Catholic king to the throne. But on the night the French fleet was about to sail, a violent storm lashed the ships' berths, ripped their sails, and toppled their masts, and the invasion attempt was abandoned. Thus repulsed at sea, the French continued to fight on land, one battle after another, while vast sums were spent and not much of anything was accomplished.

The news that France and Great Britain were locked in a fierce European war soon reached American shores. Here, it once again inflamed the long-simmering tensions between the colonists of New France and their opposing numbers in England's Atlantic colonies. These tensions had often resulted in small clashes here and there, but never an all-out war. Now, however, many of the American colonies rallied to the colors, filled with pride in their English heritage and eager to teach these annoying French a lesson they'd never forget. The English militia, filled with righteous anger, soon settled on a perfect military objective: to capture the French fortress of Louisburg on Cape Breton Island, just off the coast of Nova Scotia. After heavy fighting, they succeeded in investing the citadel.

Down south, in the West Indies, things got even more heated. Having also declared war on Spain, the British navy concocted a plan to attack the Spanish colonies of Central America from both east and west, from the Atlantic and the Pacific. The fleets sailed, but storms, disease, and a determined Spanish defense ensured that these grand designs all came to naught.

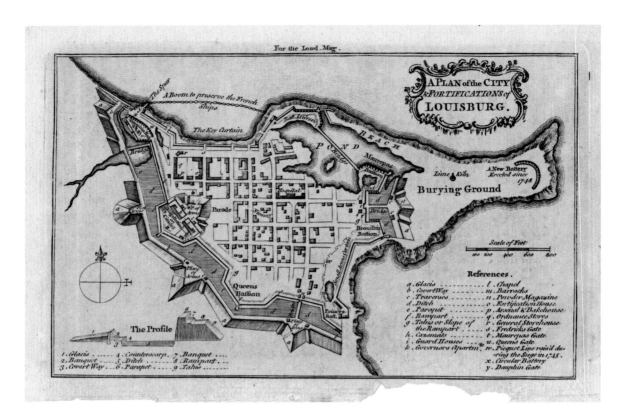

FIG. 88. Map of the French fortress of Louisburg, captured in July 1745. The fortress was returned to France three years later by the Peace Treaty of Aix-la-Chapelle, enraging the colonists of Massachusetts.

What this strange conflict did achieve is that for the first time, a continental war had spread to North America, with both French and English colonists rushing to the defense of their homelands. And while in Europe the war finally came to an end with the Treaty of Aix-la-Chapelle of 1748, in North America the fuse of European enmity continued smoldering. That was particularly true for Massachusetts, which had lost 8 percent of its male population in the war and where news of the return of Louisburg to France was met with outrage. These and other colonists decided to bide their time and wait for a spark that would once again prod the colonies to all-out war. That spark was not long in coming.

The French and Indian War (1754–1763)

In 1749, the governor of New France, Roland-Michel de la Galissonière, was fed up with repeated attempts by British traders to trespass in the Ohio Valley, which—on paper at least—was considered part of *Nouvelle France*. These interlopers sought to steal the fur trade with local Indians from under the noses of the French. In response, de la Galissonière dispatched an expedition of some two hundred French marines into the valley, more as a show of force than for actual combat, in the hope that this would rally the Indian tribes to the French side and forever end any contact between them and English colonists.

Alas, the campaign did not have its desired outcome. "All I can say," wrote one French commander, Pierre-Joseph Céloron, upon his return to camp in Montreal, "is that the Natives of these localities are very badly disposed toward the French and are entirely devoted to the English. I don't know in what way they could be brought back." Soon thereafter, news of the French maneuvers in the Ohio Valley reached the French and British capitals and once again spurred a call to arms. Thus began the French and Indian War, a conflict that would forever change the face of the North American continent.

To understand this, we should always remember that while French and English colonists had never seen eye to eye, they nevertheless shared some solidarity, some sense of a common cause. They were Europeans, surrounded by hostile natives in a foreign land, with wild animals, unusual climate cycles, and impenetrable natural barriers. In the early days, these colonists might have been rivals but never sworn enemies, not foes to the death. The war of 1754 changed that.

Men on both sides rushed to arms to defend their homesteads, their lands, and the boundaries of their colonies. That meant that now, more than ever, an exact definition of those boundaries became very important, for it was along these frontiers that the battles would be fought. Not for nothing did the French call the conflict *la Guerre de la Conquête,* "the War of the Conquest."

Another crucial factor in this conflict was knowing which Native American tribes resided in the borderlands and what side they were likely to take in the conflict. This was extremely important, because at the outbreak of war the English colonies were protected by just five British companies of one hundred men each—a pitiful number. Alliances with neighboring tribes were therefore essential to bolstering their defenses in the battles to come.

Bellin's map of the western part of New France, for example, was created to show that the French garrisons of the Great Lakes could easily be overwhelmed by the vast numbers of the Huron, the Renard, the Mascouten, the Iroquois, and the Erie tribes that surrounded them. Indeed, Bellin's map was

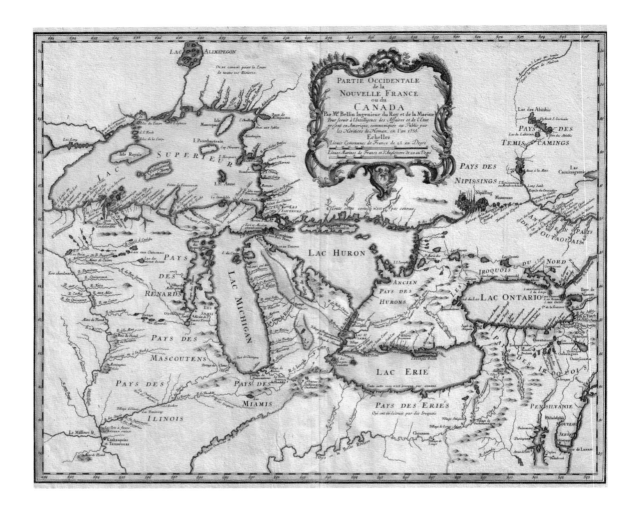

FIG. 89. Jacques-Nicolas Bellin, *Detailed Map of the Western Part of New France*, 1755. This highly influential map identified the many Indian nations who resided on its depicted land. Since the French and Indian War was very much an attempt to rally the native nations to either side in the conflict, this information was of strategic significance.

instrumental in prodding the local French commanders to conclude treaties with most of these nations, except the Iroquois. As we saw, the Iroquois tended to throw in their lot with the English colonists, who also made common cause with the Cherokee and the Catawba.

For nine years the war raged up and down the spine of New France, from Newfoundland in the north to Virginia in the south, where the local Virginian militia was led by a twenty-two-year-old officer named George Washington. Initially, the war did not go well for the English colonists. The French adroitly used their Indian allies to outwit the English forces, and several plans by the British commanding general, Edward Braddock, came to naught. Then, in 1757, the French siege of Fort William Henry, located on the border between New

York and Canada, resulted in an unspeakable massacre. After the fort's occupants agreed to surrender, the Indians rushed in and scalped the English soldiers, while the French looked on and made no effort to stop them. Women, children, and servants were taken as slaves.

This bloody event marked the nadir in the relations between the French and English in America. For years to come, the cry "Remember Fort William Henry!" would stir English hearts against all things French. It would also inspire the 1826 novel *The Last of the Mohicans* by James Fenimore Cooper, which between 1912 and 1992 would lead to a number of film adaptations, the last one starring Daniel Day-Lewis.

The British Whig government, prodded by William Pitt, was finally galvanized into action. Britain had already dispatched six thousand troops, but Pitt judged, correctly, that the French could be defeated only by striking at the heart of New France: the towns of Montreal and Quebec City.

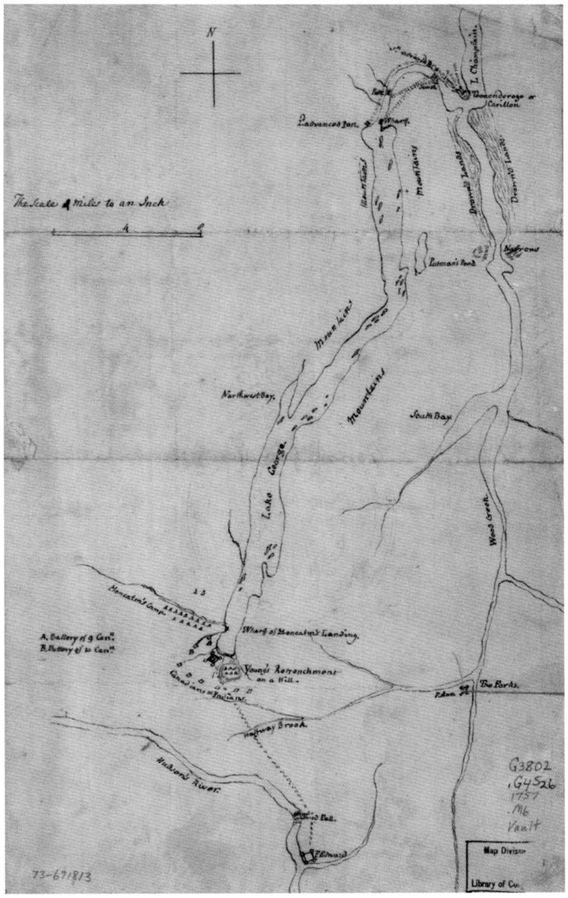

Both towns were extremely difficult to attack because of their geographical location and the harshness of the Canadian winter. Any military campaign would therefore need to know the lay of the land in exact detail and have the best possible grasp of the field. This changed the nature of mapmaking in America. The art of cartography, born from commercial and colonial interests, now became an instrument of war.

FIG. 90. A hand-drawn map of the situation during the 1757 siege of Fort William Henry by the English engineer James Gabriel Montresor, showing the position of the French camp and possible angles of attack.

London as the New Center of Cartography

No one understood that better than the mapmakers in London, a city that by the eighteenth century had succeeded Holland as the center of global cartography. In fact, that is why in 1679 a twenty-four-year-old cartographer named Herman Moll decided to pack up his belongings and move to the British capital. His actual nationality is not known. The name "Moll" is common in both Holland and Germany, but some historians believe he was born in Bremen, the ancient Hanseatic German city.[78] Moll was a gregarious fellow, with an unruly mop of dark hair, big, slightly bulging eyes, and an easy smile. This likability soon offered him an entrée in London's intellectual circles. In time he became close friends with luminaries such as the navigator and rumored pirate William Dampier, the scientist Robert Hooke, and the physicist Robert Boyle while making a living in various engraving shops. With this experience, he was able to publish his first major work, *A System of Geography*, in 1701. This was followed in 1715 by his magnum opus, an atlas of thirty large folio maps entitled *The World Described*. One of these is the map that would bring him lasting fame under the title *This Map of North America According To Ye Newest and Most Exact Observations*—also known, more prosaically, as the Codfish Map. As it happens, the map includes a pretty inset engraving of fishermen catching and drying cod along the shores of Newfoundland.

There was a good reason for that, because the codfish industry at the time was the second largest source of revenue from British America after the trade in Virginian tobacco. Moreover, fishing rights were major points of contention between the French and the British, so the identification of fishing waters carried strong political overtones as well.

Moll's maps testify to his attention to precision and detail; like many German maps of this era, they are distinctive for their elaborate cartouches, executed with Baroque flourishes and insets. Indeed, most German cartographers were devout Lutherans and dedicated their maps to the glory of God, as composers such as Johann Sebastian Bach did with their musical compositions. But few of these maps offered radically new insights. After all, the Germans were not explorers themselves. They relied on maps made by others, sometimes enhanced by reports from seafarers. For example, the Codfish Map includes the mythical Long River, that was believed to connect the Mississippi River with points in the far West. The myth of the Long River was based on observations by Louis-Armand de Lom d'Arce, baron de Lahontan, a notorious French adventurer and fraudster who claimed to have discovered this waterway in the 1690s.

Things changed in the 1740s, not only because of the ongoing contests with the French but also because Great Britain was suddenly gripped by fear

of a Jacobite rebellion in Scotland, which aimed to restore the Stuart line to the English throne. In response, the British Ordnance Survey commissioned a series of detailed maps of the country, directed by the cartographer William Roy, to aid in the defense of the realm. As military maps they were never published, but they did raise the quality of the underlying data, accuracy, and detail of geographical features to an entirely new level. The growing threat of France, including the very real danger of an invasion, further added urgency to this new type of mapmaking. There were no longer any cartouches or flowery ornaments in these maps; instead, the focus was on representing the ground as faithfully as possible.

Similarly, in 1748 the British Board of Trade and Plantations became concerned about the vulnerability of Pennsylvania and Virginia. The board ordered a new set of maps that would clearly chart these two regions with a detailed depiction of towns, roads, and topographical features such as rivers and streams. For the Virginia map the board chose two experienced surveyors, Joshua Fry and Peter Jefferson, whose son Thomas would later become a leader of the American Revolution. The first edition of these maps was delivered

FIG. 91. Herman Moll, *Map of North America*, also known as the Codfish Map, first published in 1715

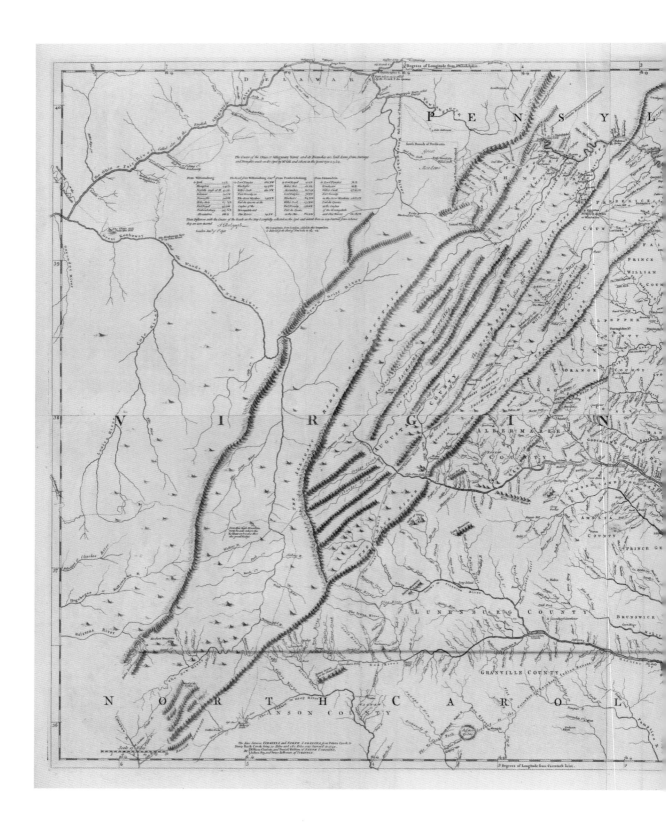

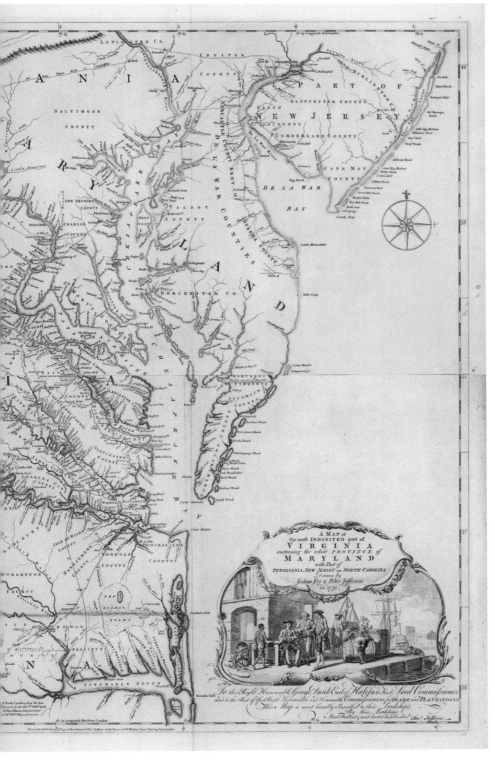

FIG. 92. Joshua Fry and Peter Jefferson, *A Map of the Most Inhabited Part of Virginia*, 1755, was the first map to show all of Virginia's four rivers and their tributaries

in 1752 and finally completed in 1755, after the outbreak of the French and Indian War.

In its final form, the map documented the living space of four hundred thousand colonists (both Whites and slaves), and the heartland of America's tobacco plantations. The map would later play an important role in the Revolutionary War for its detailed depiction of Virginia's river systems; it was the first map ever of the four principal rivers and their tributaries.

A similar map, though on a far greater scale, was published that same year by John Mitchell under the title *l'Amérique Septentrionale avec les Routes, Distances en miles, Villages et Etablissements François et Anglais* ("North America with the roads, Distances in miles, Villages and French and English Settlements"), thus clearly revealing the military purpose of the project. Not surprisingly, Mitchell's map would become the single most important artifact for debating and settling treaty disputes in the eighteenth and even nineteenth centuries.

Like Joshua Fry and Peter Jefferson, John Mitchell formed part of a new class of cartographers. These were men who were born in America and had arrived at their profession along circuitous paths that, as for their counterparts in Europe, often involved stints as natural scientists, globe makers, surveyors, physicists, or any other scientific roles. In the eighteenth century, to be a map-maker was a gentleman's calling, informed by a whole range of disciplines; the word *dilettante* did not have the pejorative meaning that it has today.

In Mitchell's case, that meant that although he was born and raised as the son of a wealthy plantation owner in Lancaster County, Virginia, he was soon dispatched to the University of Edinburgh to get his degree. Alas, young Mitchell had a hard time trying to figure out what he wanted to do (a problem that has vexed students since time immemorial), and so he wound up studying the arts, natural history, botany, and medicine. By 1735 he was back in Virginia and practicing as a physician while devoting his spare time to his love for botany. In time he married a local girl named Helen and was content.

There the story might have ended were it not that Helen was sickly and suffered greatly from the hot summers and brutal winters of Virginia. In 1746, Mitchell made the decision to return to the more temperate climate of England. Unfortunately, the War of the Spanish Succession was still raging, and the couple's ship was intercepted by French pirates on the high seas. All their belongings were taken away, including Mitchell's coveted botanical samples, so they arrived in London virtually penniless. But Mitchell was able to quickly develop a network of contacts. In 1748 he was elected to the Royal Society, a singular honor that placed him at the center of British intellectual endeavor. The official document that nominated him to this august body went out of its way to cite his expertise as someone "who from his long residence in Virginea, & from his great application to the Study of Natural history, especially Botany, is very well acquainted with the vegetable productions of North America."[79] And not just its vegetable cultivation, for Mitchell's youth in Virginia had given him a keen understanding of the geography of the Eastern Seaboard as well as the political tug-of-war that was taking place at the borders of the English colonies.

The Royal Society connection brought him into contact with an influential nobleman named George Montagu-Dunk, the Earl of Halifax. As it happened, Halifax was also the president of the Board of Trade that, as we saw, was focused on creating a new class of maps of all strategic territories under British control. It was only natural that this nobleman would share his concerns about the reliability of existing maps depicting England's American colonies, given the different administrations and the patchwork of surveys that had produced them. What was needed, Halifax argued, was a complete and thorough map of all of English North America, executed with the same level of scientific detail throughout. Mitchell, whose personal brush with French aggression still rankled, was only happy to oblige.

Modern historians have puzzled over the choice of Mitchell over far more experienced cartographers who could be found in London by the dozens, but here, as in so many other cases, the British sensitivity for class undoubtedly played a role. Mitchell was a member of the Royal Society by virtue of his work as a physician and botanist, not as a cartographer, and that gave him a leg up over his competition. What's more, by commissioning Mitchell rather than approaching the cartographers of the British Admiralty, Halifax could keep full control of the project—and claim credit if indeed it proved successful.

Our story has lingered on the life of John Mitchell for one important reason: his map would set the stage for much that was about to unfold on American soil. For both sides of the American Revolutionary War, Mitchell's map would serve as the defining reference for the field of battle.

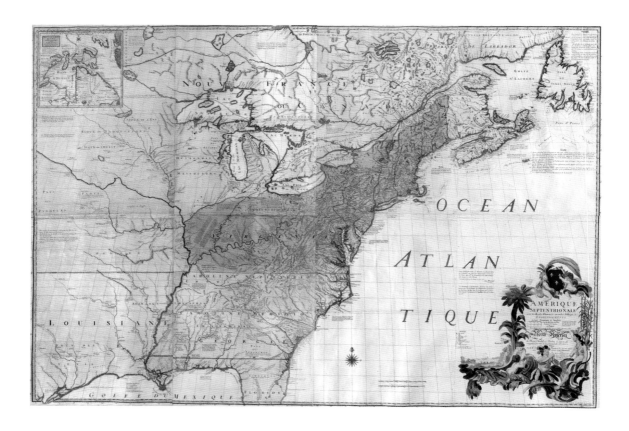

FIG. 93. Georges Louis Le Rouge, *l'Amérique Septentrionale* ("Map of North America"). This was a French version of the Mitchell Map published in 1757.

Of course, as an amateur cartographer Mitchell did not have access to any new data other than what had been published in the years before. This is where the commission by Halifax made all the difference. The board was ordered to provide Mitchell with all of their latest charts, surveys, and other data, including the map previously drawn up by Fry and Jefferson. Officers of the board even sent letters to all colonial governors in America and ordered them to provide pertinent geographical data and survey maps to Mitchell forthwith. The result of this effort is an artifact of truly awesome proportions and detail. While much of the territory west of the Mississippi is left indistinct, as was typical of the time, the Eastern Seaboard is documented with a level of detail far beyond anything that had been published before. Of course, the Mitchell Map deliberately favored the British side in interpreting areas of questionable ownership, just as French maps of the era tended to diminish English possessions. Interestingly, this did not prevent Georges Louis Le Rouge from republishing the map in French!

The great irony of the Mitchell Map is that an enterprise designed to protect British interests in North America would ultimately become the most important cartographic instrument in the pursuit of American independence. Of invaluable importance during the Revolutionary War, the Mitchell Map would also serve as the principal reference during the negotiations of the Treaty of Paris, which in 1783 ended the war and sealed the birth of the United States—the subject of our next and final chapters.

Meanwhile, the French and Indian War ground on. The French were making impressive gains, particularly in the Ohio Valley, pushing back against the colonists of Pennsylvania. This is when Major George Washington of the Virginia Regiment agreed to a parley with the commander of the French forces, Jacques Legardeur de Saint-Pierre. First, he and his party were plied with wine, in which "they dos'd themselves pretty plentifully," as he later wrote, no doubt in the hope it would give "license to their Tongues."[80]

Two days later, the young Virginian finally met the French commander himself and presented him with a written ultimatum to vacate Ohio Country. "Ah," Saint-Pierre replied in a strong French accent, "as to the Summons you send me to retire, I don't think myself obliged to obey it." Indeed, why should he? At that point, Washington confronted enemy forces that were far more numerous than those under his command—a situation that would repeat itself some twenty-odd years later. But then, back in Europe, another war broke out that raised the stakes even higher.

The Seven Years' War (1756–1763)

Once again, this brought the two superpowers of France and Britain into conflict, although this time their alliances were rearranged like a deck of cards. The French decided to enter into a "grand coalition" with Russia, Spain, Austria, and Sweden, while England allied itself with Prussia, Portugal, and various German states.

On paper, it seemed that France and its allies commanded far superior forces, particularly because most states in northwest Europe—including Denmark, Norway, and Holland—had declared their neutrality. But this appearance was deceptive because the Seven Years' War was truly the world's

FIG. 94. British warships in action: *The Capture of the French ships Alcide and Lys*, by an unknown artist, 1755

first global conflict, fought over several continents, from America to India, and from the coasts of Africa to the islands of the Philippines. And when it came to battleships, no one came close to matching the power of Britain's Royal Navy. The result was a contest in which the French coalition fought its battles the conventional way—by massing large forces on land—while British men-of-war roamed freely across the seas, ravaging French ships, bombarding French ports, and pillaging French possessions with abandon.

Britain had also made a brilliant decision to enlist one of Europe's greatest military minds, Prussia's Frederick the Great, to the British cause. This soon turned the tide on land as well. In 1757, Frederick crushed the French forces at the Battle of Leuthen, killing 10,000 Frenchmen for only 548 casualties on the Prussian side. And yet the French Crown refused to abandon the field; the prestige of France was at stake. And so the war went on, killing untold numbers of civilians while destroying towns, fields, and monuments that had stood for hundreds of years.

By 1763, most of the European powers were exhausted. Crowned heads had to admit that the war had entered a stalemate. The Austrian Empire was nearly bankrupt; her ruler, Empress Maria Theresa, had to pawn her jewels in order to maintain some measure of financial credit. Austrian citizens were asked to donate their silver. Meanwhile, the British continued to rack up victories. Their ships captured the French possessions of Guadeloupe and Martinique, as well as Spanish Havana and Manila in the Philippines. In America, British forces finally broke through in French Canada, seizing Fort Niagara and Fort Carillon during what became known as the *Annus Mirabilis*, the "Miracle Year." It culminated in the fierce battle for Quebec City, led by the British general James Wolfe. Although Wolfe was killed, Quebec was taken, and the future of New France was sealed.

The news thrilled all of London, from the lowliest beggar to the highest-born peer. Among them was an American-born artist named Benjamin West, the tenth child of an innkeeper, who was now living in London. Now a highly successful portraitist, West fondly remembered the years of his youth in Pennsylvania. According to his memoir, as a child he was introduced to painting by Native Americans, who showed him how to create pigments by mixing clay with bear grease. An autodidact like Copley, West never had a formal education; it is said that many years later, while serving as president of London's Royal Academy of Arts, he could hardly spell.[81] But as an artist, West was without peer. In London circles he was known as the "American Raphael" and would eventually become the official historical painter to the court of King George III, shortly before the outbreak of the Revolutionary War.

West never forgot his American roots. Deeply moved by the war between France and Britain, he painted his most famous work, *The Death of General Wolfe* (1770). It shows the general on the brink of victory, expiring in the arms of his loyal American lieutenants and officers of the British expeditionary army. Instantly popular, the painting inspired countless engravings, making it one of the most frequently reproduced images of the era. While no one could anticipate it at the time, it also marked the final high point in the relationship between Britain and her colonies in America.

The Seven Years' War accomplished two important things. One, it turned Britain into the world's largest empire virtually overnight. Utterly exhausted,

France's King Louis XV had no choice but to agree to the punishing terms of the Treaty of Paris, concluded in 1763. Most of New France was ceded to the British Crown. The Spanish territory of Florida, the oldest European settlement on the continent, was likewise handed over to Great Britain. In return, Spain received some of the French holdings west of the Mississippi River, but these included largely undeveloped lands ruled by Native Americans. In India, France lost most of its possessions, making way for Britain's undisputed rule of this subcontinent in the future. In one fell stroke, Britain now controlled all of North America east of the Mississippi.

The second major outcome of the war was that the bonds between Americans and their British protectors were now closer than ever. American and English soldiers had fought shoulder to shoulder and had bled for a common goal, a common vision: undisputed English rule in its American colonies. Together, they had emerged victorious for the greater glory of the British Crown and its new king, George III. "Rule Britannia" was toasted in pubs and dining rooms across the English colonies. Wherever one looked, the flag of Saint George fluttered proudly in the wind.

And then, just a decade later, it all fell apart.

FIG. 95. Benjamin West, *The Death of General Wolfe*, 1770

THE OUTBREAK
OF REBELLION

WHAT POSSESSED A SMALL GROUP OF AMERICAN COLONISTS with no standing army, and with no naval fleet to speak of, to take on the mightiest empire in the world? What prompted this foolhardy rush to history's first Brexit? After all, Britain would soon have more than thirty other colonies around the globe where for the foreseeable future colonists were content to live and prosper under the benign embrace of Britain—including those in Australia, Africa, India, and Southeast Asia. Many of these English colonies would not aspire to independence until the twentieth century. So what made the American case unique? What prompted their rush to arms against the most powerful military in the world?

By the same token, we may well ask what motivated the English Crown to expend so much of its treasure, and the flower of its youth, in a conflict more than three thousand miles away? Why did cooler heads not prevail in Whitehall, and why did its constitutional monarch, restrained as he was by Parliament, not pursue a diplomatic settlement—particularly in the early phase of the war, when such a settlement was still within his grasp? Why did King George III persist in throwing vast sums of money, ships, and armed forces at the American Revolutionary War, even when its commanders warned him that the conflict could not be won by military means?

Reams of ink have been expended on these questions, and they continue to inspire more books and arguments to this day. But one thing is clear: the dispute between the American colonies and their motherland went far beyond the motto "No taxation without representation," beyond the Boston Tea Party and all the other totems that today we attach to our foundational saga. Instead, the conflict was the result of "a long fuse," to quote a book by the historian Don Cook. [82]

To understand the cascade of factors that brought both parties to the brink of war, we must first realize the devastating impact that the European wars had on Britain's economy. True, the Seven Years' War had turned the island nation into a global empire "where the sun never set," reaching from Canada and America to the Caribbean and the Mediterranean, and from Africa to India and Southeast Asia. Giddy with victory, the British politician Horace Walpole wrote that the fantastic stream of triumphs across the globe reminded him of "the handiwork of a lady romance-writer."[83]

But the stupendous cost of shipbuilding, combined with the expense of maintaining a wartime navy as well as large expeditionary forces, had depleted the English treasury. The total bill for the war came to £122.6 million, and much of this eye-popping amount had been borrowed on the markets. As a result, the total debt of the English Government now approached a quarter billion pounds, so that half of the government's revenue went to interest payments alone.[84] That also meant that the Crown could not pay off the principal and that by 1764 the war debt had ballooned to nearly £130 million. Given this predicament, the £1 billion in taxable goods that arrived from Britain's American colonies each year constituted a vital financial lifeline. But it was not enough.

The dominant feeling in London was that the Americans, who after all were the main beneficiaries of Britain's crushing victory over the French, should do more to help the mother country cope with its war debt. As Rick Atkinson has shown, the average American colonist paid no more than a sixpence a year in British taxes, compared to the average tax bill of twenty-five shillings—fifty times more—that most Englishmen were required to pay. Already, British citizens were the most heavily taxed population in all of Europe, with sales and excise taxes approaching 25 percent.[85] It therefore seemed entirely reasonable for the British Crown to ask its American colonists to step up to the plate and to help recoup some of the immense costs that had procured freedom and security for the American colonies.

The colonists, however, saw things differently. For much of the past century, Britain had been so preoccupied with fighting its European enemies that it had allowed its overseas colonies to manage their own affairs in what Edmund Burke called a happy condition of "salutary neglect."[86] This was a deliberate policy, for as Robert Walpole, British prime minister from 1721 to 1742 had said, "If no restrictions were placed on the colonies, they would flourish." The American colonists had seized that opportunity with both hands and, as we saw, had built systems of governance and jurisdiction that paid lip service to the Crown but otherwise operated as largely autonomous states.

For example, neither Walpole nor his successors had ever enforced the odious Navigation Acts, first established by Oliver Cromwell and King Charles II, which compelled English colonists to trade only with England, Scotland, and Wales. Like a benign but mostly absent father, the Crown had allowed the settlers to manage things as they saw fit, as long as the ships carrying sugar, tobacco, rice, and fur arrived in English ports on schedule. As Alan Axelrod wrote, "the Crown and Parliament had been giving the colonies a free ride."[87] Now, that neglect had come home to roost.

Already in 1755, King George II and Parliament had begun to enforce some of the terms of the Navigation Acts by authorizing royal customs officers in America to force local governments in the arrest and prosecution of smugglers and others who traded with "unauthorized entities" outside the British sphere of influence. As part of this writ, English customs officers were given the power to enter warehouses and even private homes without a search warrant from the local courts. This practice kindled deep resentment among many of the colonial authorities, but there was little chance of making their opposition known, since most were fighting for their lives in the French and Indian War. Parliament drew the wrong conclusion from this response, thinking that the colonies had no problem with a more vigorous enforcement of the Navigation Acts.

Also generating considerable ill will were the terms of the 1763 Treaty of Paris, which had ended the war between France and Britain. In return for the help that the Seneca, other Iroquois tribes, the Ottawa, and the Shawnee had provided the English army in their fight with the French, the British Crown had promised these nations that white settlement would not go beyond the Allegheny (part of the Appalachian) Mountains. When American settlers pushed across the mountain range regardless, King George III's Proclamation of 1763 sternly ordered them to vacate these lands, and move back even farther, to the east of the Appalachian Mountains! Outraged, the colonists in the trans-Appalachian frontier refused to leave, thus inviting repeated raids by Indian tribes who believed they had the English king on their side. Calls went to London to send troops to assist the settlers, but of course the king could not go back on his word and refused to intervene. As a result, the trans-Appalachian region became a Wild West territory where settlers had to fend for themselves with whatever arms and militia they had at their disposal. The local colonial governments backed them to the hilt and refused to enforce the 1763 Proclamation. Thus, the first fault lines between king and colonists were drawn.

It was the tragedy of both Britain and its overseas settlers that George III, a deeply insecure man with a mediocre mind, found himself at the head of a constitutional monarchy rather than an absolutist one. Had he ruled in Russia, France, Prussia, the Habsburg domains, or any of the other absolutist monarchies of his time, he would have been able to indulge in his penchant for autocratic governance without constraint. Alas, in 1760 he rose to the throne of a country blessed with a parliamentary democracy that sought to contain royal privilege at every turn. This had the unfortunate consequence of stirring the king's innate obstinacy, a reluctance to listen to reason, and a determination to persist with policies, no matter how ill-advised, lest he create an impression of weakness. William Pitt the Elder, the de facto prime minister from 1756 to 1761, was one of the first senior officials to discover the king's intolerance for dissent, when he was ousted from his position simply because he had advocated a policy of moderation toward the American colonies. The king would have none of such talk. English soldiers and sailors had bled to keep these colonies safe from her enemies, and now the colonists would have to pay for the privilege.

As a result, the position of prime minister was vacant for most of 1766–1768 while the king searched for a pliant yes-man who would execute the royal wishes without demur. He found such a man in Sir Frederick North, who would serve the king as his prime minister throughout the conflict with America. The king's unwillingness to listen or to seek a compromise could not have come at a worse time for Britain and her colonies and became a major factor in the inevitable slide toward war.

The British Acts of Trade

All this may explain why, from 1764 onward, George III's chancellor of the Exchequer, George Grenville, initiated a series of acts with the goal of sharply increasing revenues from the overseas colonies. As he stated in Parliament, the purpose of these acts was for "new provisions and regulations" to be established "for improving the revenue of this Kingdom" and "for defraying the expenses of defending, protecting, and securing the same."

First, the Sugar Act set tariffs on a large number of products imported from countries outside of Great Britain, including silk, iron, hides, and textiles. Next, the Currency Act restricted the issue of paper money by the local colonies, such as bills of credit, which had been used to pay for military expenses during the French and Indian War. These local bills tended to depreciate relative to the pound sterling and thus produced an inflation that was detrimental to merchants back in England.

While local governments could still issue bills of tender for local public debt, the Currency Act decreed that these notes could *not* be used for private debt related to overseas trade with Britain. Of course, that deprived these notes of their value and created acute problems for local colonial governments who had only limited access to hard currency such as the British pound, let alone gold or silver.

Worse, the act essentially deprived the colonies of the ability to control their own funding. This made a deep psychological impact on communities that were used to managing their own affairs, financial and otherwise. It fostered the sense that the English Parliament, more than three thousand miles away, cared little for the real hardships of colonists on the frontier of the New World and ignored the great sacrifices that the colonies had made during the war.

Thus, when Parliament fired its next salvo, in the form of the 1765 Stamp Act, resentment among the colonies grew into outright opposition. The Stamp Act was perceived as particularly heinous, precisely because of its indiscriminate effect on anything that involved printed paper. Newspapers, pamphlets, wills, marriage licenses, even playing cards were now subject to a tax. It mattered little that similar stamp taxes had previously been levied in other European countries, including Britain itself, which had introduced a stamp tax on its citizens in 1694. The Americans responded by boycotting English products and impeding English tax collectors in any way they could. In the end, the act raised only a paltry £45 at the cost of inflaming much of the colonial population. Opposition also rose in British Parliament, particularly when British manufacturers complained of losing business in the colonies. One parliamentarian, Isaac Barré, referred to the colonists as "these sons of liberty"—an epithet that Samuel Adams would later embrace as a title of honor. In 1766, Parliament reluctantly repealed the Stamp Act.

FIG. 96. A thirty-shilling note, issued by the colony of New Jersey in 1764. This is the earliest surviving example of colonial currency and is now in the British Library.

The news was greeted with relief throughout the colonies. It seemed that a dangerous confrontation had been averted. New York commissioned an equestrian statue of George III, the "best of kings," modeled after that of Marcus Aurelius on the Campidoglio in Rome. But the reprieve was short-lived.

All of this reckless brinkmanship, so at odds with Britain's erstwhile hands-off policy, was observed with alarm by the former English governor of Massachusetts Bay, Thomas Pownall. Though a product of British gentry who had been educated at Trinity College in Cambridge, Pownall was an avowed Americanophile who after 1753 had traveled widely through the colonies. Along the way he became good friends with Benjamin Franklin and Massachusetts governor William Shirley, and was particularly attracted to the problem of how to deal with the rising tensions with the Iroquois nations bordering New York and Pennsylvania. After he befriended an émigré cartographer named Lewis Evans, he decided to create a map that would clearly identify the territory of the Iroquois tribes vis-à-vis the lands claimed by the American colonists. Though lacking in the beauty and ornament of the French maps of this period, the Evans-Pownall map of 1755 more than made up for it in detail, providing a minute depiction of individual tribal lands in relationship to colonies from Rhode Island to Virginia.

Pownall nurtured a deep desire to be appointed by the Crown to the governorship of one of the colonies, and this ambition was satisfied—at least in part—when he was given the position of lieutenant-governor of New Jersey in 1755. That left him with very little to do, since His Majesty's governor of New Jersey, Jonathan Belcher, was a hands-on administrator who did not brook

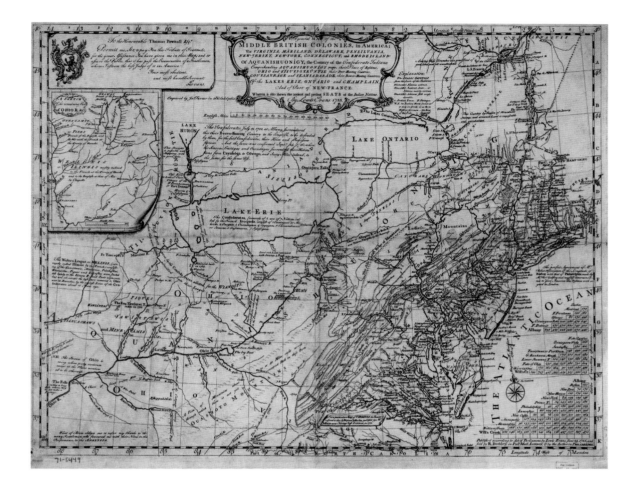

much interference and had no plans to retire anytime soon. Pownall returned to London, where he ingratiated himself with the prime minister, the Duke of Newcastle, and in 1757 realized his dream by being appointed the governor of Massachusetts.

For the remainder of his tenure in Massachusetts and his subsequent service back in London after 1763, Pownall continued to plead for moderation and compromise with the American colonists. He had observed these proud people firsthand and grasped their determination to build a just and honorable society, provided they were given the freedom to do so. This prompted him to write a book, *The Administration of the Colonies,* in which he argued how the tensions between colonists and their motherland could be defused and how Americans could be encouraged to prosper as loyal citizens of the British

FIG. 97. Lewis Evans, *Map of the Middle British Colonies in America and the Country of Confederate Indians*, also known as the Evans-Pownall Map, 1755

A View of the Falls on the Pasiaick or second River in the Province of New Jersey.) Vue de l'Cataracte du Pasiaick, on seconde Riviere, dans la Province du Nouveau Jersey.
The height of the Fall between Eighty and Ninety feet, the River about Eighty Yards broad. La Hauteur de cette Chute est de Ixo a 90 pieds, et la Largeur de la Riviere d'environ 80 Toises.
Sketch'd on the Spot by his Excellency Governor Pownal. Painted and Engraved by Paul Sandby.
London Published according to Act of Parliament, 20 May 1761 by Tho. Jefferys, the Corner of St Martins Lane.

FIG. 98. Thomas Pownall, *The Great Falls of the Passaic River*, 1761

Empire. In this, he tried to seek an equitable and honorable compromise. For example, while he defended the obligation of the colonies to contribute to the cost of maintaining a military presence against their enemies, he also argued that Americans were entitled to the same type of representative government that English, Irish, and Scottish citizens enjoyed.

One wonders what would have happened if Pownall's incisive analysis had been taken seriously by King George III. The history of America might have been very different—perhaps similar to that of Canada and Australia, nations that achieved their independence from Great Britain in 1867 and 1901, respectively. Unfortunately, Pownall was not a skilled author, and his book made little impact. On the other hand, he was quite an accomplished artist, as the images in this chapter attest, so his depictions of his beloved America left a far more favorable impression.

The Fuse Is Lit

The Stamp Act had galvanized the colonies, but an even more grievous act, the Mutiny Act of 1765, brought them together in a unified front of opposition. This act decreed that English troops could be quartered in private homes, thus treating the American colonies as "occupied territory" rather than an extension of English lands and law. Adding insult to injury, it also forced the colonies to pay for all costs of feeding and supplying British troops. Most colonial legislatures were outraged by these demands and simply refused to comply. There was, as yet, no talk of armed resistance; the colonies simply felt that their needs were not being adequately understood and that the acts issued by Grenville had no process of grievance, which therefore made them undemocratic and unconstitutional.

This would have been a great opportunity for the parties to arrange for a parley to see if some form of compromise could be reached. It was exactly for this purpose that delegates from nine colonies convened on October 25, 1765, in New York's City Hall for the so-called Stamp Act Congress, where they drew up a fourteen-point "Declaration of Rights and Grievances."

The document argued that if the American colonists owed to the Crown "the same allegiance" owed by "subjects born within the realm," then they should also possess all the rights of Englishmen, including due process in the English court of law (rather than the arbitrary jurisdiction meted out by the Admiralty courts), as well as voting rights in Parliament. There should be no taxation without representation, the signers stated. And if the colonies were not granted any representation, except in the form of their local colonial assemblies, then it followed that only those assemblies had the right to levy taxes.

Legally, it sounded like a very logical and persuasive argument, and not surprisingly it made quite an impact when it reached London two months later. William Pitt declared his support for the declaration and began to push for a repeal of the Stamp Act. He knew that the government was under pressure to do something, because Britain's economy continued to suffer from American boycotts. As we saw, on March 18, 1766, the Stamp Act was officially repealed, but the king's vindictiveness ensured that there was little cause for celebration. That same day, Parliament issued the Declaratory Act, which affirmed its right to make laws binding on the American colonies "in all cases whatsoever." The appeal for "no taxation without representation" was therewith roundly rejected.

With that declaration, the die had been cast. By denying Americans the rights of Englishmen, the British Crown deprived its colonists of their legitimacy as citizens. They were now, essentially, stateless persons. And if that was the case, then the only option for the colonists was to acquire a legitimacy of their own—not as Englishmen but as Americans, as citizens of the land where they were born and had lived and worked all of their lives. In many ways, then, it was the British Acts of 1765–1766 that pushed the American colonists on their path toward independence. Fittingly, the Stamp Act Congress is often seen as the first political act in the drama of the American Revolution, even though for many delegates the idea of a break from Great Britain was still far from their minds. They had appealed to the British Crown for redress, and that appeal had been denied. Now there was only one course left to pursue.

From Tea Party to Open Resistance

From this point on, Britain and her colonies began their slow slide to war. Parliament decided to rub salt in the American wound with a new series of acts, this time dreamed up by the new chancellor of the exchequer, Charles Townshend, who was desperately trying to improve Britain's dire finances. The resulting Townshend Acts of 1767 were even more punitive than anything that Grenville had thought of, because they taxed a whole range of basic, everyday commodities such as glass, paint, lead, paper, and even tea, all of which had to be imported from Britain. Once again, the colonies were unified in their opposition, and several ports simply refused to offload the goods in question from British ships. Too late, Parliament realized that they had shot themselves in the foot by jeopardizing the very imports on which the British treasury had become so dependent.

On January 1, 1768, Boston merchants took a step further by pledging to boycott *all* British goods, a move that was soon joined by New York and Philadelphia. Other cities, however, refused to go that far. This explains why, even if the volume of exports to the colonies was declining, the boycott movement did not have the catastrophic effect it was hoping for. But in the end, it didn't matter. In Boston, the Royal Customs Board decided to enforce the Townshend Acts by any means possible and, well aware of the increasingly restive mood of the city, asked for military assistance. In response, the supreme commander of all English forces in North America, General Thomas Gage, dispatched a force of four regiments to restore order in the city. When on March 5, 1770, these English redcoats found themselves confronted by an angry mob, they opened fire, killing five unarmed civilians.

News of the Boston Massacre ricocheted through the colonies, but in London Parliament was blissfully unaware of this sudden escalation. As it happened, on that same day, March 5, Prime Minister Lord North presented a motion in the House of Commons to repeal parts of the Townshend Act. The motion was carried and the most odious taxes were removed, but the principle of absolute British sovereignty over the life of American colonists, including the power of the Board of Customs and the right to levy taxes, remained.[88] Almost as an afterthought, the tax on British tea, three pence per pound, was retained as well. This was probably due to extensive lobbying by the English East India Company, which had seen its revenues drop alarmingly as a result of competition from the Dutch East Indies. The new Tea Act now gave the East India Company an absolute monopoly on the sale of tea to the American colonies, even bypassing English merchants and wholesalers in Britain proper.

On December 16, 1773, a small party of men, some disguised as Native Americans, boarded three British ships that were moored at Griffin's Wharf in the port of Boston. Using block and tackle, they brought up large chests containing some forty-five tons of tea, broke the lids, and dumped the aromatic contents into Boston harbor. "By morning," Rick Atkinson wrote, "almost £10,000 worth of soggy brown flakes drifted in windrows from the wharf to Castle Island and the Dorchester shore."[89]

King George III was shocked when he heard the news. British merchants, fearing an all-out embargo of British goods, urged caution. But Parliament knew that the king would not be in a forgiving mood and rushed to comply with George's desire for revenge. From March 1774 onward, the House of Commons adopted four laws that became known as the Coercive Acts and that in America would be derided as the Intolerable Acts. Their terms were exceedingly harsh. Self-government in Massachusetts was dissolved. All of Boston's

FIG. 99. This print of the Boston Massacre was engraved
and printed by Paul Revere.

commerce was shut down, and a blockade was thrown around its harbor. In a further vindictive move, the English province of Quebec was extended into Ohio Country west of the Appalachians, with the goal of displacing American colonists there with French Catholics.

The Coercive Acts were inspired by a fatal misreading of the American colonists' motives and their plea to be treated as equals. A wiser and more perceptive king might have seized this moment to call for moderation and to seek a way to admonish the Americans without impugning their human dignity. Prudent counsel might have reminded him that the thirteen colonies now comprised a population of 2.5 million that was doubling every quarter century and that soon America would be a political and economic power in its own right. It would have behooved Britain to do everything in its power to keep that growing strength within the British sphere of influence and to seek a middle course between English sovereignty and the American desire for autonomy, which at this stage was still in the realm of possibility.

The able Doctor, or America Swallowing the Bitter Draught!

FIG. 100. This 1774 political cartoon shows evil Englishmen forcing tea down the throat of a heroic maid, a symbol of America. It was part of the effort to rally opposition to the Intolerable Acts.

But the king's mind was made up. For him, the American colonists were unruly children who needed to be sternly disciplined into obedience. Addressing Parliament in March 1774, he "lamented the dangerous spirit of resistance displayed by the people of Massachusetts Bay," according to one witness, and expressed "my most anxious desire to see my deluded subjects, in that part of the world, returning to a sense of their duty, acquiescing in that just subordination to the authority, and maintaining that due regard to the commercial interests of this country."[90]

The Coercive Acts had the opposite effect, as many observers, including Thomas Pownall, must surely have anticipated. In September 1774, fifty-five delegates from every colony except Georgia gathered in Philadelphia for the First Continental Congress. Here, the delegates agreed to halt all trade with Britain, and to resist the sale or trade of any British goods, until the Coercive Acts were repealed. Many hoped that this economic pressure would bring the British Crown to its senses and avoid a break with the motherland, as some more radical protesters were now advocating. After all, it was because of similar tactics that Parliament had previously repealed the Grenville and Townshend acts. But King George was not to be moved. "A most daring spirit of resistance and disobedience to the law" had spread through the colonies, he declared to Parliament. Its members, eager to please their warlike king, brayed their support. As far as Britain was considered, Massachusetts and various other colonies were now in a state of open rebellion, and only a military response could set matters right.

The First Clashes

For British strategists, the focus was Massachusetts. That was where, in their eyes, the rebellion was born and where the British military needed to set an example. And with good reason, for this time around, the boycott of British imports succeeded beyond the colonists' wildest dreams: between 1774 and 1775, imports dropped 97 percent, to the great distress of British merchants. This is why Parliament declared Massachusetts to be in a state of rebellion and ordered a blockade of the colony, depriving it from any other sources of trade and supplies. In addition, General Thomas Gage—who served as both commander in chief of British forces and the military governor of Massachusetts—prepared a plan to disarm all of the local militias.

Though he was a gifted administrator, Gage's acumen as a military strategist was less distinguished, as his rather checkered record during the French and Indian War may attest. Moreover, he was now in his fifties and was looking forward to spending the final years of his service in peace and quiet, together with his American wife. But he was the man on the scene, and so Gage directed Britain's military movements in the opening salvos of the war—or what many Britons and loyalist Americans hoped would be little more than a police action to put the New England rebels in their place. On that score, at least, Gage was brimming with confidence. In 1774, he had assured George III that when push came to shove, most of the other colonies would not come to Massachusetts's defense. They were too different socially, culturally, and economically, he told the king, which was certainly true. As a result, Gage believed that four regiments of around five hundred men each would be sufficient to settle the matter—a fateful miscalculation, as events would soon bear out.

As a case in point, on April 18, Gage sent seven hundred redcoats led by Lieutenant Colonel Francis Smith on a mission to confiscate what was believed to be a large cache of weapons in the town of Concord, eighteen miles from Boston. On the night before the raid, however, a local network of informants had gotten wind of Smith's plans and had dispatched riders to all militias in the area, one of whom was Paul Revere. After an initial skirmish between the militia and the British regulars at Lexington, the redcoats continued on to Concord, confident in their ability to seize the suspected arms.

Fortunately, most of the military stores had already been dispersed to surrounding villages, but the British were still able to seize barrels of flour, musket balls, gun carriages, and other implements. A small party of one hundred regulars was then ordered to secure the North Bridge, where a force of four hundred American militia lay in ambush. They had seen smoke spiraling up from their homes in Concord and had concluded—incorrectly, as it turned out—that the British had set their houses to the torch. Enraged, they stood up and fired volley after volley of musket fire until the field was aflame with the bright flashes of ball. This was, as Ralph Waldo Emerson later wrote in his poem "Concord Hymn," the "shot heard round the world."

Within mere minutes, eight British regulars lay wounded, including four officers, and the company was forced to retreat. That twenty-mile retreat lasted all day, under constant harassing fire, until a relief force led by General Hugh Percy brought the redcoats back to the safety of Charlestown, a suburb of Boston.

The American forces, as improvised as they may have been, were determined to make use of the sudden turn of events. All of the militia in the surrounding regions converged on Boston with the aim of throwing a siege around the British military. The vulnerability of these forces was obvious now that they were bottled up in the narrow peninsula of Boston Harbor. In fact, that was made eminently plain in a map drawn up by a witness on the scene, Lieutenant Thomas Hyde Page, a member of His Majesty's Corps of Engineers.

In order to deprive the regulars of supplies, colonial teams went around the surrounding territory, evacuating any foodstuffs or lumber that could be raided by the British. In desperation, the naval commander on the scene, Samuel Graves, ordered a loyalist merchant, Ichabod Jones, to dispatch a sloop to Machias, in Maine, in the hope of securing timber from that territory. A

FIG. 101. Battle map of the action at Concord, which was rushed to London and engraved on July 29, 1776, for use by the king in following the progress of the war. The map shows the position of militia and minutemen south of Concord and the location of the king's troops they faced. The map explicitly shows the militia fighting from behind rocks and walls, while the British redcoats are pictured fighting out in the open.

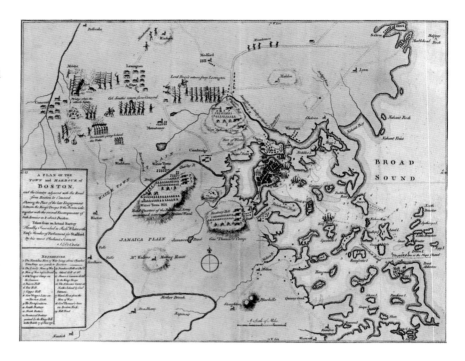

FIG. 102. (*Opposite page*) Thomas Hyde Page, *The Town of Boston with the Intrenchments of His Majesty's Forces, 1775.* The map revealed the vulnerability of British forces behind their entrenchments.

British schooner, the HMS *Margaretta*, was to sail alongside and provide protection against any American ships. But the people of Machias refused to meet the British demands, while a small group of courageous rebels then seized the *Margaretta* in an altercation that killed her captain, Lieutenant Moore. It was the first instance of a British naval defeat at the hands of American patriots.

News of this daring capture ran all through New England, and it had serious repercussions. Graves retaliated by ordering that the town of Falmouth (today known as Portland, Maine) be entirely destroyed by the British fleet.

The so-called Burning of Falmouth took place on October 18, 1775, but the wanton destruction of this undefended town by overwhelming British naval firepower merely served to outrage the colonists and push many wavering Americans over to the rebel cause.

The brutal deed had other, even greater consequences as well. Back in Philadelphia, the Second Continental Congress had emerged as the de facto national assembly for managing the Revolutionary War. It now authorized the development of a Continental Navy—a service arm that would play a key role in the battles to come. Earlier, on June 14, the Congress had voted to create a Continental Army by fusing the many disparate colonial militias into a cohesive

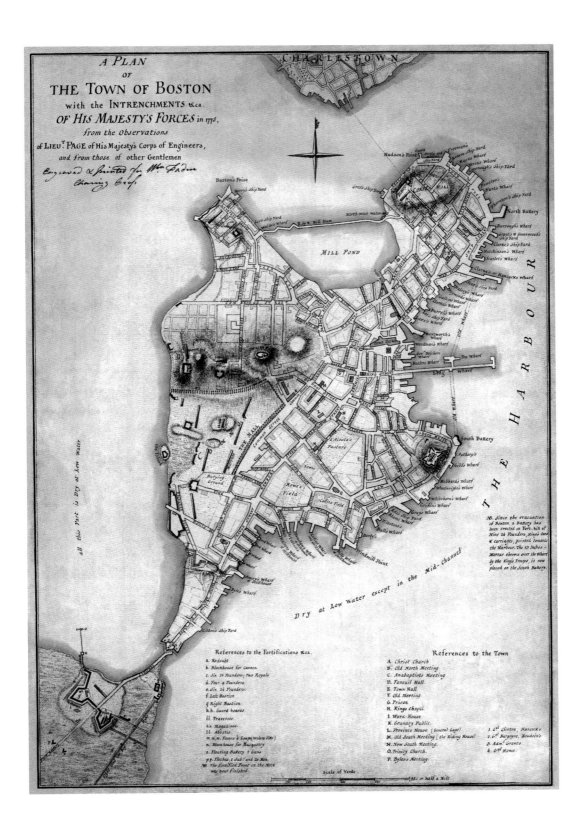

FIG. 103. A 1782 engraving
of the Burning of Falmouth

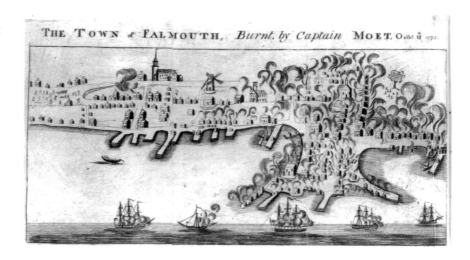

force. This new army needed a commanding general, and for that the choice fell on George Washington of Virginia.

Washington had previously risen through the ranks of British Continental forces during the French and Indian War, eventually reaching the rank of lieutenant colonel. Ironically, he had served under Thomas Gage during the 1755 Battle of Monongahela, when Washington had two horses shot from under him and ended up with bullet holes in his hat and coat. His impressive sangfroid during this engagement was much commented upon and earned him a favorable reputation, so that he eventually rose to command the royal forces of Virginia. In 1758 he was promoted to the rank of brevet brigadier general and led an attack on the French fort of Duquesne, but the French abandoned the fort before the assault could be launched. Washington eventually retired to his beloved plantation on Mount Vernon, where his wife, Martha Washington, was waiting for him.

As soon as the tensions with Britain escalated, however, Washington threw himself into the fray, sharply opposing the Stamp Act and other acts while pushing for Virginia to boycott all British imports in imitation of other colonies in revolt. He saw the battle against George III as a fight against tyranny, whose "custom and use shall make us . . . tame and abject slaves." On August 1, 1774, he was elected as Virginia's delegate to the First Continental Congress and soon thereafter launched himself on the recruitment and training of Virginia militias.

Still, news of the outbreak of actual hostilities between Britain and her American colonies took him aback. Like many other Americans who had served with British forces in the wars against the French, he had hoped that sufficient saber-rattling would bring the king to his senses. "Sobered and dismayed," he made his way to Philadelphia on May 4, 1775, to take the lead of America's Revolutionary War.

FIG. 104. *(Next page)* Auguste Jacques Régnier, *Washington the Soldier at the Battle of Monongahela*, 1854

The Battle of Bunker Hill and Gage's Response

News of the defeat at Concord shocked the king, who had trusted Gage's assurances that he could suppress the rebellion with the forces at his disposal. In response, a British flotilla soon brought reinforcements of two thousand men, led by three generals who would play a key role in the battles to come: forty-six-year-old William Howe, the fifth Viscount Howe, with a distinctive record in the Seven Years' War; forty-five-year-old Sir Henry Clinton, an officer and a member of Parliament; and fifty-three-year-old General John Burgoyne, an amateur playwright of some note and likewise a member of Parliament since 1761. Together, they weighed the situation in Boston and agreed that the position was untenable.

The British forces needed to break out and regroup, so that they could fight the Continentals on more favorable terrain. As a first step, they decided to take control of the hills surrounding the city so as to protect the ships that would have to enter the harbor and board the troops. This required maneuvers that could be scarcely hidden, so that as soon as the redcoats began to prepare for their evacuation, news was relayed back to the Continental Army.

As it happened, the Boston colonial forces were led by a highly capable officer named General Israel Putnam. He instantly realized the need to take possession of the hills, and particularly Bunker Hill, so as to fortify them and frustrate the British plans. Thus, after the sun had set on June 16, 1775, some twelve hundred men led by Colonel William Prescott swarmed over Bunker Hill with the intent of building redoubts. Unfortunately, they got lost in the dark and mistakenly occupied a nearby mound known as Breed's Hill. There, the men dug, hammered, and sawed all night long to erect breastworks, which of course did not go unnoticed. At daybreak, Gage observed the hastily built

FIG. 105. An extremely rare hand-drawn colored map of the situation after the Lexington and Concord battles, showing the lines, batteries, and encampments of the British and American armies, June 1776. The map clearly reveals the difficult position that the British forces found themselves in after the action at Concord.

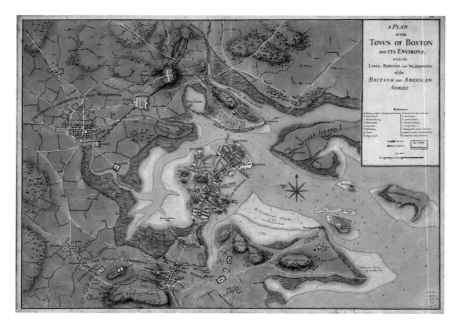

fortifications through his spyglass, shrugged, and ordered his regiments to attack. High on the hill, nervous Continentals gripped their muskets and loaded them with ball. For the first time, a Continental Army was about to come to grips with a large and indeed superior force of redcoats. "Do not fire until you see the whites of their eyes," Preston urged his men, knowing that many of his inexperienced militia would want to fire long before the enemy was in range. Preston knew that American stocks of ammunition were limited, in contrast to the bountiful stores that the British were believed to possess.

As it was, the American troops could hardly be contained. High overhead, billowing clouds of smoke rose to the sky as British ships unleashed a massive bombardment on Charlestown, in another entirely spurious attempt to intimidate the rebels through terror. This was not the way gentlemen were supposed to fight. All that was achieved by this form of ruthless, unrestricted warfare was that any remaining feelings of kinship between Continental officers and their erstwhile brethren were dissipated forever. The pointless destruction of Charlestown filled the defenders on Breed's Hill with a righteous rage and a determination to make the redcoats pay in blood.

This they proceeded to do. Twice, Howe's corps launched an assault across difficult, uphill ground, with redcoats struggling through high grass to get close

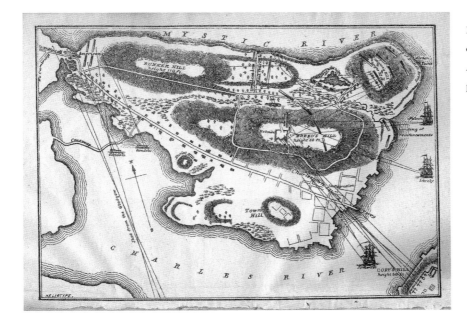

FIG. 106. Map of the Battle of Bunker Hill, showing the American breastworks and the position of British forces.

to the rebel breastworks. As soon as they were in range, the Continentals let loose a most fearsome barrage, firing with exceptional discipline, making every shot count. The effect was devastating. Scores of British soldiers were killed or wounded, many fatally. As one survivor wrote, "Most of our Grenadiers and Light-infantry, the moment of presenting themselves lost three-fourths, and many nine-tenths, of their men. Some had only eight or nine men a company left." Wounded British soldiers covered the hill, filling the air with moans and cries for help. It was a stunning reversal for an army that had begun to believe it was invincible, certainly when fighting against a motley group of farmers and tanners.

Desperate to rectify the situation, Howe called for reinforcements from Clinton's regulars while ordering the walking wounded to pick up their muskets and line up for a third assault. Behind the Continental barricade, there was disarray as well. Many men decided that they'd had enough fighting for the day and were beginning to leave the field, only to be ordered back by their officers at gunpoint. Thus, when Howe flung his remaining forces at the American lines for a third attempt, the defense began to break. Many fighters had run out of ammunition, which made further resistance pointless. Worse, the British were equipped with bayonets for close-quarters fighting, which the Americans lacked. As most of the Continentals stole away, Prescott remained in the breach, parrying the bayonet thrusts of the redcoats with his saber. Fortunately, the American retreat was an orderly affair, so that even General Burgoyne was heard to mutter that their withdrawal was "no flight; it was even covered with bravery and military skill."[91]

Bravery and skill had indeed dominated, even though in the end the British took command of the field and the Continental Army withdrew to Cambridge. This "victory" had come at a horrific cost. In all, Howe, Clinton, and Burgoyne had suffered 1,054 casualties, including 226 killed. Many of these, including one lieutenant colonel and two majors, were veteran officers whose experience made them difficult to replace. In British eyes, then, the assault had been a dismal failure, even if in the end they had carried the day. Indeed, the number of dead and wounded was the highest the British would suffer at any point in the Revolutionary War. "A few more such victories," Clinton wrote bitterly in his diary, "would have shortly put an end to British dominion in America."

On the Continental side, casualties amounted to 140 killed and 310 wounded, further underscoring the lopsided outcome of the engagement. Among the officers killed was Joseph Warren, president of the revolutionary Massachusetts Provincial Congress, who had just been commissioned a major general. But rather than exercising his rank, Warren chose to fight in the ranks as a private soldier and was killed when British troops finally succeeded in reaching the American line. Thirty men had been captured by the British; most of them would die from their wounds or from cruel treatment by their captors.

News of the battle soon spread through the colonies, and by fast ship to London, where it was received with mixed feelings. The Pyrrhic victory prompted King George III to reject a last attempt by the Continental Congress to seek a mediated resolution to the conflict.[92] It also hardened feelings in Parliament. "The sooner they are made to Taste Distress," a Tory politician named James Oughton wrote, "the sooner will [Crown control over them] be produced, and the Effusion of Blood be put a stop to." It was a sentiment widely shared in the House of Commons; now, only the bitter taste of steel and cannon could restore order in the colonies.

General Gage did not escape the wrath of his sovereign. Three days after the report of the Battle of Bunker Hill was received in London, he was

FIG. 107. John Trumbull, *The Death of General Warren at the Battle of Bunker Hill*, 1786

dismissed from his post as commander in chief, to be replaced by General Howe. Howe received the news with equanimity. In Boston he had taken a measure of his foe, and had come to the conclusion that Gage's early optimism was entirely misplaced. "A large army must at length be employed to reduce these people," he wrote soberly to Parliament. The problem was, Britain did not have such a "large army" at its disposal, as Howe well knew. An island nation, it had always placed its strength in its navy, rather than in large standing armies. While at the peak of the Seven Years' War Britain had fielded over two hundred thousand men, that number had now dwindled to thirty-six thousand active-duty regulars.[93] There was only one way to solve that problem: the hiring of foreign troops.

For George Washington, however, the outcome of Bunker Hill was a reason for hope. His largely untrained and undisciplined army had fought surprisingly well against the best forces that England could put in the field. There was now an even chance that the Continental Army might yet prevail.

THE BATTLE FOR INDEPENDENCE

IX

IT WAS A SIGHT TO STIR THE HEART OF EVERY ENGLISHMAN. AT 8:00 a.m. on February 12, 1776, as a watery sun chased away the night, forty-four ships unfurled their topsails, weighed their anchors, and majestically sailed out of the stone haven of Cork on the southwest coast of Ireland. With flags and pennants snapping proudly in the breeze, three men-of-war took up station at the head of the convoy, followed by three ordnance ships, seven victuallers, a tender, a storeship, and twenty-seven transports carrying five regiments of British regulars.[94] It was a magnificent sight, this huge concentration of Britain's naval power, as it confidently slipped into the Atlantic for the long voyage west.

But looks could be deceiving. Lord North and his opposite number in the Royal Navy had to move heaven and earth to get anywhere near the number of troops the king wanted, which was a minimum of seven regiments of about 670 men each. Recruiting parties had scoured every pub, alehouse, and inn looking for miscreants who could be pressed into service, even stooping as low as to haul inmates out of Shrewsbury jail. "The Ardor of the nation in this cause has not hitherto arisen to the pitch one could wish," Lord George Germain, British secretary of state, ruefully confessed to George III. "It certainly should be encouraged wherever it appears."[95] More to the point, the desired ardor was almost entirely absent in a nation that had grown tired of Britain's endless wars, except in the chambers of Parliament, where righteous anger against the American colonists still ruled the day.

It was all well and good for colonial governors to beg for a massive influx of British troops, if for nothing else than to buck up the spirits of American loyalists to the Crown—but shipping an expeditionary force of five thousand men across three thousand miles of ocean was hard. In fact, the loyal population

FIG. 108. A 1777 map of the British-held fort of Ticonderoga, revealing the placement of cannons and defensive lines

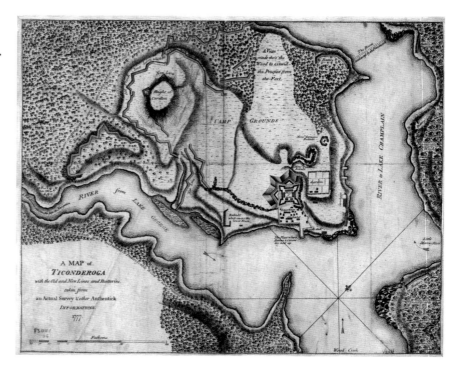

in the colonies was much smaller than what these governors were claiming in their missives to London. Even among historians today, the most optimistic estimates put the number of loyalists in the colonies at no more than 20 percent—hardly a constituency that could tip the scales.

The real problem, as General Howe well knew, was how to keep this force supplied and fed while operating in hostile territory. If his calculations were correct, he would soon command an army of thirty-five thousand troops and four thousand horses, which together would consume thirty-seven tons of food and thirty-eight tons of hay and oats per day—a staggering amount, which for the most part would have to be imported using the tenuous transatlantic supply line from Britain.[96] Worse, a Treasury report revealed that of the 950 horses shipped to American shores, nearly half didn't survive the journey.[97]

As if these problems weren't enough, the weather in Cork was atrocious, so that the expedition's original departure date of December 1, 1775, was delayed by more than two months, severely testing the king's patience. Worse still, by year's end the requisite number of troops had still not been secured.

In desperation, the Admiralty then diverted two full regiments destined for Quebec to the expeditionary force gathering at Cork, in order to obtain the seven regiments that the king insisted upon. Bad luck then continued to shadow the flotilla as it fought the stormy seas of February. Barely a day had passed since their departure when a huge storm struck the armada, damaging nine ships so severely that they had to return to safe harbors on the Irish and British shores. Twenty-four days later, the ships had not moved much farther than the Portuguese coast. More vessels would be lost in the weeks to come, so that of the original forty-four ships, only eight would eventually make it to North America.

Back in the colonies, news of the coming convoy was not yet cause for alarm. So far, the American militias had given a good account of themselves against the superior forces of the Crown. Apart from the heroic stand during the Battle of Bunker Hill, a small force of militiamen from New Hampshire, known as the Green Mountain Boys, had executed a daring coup de main near the south end of Lake Champlain. Led by the politician Ethan Allen and a daredevil military officer named Benedict Arnold, the group had surprised and overwhelmed the small British garrison of Fort Ticonderoga, as well as the nearby fort of Crown Point.

Flushed with victory, Arnold and his men set out again seven days later, on May 18, 1775, and succeeded in raiding Fort Saint-Jean on the Richelieu River of Quebec. They absconded with chest loads of muskets, cannons, and ammunition, as well as a British navy vessel. Around sixty of these cannons, including mortars, were carted to Boston where they served in the Battle of Bunker Hill.

Not all of the Continental exploits met with military success. Just a month before the Ticonderoga raid, Congress had authorized an ill-advised invasion of Quebec, in the hope of deterring the British from using Quebec as a major base and in the mistaken belief that the French population would welcome the American colonists with open arms.[98] The Continental expedition, led by General Philip Schuyler, General Richard Montgomery, and Colonel Arnold, was successful in investing the city of Montreal. But when the invading force finally arrived before Quebec City on New Year's Eve, 1776, after a harrowing march through severe blizzards, a stout defense by British regulars stopped the Americans in their tracks.

FIG. 109. John Trumbull, *Death of General Richard Montgomery during the Battle of Quebec*, 1786

Already worn out by the long march, the Continental force was forced to withdraw. Among its casualties was Montgomery, whose death became the subject of a famous 1786 painting by John Trumbull. Arnold was hit in the leg but refused to leave Canada. He and a small force decided to stay in the area with the hope of exacting revenge. In the end, that decision would have a tremendous strategic significance for the future conduct of the war.

Better news arrived in March of 1776 in Boston, where the British were still quartered. On March 2, Continental troops at Roxbury and Cobble Hill decided to remind the British that they were still there and opened fire with their excellent British cannons, some of which had been captured at Ticonderoga. For several hours cannonballs roared over the city, doing little damage other than terrorizing the population, which was fine with Washington. The whole point of the exercise was to distract the British while twelve hundred Continental soldiers got ready to seize Dorchester Heights, a prominent hilltop in South Boston. Cloaked by darkness and the sound of earsplitting cannon fire, the action succeeded brilliantly. On March 11, the British woke up to the terrible realization that American artillery was now in place on the highest point of Boston, from which Washington could direct plunging fire on the town as well as British ships at will. General Howe's immediate impulse was to order a counterattack, but soon thereafter Boston was flayed by the worst possible winter storm, damaging both British and American positions. It broke Howe's will to fight. Much to the surprise of his officers, Howe ordered a complete evacuation from Boston.

Nine thousand troops were loaded on what remained of British naval power in the bay and were then taken north to Halifax to await the promised flotilla from Cork. On March 17, the first company of Continentals liberated the city, followed by a triumphant General Washington on his silver steed.

There was therefore every reason to be optimistic, but Washington knew that the British withdrawal was no Dunkirk, in modern parlance. Howe's force had left the field in good order, with much of its stores and ammunition, all under the protection of two hundred cannons on their navy escorts. Moreover, the full fury of Britain's military might would soon descend on American shores. Washington wondered if Congress would be able to give him the forces necessary to stop it.

FIG. 110. Hand-colored map of Boston, showing the British encampments in Boston in red and the Continental artillery poised on Roxbury Hill and Dorchester Heights on the bottom

The Declaration of Independence

On July 4, 1776, the Second Continental Congress took a giant leap: it formally declared itself an alliance of thirteen sovereign states that no longer recognized British rule. The decision to do so was not one that was made overnight. More than a year had passed since the outbreak of war, during which many prominent American colonists still hoped that economic and military pressure would bring the British to the bargaining table. The social and emotional ties to the mother country were strong, particularly in the

FIG. 111. John Trumbull's *Declaration of Independence* of 1819 depicts the five-man drafting committee presenting the declaration text to Congress.

south, where many plantation owners modeled themselves after the British gentry and had built sprawling mansions to match. "Believe me, dear Sir: there is not in the British empire a man who more cordially loves a union with Great Britain than I do," Thomas Jefferson had written on November 29, 1775. "But, by the God that made me, I will cease to exist before I yield to a connection on such terms as the British Parliament propose; and in this, I think I speak the sentiments of America."[99]

When in February 1776 the English Parliament passed the Prohibitory Act, ordering a blockade of American ports while declaring all American ships, whether civilian or military, to be enemy vessels, most members of Congress realized that there was no turning back. Still, many delegates were apprehensive, in part because their constituencies had never authorized them to take such a drastic step. Therefore, between April and July 1776, a period of intense consultation took place before the thirteen colonies were ready to formally separate themselves from the English Crown.

In seeking a legal foundation for its decision, Congress cited twenty-seven grievances against King George III, including his persistent opposition to laws that the colonies deemed absolutely vital for their peace and security and his decision to burden the colonial commonwealth with unwarranted taxes and levies. But the core of the argument went deeper. Jefferson, the ranking intellectual among the Founding Fathers, had read the works of a movement called the Enlightenment, which originated after the devastation of the Thirty Years' War between Catholic and Protestant states. Among European scholars, the ravages of this war prompted a deep skepticism about the lofty ideals of Christianity. If the purpose of the Christian faith was to foster love and compassion, how then could Christians engage in such wholesale slaughter? In response, a group of philosophers sought to develop a new moral and ethical foundation for humankind, using humanist principles first developed in the Renaissance. They included the Dutch philosopher Baruch Spinoza, the German author Immanuel Kant, the French philosophers Denis Diderot and Voltaire, and the English philosopher John Locke.

Locke was particularly taken with the idea of the Enlightenment as a tabula rasa by which humankind could "reset" the purpose of its existence. He believed that no single religion could ever claim to be absolutely perfect in its revelation; therefore, all nations should grant their citizens complete freedom in conscience, thought, and faith. A fellow empiricist, Thomas Hobbes, took this principle a step further by arguing that each individual possessed human rights that no sovereign could put aside. Denis Diderot used these ideas as the basis for his *Encyclopédie* project, an ambitious undertaking to catalog all human knowledge, by calling for full equality and intellectual liberty of all people, unfettered by religion.[100]

Initially, aristocrats throughout Europe were smitten with these high ideals and eagerly discussed them in salons, hoping for some reflected intellectual glory. The fact that France had replaced Spain as the dominant power in Europe, and Italy as the center of European culture, played a major role as well. French, rather than Latin or Italian, had now become the lingua franca of European science, diplomacy, music, literature, and art. This magnified the impact of the French philosophers, and particularly Voltaire. From 1736 onward, Voltaire corresponded regularly with King Frederick the Great of Prussia as well as the most powerful autocrat of all: Czarina Catherine the Great of Russia. But the affection of these monarchs for Enlightenment ideals went only so far. While they liked to flirt with concepts such as equality and freedom, none dared to actually implement them as a matter of state policy.

This is why the American Founding Fathers would make such a crucial difference. Thomas Jefferson was well-read and fully aware of the Enlightenment's ethical and political debates. During his time in college, he had immersed himself in the work of Deist authors who argued that rational thought, rather than divine revelation or mysticism, could prove the existence of God. English Deists such as Matthew Tindal believed that while God created the universe, he did not intervene in human affairs, for he had given humans the gifts of reason and free will. This explained, in the Deist view, why there was so much violence and evil in the world despite God's innate goodness and why it was up to humankind, guided by rational thought, to create order in the chaos. Jefferson embraced this view wholeheartedly, believing, as he later wrote, that in "every age, the priest has been hostile to liberty . . . they have perverted the purest religion ever preached to man into mystery and jargon."[101] Many years later, this prompted him to study Jesus's moral teachings, rather than Christian doctrine, which he compiled in a book entitled *The Life and Morals of Jesus of Nazareth.*

FIG. 112. Rembrandt Peale, *Portrait of Thomas Jefferson*, 1800 (Courtesy, White House Collection)

Above all, Jefferson embraced Locke's and Hobbes's argument that every human being, man or woman, was endowed by God with certain core rights and that no sovereign should ever seek to suppress the full enjoyment of those rights. This is what inspired him to write the famous opening passage of the Declaration of Independence: "We hold these truths to be self-evident, that all men are created equal, that they are endowed by their Creator with certain unalienable Rights, that among these are Life, Liberty and the pursuit of Happiness."

The colonies had formally broken with Britain, but they were not yet fused as a sovereign nation, as a "United States." The question of whether they would actually survive as an independent people was still very much in the air. And to underscore that unsettling notion, the first ships of the British invasion fleet were landing their troops on Sandy Hook, off the coast of New Jersey, as the ink on the Declaration was not yet dry.

The Battle for New York

General Howe stood at the rail of his flagship and watched the disembarkation of his soldiers with a deep sense of satisfaction. He recognized that the first months of the war had been difficult, largely due to blunders by English commanders on the scene. He knew that these mistakes had tested the patience of Parliament and his king, George III. Yes, serious errors had been made, but in his heart he couldn't fault his officers, who had done their best. It was always difficult to fight a determined native insurgency on *their* ground, in hostile territory, where every home or farm might harbor men with muskets ready to shoot you in the back. What was more, it was just fifteen years since this new global empire had been dropped in Britain's lap. Parliament might crow about its sudden fortune, its mastery over so large a realm, but professional soldiers like Howe knew that Britain would need to build a vastly expanded military if it wanted to hold on to such an empire. The navy might secure the routes, but to pacify the interior of Britain's new domains, with its millions of restive subjects, would require a force that no one in Parliament could yet fathom.

True, the first year of the war had not gone well for Britain, but now that was going to change. Now, at long last, Howe's ships were arriving off the shores of New Jersey with a fully rested force of ten thousand men, and he had been assured by Secretary Germain that a second armada was on its way from Ireland with an even greater force of twenty thousand men. Over a hundred ships were now at sea to carry this expeditionary army to his shores—a stupendous armada, commanded by none other than his older brother, Admiral Richard Howe. Further, the king had agreed to hire an additional seven thousand German mercenaries—Hessians, mostly—which in hindsight was perhaps not surprising, given that George III and his predecessors were from the House of Hanover. If all this came true, then soon he would command the

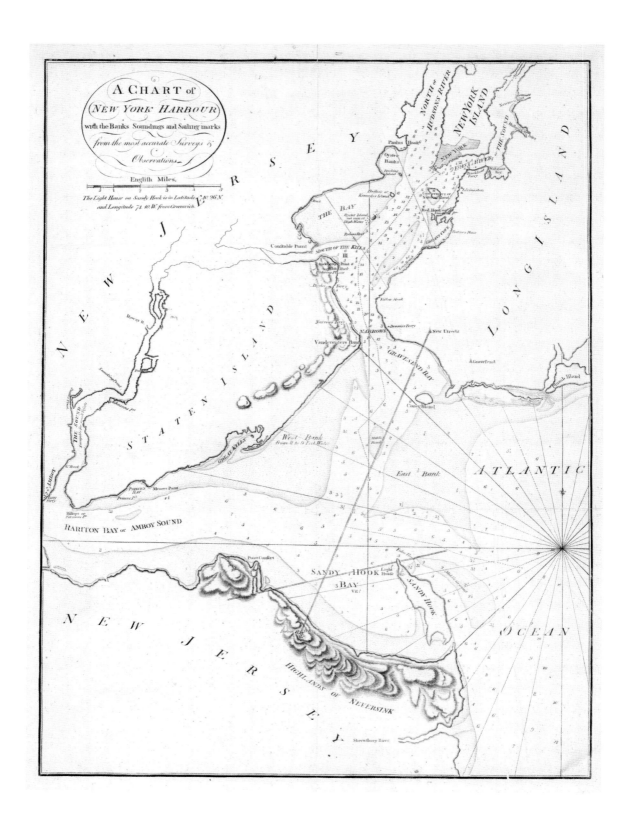

A CHART of
NEW YORK HARBOUR
with the Banks, Soundings and Sailing marks
from the most accurate Surveys &
Observations

English Miles.

The Light House on Sandy Hook is in Latitude N.40.26.N
and Longitude 74.10.W. from Greenwich.

largest expeditionary army that Britain had ever put into the field: thirty-seven thousand men, backed by nearly 250 cannons. It would dwarf any force that Washington could put in front of him, if his intelligence reports were on target. So far, the Continental Army in New York, augmented by various militia, was believed to be no more than eighteen thousand ill-trained and ill-equipped men, an estimate that was not far from the truth.

FIG. 113. *(Opposite page)* Chart of New York Harbor on the eve of battle, August 1776

Perhaps, Howe wondered, just the sight of such an awesome force would be enough to make these colonists see reason. Perhaps the prospect of seeing their homes, their fields, and their livestock destroyed as his troops swarmed over their lands would make them desist from their folly. He would welcome it. They were English descendants, after all. Perhaps, common sense might still prevail. The king thought so, too, and had expressly granted him and his brother Robert the authority to negotiate a peaceful settlement, if such was in prospect. The king doubted that this would be the case, but, as he said, "I think it right to be attempted, whilst every act of vigor is unremittingly carried on."

With that idea in mind, Howe had sent a messenger under white flag across New York harbor with a letter addressed to "George Washington, Esq." Escorted to Joseph Reed, Washington's adjutant, Reed thanked the emissary for his trouble but confessed that he knew of no man with that title. When appraised of this diplomatic faux pas, Howe was deeply annoyed and simply added "etc.", so that the letter was now addressed to "George Washington, Esq., etc." This, if anything, was an even greater affront to the dignity of the American general, and the letter was once more politely declined. Washington, however, saw the wisdom of at least appearing to give peace a chance. The messenger was informed that if Howe wished to parley, Washington would be willing to receive his emissary. That meeting took place on July 20, but since Howe's remit was limited by royal decree to the granting of "general and special pardons," nothing much was accomplished, and the meeting broke up. That was the penultimate attempt to seek a peaceful resolution to the conflict.

Howe would try one more time, by meeting with a Congressional delegation during the Staten Island Peace Conference of September 11, but once again the discussion failed to bear fruit. The colonies were determined to be in control of their future and no longer wished to be subjects of a cruel and insensitive tyrant—it was as simple as that. "Directing pardons to be offered to the colonies, who are the very parties injured," wrote Benjamin Franklin, who had joined the delegation, "can have no other effect than that of increasing our resentments." He added, "It is impossible we should think of submission to a government that has with the most wanton barbarity and cruelty burnt our towns, excited savages to massacre our peaceful farmers, and is even now bringing foreign mercenaries to deluge our settlements with blood?" Clearly, the answer was no. And so, after three hours, the meeting ended and the parties went their way.

Lord Germain was true to his word. By August 6, Sandy Hook Bay had become a veritable forest of masts, including 130 ships of Howe's own force that had sailed from Halifax; his brother Robert Howe's expeditionary force of 150 vessels that had arrived in July; and, finally, General Clinton's flotilla of forty-five ships that had limped back from Charlestown after an ill-fated invasion of North Carolina. Then, on August 12, yet another hundred ships dropped anchor in the now crowded bay, bringing German mercenaries as well as Highlanders and various other assorted troops. The horizon was now covered from end to end with battleships, troopships, brigs, and corvettes—a breathtaking sight, sure to enfeeble even the most stouthearted colonists on Long Island, on the other side of the bay.

Germain had urged Howe not to proceed with the invasion of New York until his entire force was assembled, and now, at last, that time had come. On August 22, the first redcoat companies were rowed across Gravesend Bay to the southern shore of Long Island, on flatboats that Robert Howe's armada had brought along just for this purpose. By the end of the day, twenty thousand British troops had landed on New York soil and were marching in the direction of the town of Gravesend.

Up to this point, Washington had been fully in the dark as to the intent of British strategy. Would they land in New Jersey, cross over to Long Island, or sail up the Hudson to strike Manhattan from the rear? He suspected the last, which is why he had ordered two fortifications to be built—Fort Washington on Manhattan's side, and Fort Lee on the New Jersey shore—in order to blast any British ships that might endeavor to sail up the river. In Washington's mind, given Howe's overwhelming naval power, such a move made a lot more sense than a frontal assault on land. This is why, when told of

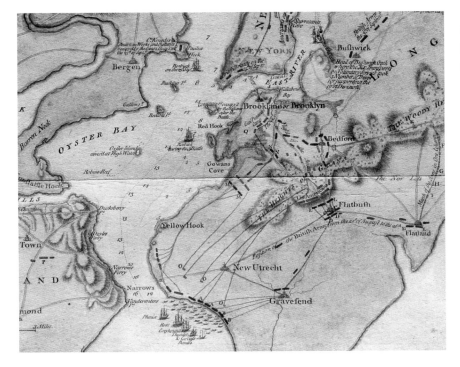

FIG. 114. The British invasion fleet lands on Long Island, from a 1776 map printed in London

the Gravesend landings, Washington couldn't bring himself to think that this was anything other than a mere feint. Thus, fatefully, he distributed his forces over Long Island, Manhattan, New Jersey, and other locations, in violation of the principle of concentration of force. In the end, only four regiments were sent to reinforce the defenders now facing the growing British host on Long Island. Already, these soldiers had built several defensive lines, beginning with the Heights of Guana, beyond which lay the more heavily fortified ridges of Brooklyn Heights. Obviously, whoever was in control of these heights would control the battlefield.

Howe's strategy of demonstrating around New York Harbor, giving Washington no clue as to where he might strike, succeeded brilliantly. Once the British infantry launched their attack, they easily brushed aside the outnumbered defenders and took control of the Heights of Guana, pushing the Continentals back to their fortifications on Brooklyn Heights. It was a rapid and stunning maneuver, executed with great discipline, and by rights Howe should now have pressed his advantage. Here, for the first time, the future of the United States hung in the balance. With his overwhelming superiority in men and materiel, Howe could have easily cut off the Continental regiments on Long Island from their base in Manhattan, after which he could leisurely proceed to destroy them in detail.

But, shockingly, he did not. Though historians have long debated his motives for doing so, Howe called an end to the day's fighting and ordered his troops to encamp. A golden opportunity for the British Empire went begging. General Clinton, who was ready to lead the assault on Brooklyn Heights, was stunned. "If we succeeded," he later wrote, "everything on the island must have been ours."[102] That, and much more.

In the meantime, Washington had come to his senses and now realized that the Long Island assault was indeed the principal axis of Howe's attack. When it transpired that the British were not going to push their advantage and pursue, he immediately recognized Howe's error for the gift that it was to save his forces. Under cloak of darkness, he skillfully withdrew his troops from Long Island and had them ferried across the East River to the relative safety of Manhattan. Amazingly, the British were too busy celebrating their triumph of the day to notice.

As dawn broke, Howe was stunned to hear that Washington had successfully withdrawn his forces. Clearly, these rebels did not intend to fight as gentlemen but preferred to sneak away in the dark of night. It didn't change the greater strategic picture, but it did confront him with a dilemma. With virtually all of the Continental Army now in New York City and beyond, there was little point in continuing to advance in Long Island. Or was there? Should he first consolidate his forces, or rush headlong after the elusive game? A more incisive and creative commander would have decided to invade Manhattan forthwith, but Howe was not that man. Always inclined to caution, and secure in his overwhelming military superiority, he settled in to wait and see what Washington would do next.

Indeed, Washington realized that in taking his army into Manhattan, he had merely exchanged one trap for another. As an island bounded by the East and Hudson rivers, Manhattan was highly vulnerable if Howe chose to surround it with his battleships and simply blast Washington's forces to bits. "It is now extremely obvious from all Intelligence," the American general wrote on September 8, that "they mean to inclose us on the Island of New York." There

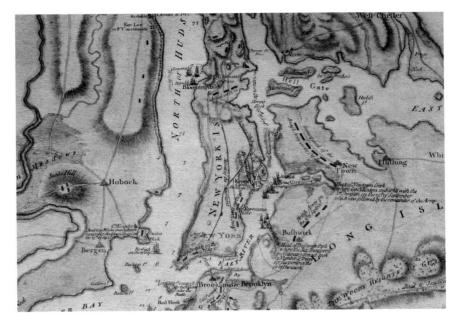

FIG. 115. The British transfer of troops from Long Island to "Kepps Bay" in Manhattan, from a 1776 map printed in London

was only one way out of this quagmire: he had to evacuate his forces from New York and into the safety of New Jersey, across the Hudson. The roles were now reversed: just as Howe had been compelled to abandon Boston under pressure from the Continental Army, so, too, was it now Washington's turn to evacuate one of the most important cities of colonial America. It was a bitter pill to swallow, but there was no alternative. Washington briefly considered the "scorched earth" policy of burning Manhattan to the ground, but Congress vetoed such a drastic move. Still, when the evacuation finally got under way on September 12, everything that could be of any value to the British was either taken, burned, or tossed into the river. Even the church bells were removed, lest they be cast into cannons by the redcoats.

Once again, Howe did little to interfere. An army is never as vulnerable as when it is in retreat, with its back turned, and with every man's mind on the safety of what lies ahead, rather than the defeat of the enemy in the rear. But Howe decided to take his time. Only on the evening of September 14, when the American evacuation was in full swing, did he order the first flatboats to leave Long Island for Kip's Bay on the southeast shore of Manhattan.

The British troops were ready and eager for a fight. Once landed in Manhattan, they set off in hot pursuit of the Continentals while British frigates

FIG. 116. Thomas Mitchell,
*British Battleships in Action
on the Hudson River off
Manhattan,* 1799

moved up the Hudson, sails unfurled and cannons run out. Deep down below, powder boys were busy bringing up bags of gunpowder from stores in the hold. Gun crews rammed the shot into the barrels, added a wad of cloth, and then quickly stepped aside as the gun captains yanked the lanyard, igniting the flintlock and sending the cannonball on its trajectory to the shore. Salvo after salvo thundered from the ships until the sky was rent with the roar of spitting cannon, casting the ships in bluish-gray smoke. Ashore, countless homes, stores, stables, and churches, some dating back to the Dutch era, were methodically smashed to bits.

All this mayhem had its intended effect: it robbed the Americans of their will to fight and prompted them to flee. Washington valiantly tried to organize a defensive stand at Murray Hill, but "the men ran to the walls and some into the cornfield in a most confused and disordered manner."[103] Incensed, Washington had to be removed from the field by his aides, lest he be captured by the enemy.

The headlong flight of their enemy hardened the British into thinking that the Continentals were little more than an undisciplined rabble, unworthy of battle with the cream of His Majesty's forces. "The dastardly Behaviour of the Rebels . . . sinks below Remark," wrote Howe's secretary. Some British and Hessian soldiers showed their contempt by killing the American wounded with their bayonets.

Once again, Howe held victory in his grasp—a strong dash, a vigorous pursuit, and he could have bagged George Washington, his officers, and a good many of his soldiers. It could have put an end to the war. And yet, once again, Howe desisted. He rested his troops—according to one apocryphal story, he paused to enjoy the wonderful pastries offered by a Quaker woman—while Washington led his forces up the Harlem Heights. This time, he succeeded in persuading his troops to make a stand, so that the next day, September 16, the Continentals successfully fended off an attempt to dislodge them from the heights.

Nevertheless, Washington's position was now extremely tenuous. Every day, new redcoats poured into Manhattan, adding to the pressure. Congress, which had previously urged Washington to hang on to the city at all costs, now relented in the face of these overwhelming odds and gave him leave to evacuate the city at a time he saw fit. This became even more urgent when it appeared that Howe was executing a flanking maneuver by landing troops in Westchester County, north of New York City. Anticipating this

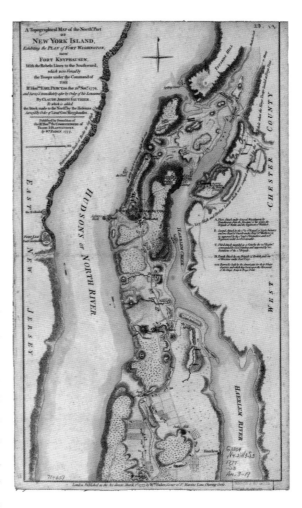

FIG. 117. The position of the Continental Army in upper Manhattan, north of Port Washington, is shown in this British map from March 1777.

pincer movement, Washington withdrew farther north, toward White Plains, but this meant that he lost all contact with the three thousand Continental soldiers remaining in the city. This time, Howe's strategy paid off, and by November 16 the British forces had not only captured all remaining American soldiers in the city but had also taken control of Fort Washington. From there, the redcoats sallied across the Hudson and took Fort Lee, thus eliminating all remaining American strong points in New York City.

There was no way around it: the Continental Army was on the run, as Howe had always believed it would be, if only he could bring his full force to bear. But instead of pursuing the fleeing Americans with everything he had, Howe made another critical mistake: he split his troops. One group under General Clinton

FIG. 118. This extremely rare
hand-drawn map shows the
position of British, Hessian, and
"Rebel" forces in and around
White Plains. It was drawn by
an officer identified as Captain
Blaskowitz.

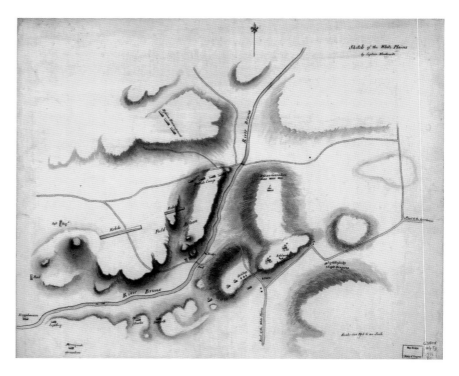

was sent away to take Newport, Rhode Island, hardly an urgent objective at this point in the battle, while General Cornwallis was dispatched with a force of redcoats and Hessians to run down George Washington, who had crossed the Hudson into New Jersey.

The Battle of Lake Champlain

Meanwhile, the Royal Navy had been busy building up its strength near Lake Champlain, so that it would be ready to carry General Guy Carleton's British forces stationed in Canada to the main battlefields down south. As we saw previously, Benedict Arnold was still in the theater, having decided to remain in the region after the retreat from the Quebec campaign. He now pondered whether it would be possible to thwart the British passage across the lake in any way.

To that end, he worked with a shipwright named Hermanus Schuyler in the construction of a handful of sloops, or "gundalows," but whether these could somehow stop British naval might was of course highly debatable.

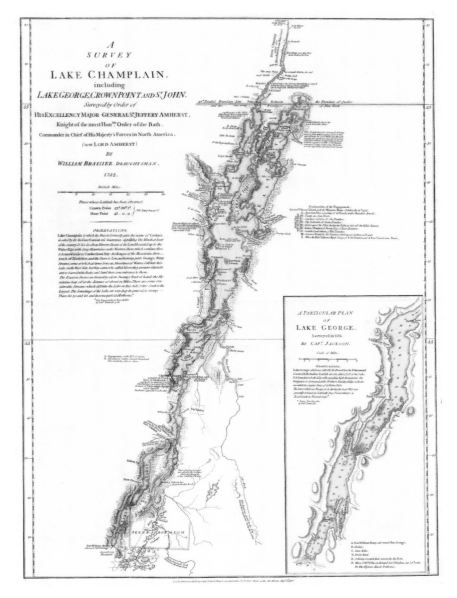

FIG. 119. A survey map of Lake Champlain and Lake George, drawn by William Brassier in 1762. Valcour Island, where the action took place, is located to the left of *La Grande Isle* in center.

These eight gunboats were small wooden affairs that at best could hold two 9-pounder cannons broadside, unevenly spaced so the crew could walk around them, plus one 9- or 12-pounder cannon in the bow. The gunboats also had twelve positions for oarsmen, its main form of propulsion, in addition to a single mast with a square mainsail and topsail. Though none of these boats have survived, the wreck of one of them, the *Spitfire*, was located in 1997 by the

FIG. 120. Engraving of Benedict Arnold

Lake Champlain Maritime Museum, while a similar vessel, the *Philadelphia*, is exhibited in the National Museum of American History.

As soon as this flotilla was assembled, Arnold dispatched it to the northern part of the lake, there to lay in wait and raise the alarm as soon as the British ships were sighted. At the same time, Arnold sent reconnaissance parties ashore, in an effort to divine what the British were up to.

Along the way, he was fortunate to gather seven more vessels, including schooners and galleys of variable size and reliability, thus raising America's first "naval force" to fifteen ships. On September 8, 1776, Arnold was in Isle La Motte, the most remote of the Champlain Islands, when news reached him that the British were on their way. That was the good news.

The bad news was that the enemy's naval force, led by Thomas Pringle, was much bigger than he had anticipated: the 180-ton battleship *Inflexible*; three corvettes, *Maria, Carleton*, and *Thunderer*, each equipped with 12 six-pounders; twenty-four heavily armed gunboats; and forty-eight flat-bottomed boats carrying British infantry. Arnold now took stock of the situation. Born in the colony of Connecticut, he had enjoyed a profitable career as a captain and merchant on the transatlantic route and was therefore familiar with naval technology and British shipping traditions.

One thing he had learned was that while English ships were certainly bigger and more heavily armed than his paltry force, their captains tended to move cautiously in waters with which they were not familiar. He therefore decided to take his hardscrabble collection of boats and position them in the narrows between the mainland and Valcour Island. This was a brilliant stroke, for it served two purposes: first, it hid his vessels from British eyes as their main force sailed by, and, second, it forced the Crown's ships to turn and sail against the prevailing north winds in order to come within striking distance of the American vessels. The British gunboats certainly had oarsmen and were able to maneuver regardless, but not the big ships, which, as he had hoped, flailed about as soon as they discovered the position of the American boats. Thus, the overwhelming British superiority could not be brought to bear, and the initial clash was fought on more equal terms. It became a contest of gunboats, each trying to load, aim, and fire as fast as it could.

Still, the British had more ships, and many more cannons. By the end of the day, two American schooners were lost while almost all gunboats had suffered considerable damage. As the British ships withdrew to lick their wounds and prepare for battle on the morrow, Arnold weighed his chances. There was no question that if the full British flotilla was brought into action, his gunboats wouldn't stand a chance. They would be shredded by broadsides from the British warships. Better, then, to withdraw to the south and see if the British would take the bait, further delaying the transit of their badly needed troops.

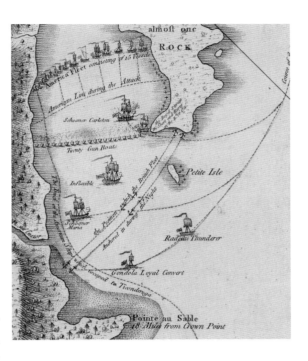

FIG. 121. Detail of a 1776 British map showing the line of American ships in the narrows and the British trying to position themselves for the assault

Amazingly, the plan worked. Arnold led his battered flotilla to Crown Point, using muffled oars to slip past the British fleet on the night of October 11. The next day, the British discovered that they had been outfoxed and immediately ordered a pursuit. During the headlong chase that followed, the ships continued to trade fire, and inevitably, America's tiny naval fleet ceased to exist. Arnold escaped by the skin of his teeth with a few small vessels in tow, while 60 of his men were killed and 110 taken prisoner. But the sacrifice was not in vain: the British ships suffered grievously as well, so that only five British warships were able to limp in to the fort. Most critically, the British plan to sever the Continental supply line by having its Quebec forces link up with Howe's New York troops was foiled. For just a week later, on October 20, the first snow began to fall, and General Carleton had second thoughts about his mission. If winter was already upon them, then he had little choice but to turn his battered fleet around and sail back to Quebec. Friedrich Riedesel, the officer commanding the Hessian forces, was furious. "If we could have begun our expedition four weeks earlier," he wrote, "I am satisfied that everything could have ended this year."[104] He was not wrong. If the British had succeeded in intercepting the badly needed flow of men and matériel to Washington, the revolution might have ended right there. Fortunately, the heroic stand of Arnold and his men had eliminated that threat.

Unperturbed, Howe's army settled down in New York to enjoy the comforts of the city, which the British would continue to occupy until the very end of the war. Howe even extended generous terms of amnesty to anyone, soldier or citizen, who now pledged loyalty to the Crown. Some three thousand people took him up on his offer—including former New York militiamen and at least one signer of the Declaration of Independence.[105]

Thus, New York became not only the center of the British high command but also a stronghold of American loyalist sentiment and resistance against the revolution for the duration of the war.

Needless to say, the king was ecstatic upon hearing the news of Washington's defeat in New York. He promptly awarded Howe the Order of the Bath, a singular honor. This shielded Howe from criticism in Parliament that his rush to offer amnesty had been too lenient, allowing soldiers who had previous fired on British troops to get off scot-free. What was more, Howe's firm control of New York also allowed the British command to paper over the failed attempt to capture the Hudson Valley. Not everyone agreed with that idea. The captains of several British warships, including the *Inflexible, Maria*, and *Loyal Convert*, wrote a letter condemning Captain Thomas Pringle for allowing Arnold to escape, arguing that he should have immediately blockaded the island with the full naval force at his disposal. But it was all water under the bridge, and eventually Pringle was raised to the rank of admiral. General Carleton was even awarded the Order of the Bath, the same honor given to Howe, for his "victory" at Valcour Island.[106]

The Battle for Trenton

"These are the times that try men's souls," the Anglo-American activist Thomas Paine wrote in one of the sixteen pamphlets, *The American Crisis,* with which he kept the colonies appraised of the war. He was right. Washington was now down to an army of five thousand men—an army, moreover, that suffered from

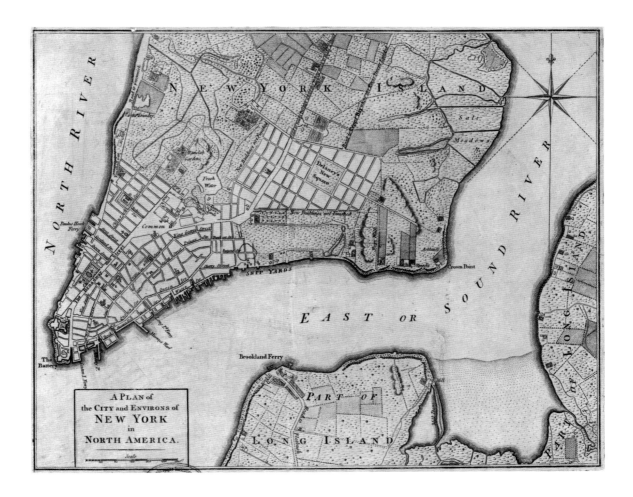

bad morale and would soon be reduced further by defections and illness, as well as the end of enlistments that would release hundreds of men to their home colonies. The decision of Congress to evacuate Philadelphia for fear of being captured by Cornwallis's expedition, now on the march in New Jersey toward Pennsylvania, didn't help matters either. And to make matters worse, one of Washington's senior officers, General Charles Lee, strayed too far from his command one night and was captured in a surprise raid by a British unit. He was found in bed with a prostitute at White's Tavern in Basking Ridge. English-born, Lee had hoped to be appointed commander in chief of the Continental Army, given his impressive military record while serving in the British Army during the Seven Years' War. Washington was chosen instead, and this had led to an increasingly fraught relationship between the two officers.

FIG. 122. Map of New York, 1776. For the remainder of the war, the city and its surrounding area would remain in British hands.

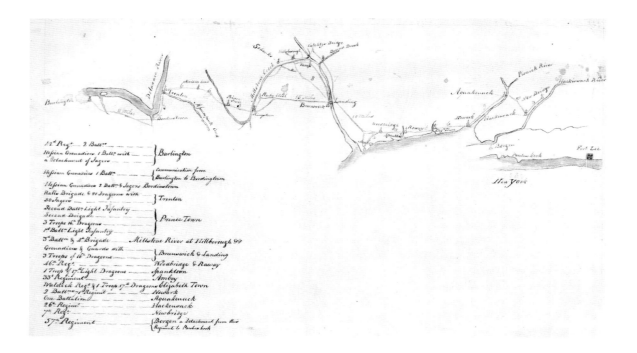

FIG. 123. Extremely rare hand-drawn map of British positions in New Jersey near the end of 1776, specifying the number of troops laagered at each strongpoint.

Though Lee had ably acquitted himself in the defense of Charleston against Clinton's unsuccessful sally in North Carolina, he deliberately dawdled with his forces in New Jersey despite Washington's urgent missives to join him as soon as possible. Lee even wrote letters to members of Congress, urging them to sack Washington and make him commanding general instead. Thus, his capture by astonished British soldiers may have been a blessing in disguise.

Confident that the campaign was as good as won, Howe now satisfied himself by building a string of outposts in New Jersey, from Bordentown to Perth Amboy, which is illustrated in a remarkably detailed, hand-drawn map. The map even identifies the troops allocated to each of these strongpoints, including the city of Trenton, which held "820 Dragoons with fifty *Jäger* ("hunters"), mostly Hessian, under the command of *Oberst* (Colonel) Johann Gottlieb Rall."

By scattering his force over so wide a territory, rather than racing pell-mell for the heart of the insurgency in Philadelphia, Howe once again underestimated the resilience of his opponent. It also left each strongpoint vulnerable to a surprise assault. Here was the opening that Washington had been looking for: an opportunity to snatch a quick and easy victory, thus boosting the morale of his troops, now down to three thousand men.

It was now December, and the American army was camping out on the western bank of the Delaware, using the river as a moat against any sudden British movements. Washington's intelligence kept insisting—erroneously, as it turned out—that Howe still intended to attack as soon as winter set in and the Delaware froze over. Reports trickled in of atrocities committed by the Hessians. These Germans were mostly illiterate conscripts whose only motive in this war was to loot, burn, and rape. This further got Washington's blood up and convinced him that some action had to be taken.

On Christmas night, 1776, the American general led a force of about twenty-four hundred men across the ice-choked Delaware River. It was bitter cold, with winds whipping up to gale force. That cloaked his movement but also slowed down his troops.

Washington had originally hoped to launch his attack before daylight, but the cannons didn't make it across the river until 4:00 a.m., and then it was a long and difficult slog to Trenton, which they didn't reach until shortly before 8:00 a.m. Washington's artillery officer, Alexander Hamilton, quietly unlimbered his artillery on King and Queen streets, sighted his guns, and let loose a volley of fire. Shocked, the Hessians poured out of their commandeered billets, only to see their commander, Colonel Rall, struck down by a bullet. American musket fire now entered the fray, further confusing the mercenaries, who were either too sleepy or too clueless to organize themselves into a cohesive defense. Sensing their advantage, the Continental men unsheathed their bayonets and plunged into the melee, hollering and screaming while slashing left and right, thrilled to be able to exact punishment on these odious foreigners. Within an hour it was all over. Washington had bagged one thousand stunned Hessian prisoners, while twenty-two lay dead and ninety-eight were wounded, many seriously.[107]

And yet, it was an incomplete victory. One American column, led by General James Ewing, had failed to cross the river at Trenton Ferry so as to close off the Hessian line of retreat, allowing five hundred Germans to escape. Nevertheless, the action heartened all American patriots. Better still, it convinced Congress that Washington was still the man to have on the scene. Best of all, he had captured forty howitzers that would be put to good use in the battles to come, for no one expected Howe to take this slap in the face lying down.

Sure enough, as soon as the British commander was told of the Trenton

FIG. 124. Emanuel Leutze's iconic *Washington Crossing the Delaware,* 1851

disaster, he ordered General Cornwallis to take fifty-five hundred regulars and chase down the Americans with everything they had. The only way to do that, though, was to march down Princeton Road, as Washington well knew. As soon as the British were sighted, small groups of militia hid in ambush along the road and proceeded to pick off redcoats as they passed. Although these skirmishes were small, they did sap the strength of the British soldiers, who loudly complained over this very ungentlemanly way of waging war. Worse, when they finally met up with Washington's main force, they discovered to their discomfort that the Americans were drawn up along a strong defensive position, the Assunpink Creek. Cornwallis sent out several probing attacks, but all of these were repulsed with a hail of cannon and musket fire. The answer, clearly, was to wait for daybreak and then to attack the Continentals with overwhelming force. But that night, Washington once again skillfully led his army off the field, leaving a few hundred brave souls to keep the campfires lit while making as much noise as possible. Thus, when the sun rose the following day, Cornwallis discovered to his dismay that his quarry had escaped once more.

This time, Washington marched his army to Princeton in an effort to stay well clear of Cornwallis. As the hand-drawn map below shows, he then split

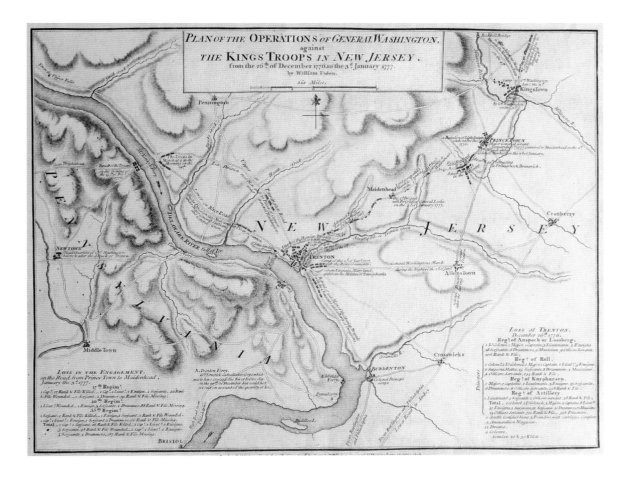

his army into two spearheads—one commanded by General Sullivan, taking Saw Mill Road, while General Greene led his units up the main road into town.

But as soon as they approached Princeton, Greene's advance guard, led by General Hugh Mercer, stumbled on two British regiments led by Lieutenant Colonel Charles Mawhood. A bitter battle ensued. Some British regulars believed that the action was led by none other than George Washington himself. In actuality, it wasn't Washington but Hugh Mercer who rode around on his white horse, urging his troops to keep up their fire until he himself was shot from his horse. Convinced that they had shot the American commander in chief, a group of redcoats ran forward and clubbed him to death with their muskets. When, days later, Washington was told of the news, he was deeply aggrieved, for the Scotsman had been a close friend and a steady hand he could ill afford to lose.

FIG. 125. William Faden, battle map of Washington's operations against "the King's Troops" in Trenton and Princeton, December 26, 1776–January 3, 1777. The map, engraved for the king's benefit, documents the casualties of British and Hessian forces in minute detail.

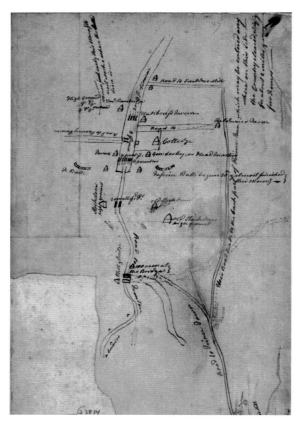

FIG. 126. Very rare hand-
drawn sketch of Princeton,
illustrating Washington's
advance on the city

With Mercer down, it looked for a moment as if the British might gain the upper hand in Princeton, but then General John Cadwalader appeared with his Pennsylvania militia, and that turned the battle (see his name scribbled on the bottom of the map shown above). The redcoats withdrew in the direction of Trenton, all the while harassed by Continental units. "It's a fine fox chase, my boys," Washington roared, overjoyed at finally giving the British a good licking.[108]

It was a fine moment indeed, but Washington knew there was no chance of holding Princeton while Cornwallis's force was still in his rear. He ordered his troops to take anything of value they could find, knowing that all civilians had previously been evacuated, and left the town around noon, mere hours before the British returned to occupy the city. The Continental Army was now tantalizingly close to New Brunswick, a major British depot stocked with arms and provisions that Washington desperately needed. Cornwallis knew that, too, of course, and so rushed to invest the town before the Continentals could come too close.

Thus, the fighting of 1776 ended in somewhat of a draw. On the one hand, the British had succeeded in evicting the Continental Army from New York and its strategic harbor, inflicting heavy casualties in the process. But on the other, Washington had shown that his patriotic forces were far from defeated and could still inflict heavy blows, by using what today we would call the classic guerilla tactics of a native insurgency. While these may not have mattered in the grand scheme of things, they did restore American morale, not to speak of the confidence of Congress in its commander in chief. Indeed, some historians believe that the Jersey campaign, though inconclusive, saved the revolution by proving that the Continental Army could hold its own in a pitched battle with the world's greatest military power. As King Frederick the Great, the leading military genius of the day, would write, "The achievements of Washington and his little band of compatriots between December 25 and the 4th of January, a space of 10 days, were the most brilliant of any recorded in the annals of military achievements."[109]

In London, meanwhile, the reports of Washington's daring raid in Trenton shocked the British, who believed, based on Howe's soothing reports, that the American rebels were all but beaten. Nor was this news well received in Potsdam, capital of Prussia. When the Hessian commander, Leopold Philip von Heister, confessed to the sovereign of Hesse-Kassel, *Landgraf* Frederick II, that an entire brigade was lost to the Americans, including all of their flags and artillery, Frederick flew into a rage. For him, the defeat struck painfully close to home. Everyone knew that he had originally been married to King George III's sister Mary, but the couple could not get along, so they had separated in 1755. Still, he had lost face in front of his former brother-in-law, the British king. Needless to say, von Heister was relieved of his command and replaced by German general Wilhelm von Knyphausen.

Both sides now faced the hardships of winter and the challenge of keeping their soldiers fed and sheltered. To that end, Howe withdrew most of his forces from New Jersey except for New Brunswick, thus ceding much of the colony to the Continental Army, which chose to winter in Morristown.

The stalemate would continue into 1777. While Howe kept hoping for a great and decisive battle that would settle the matter, Washington stuck to his strategy of fighting a defensive war, refusing to fight the British in the open. Exasperated, the British then decided to launch a major operation that Washington could not afford to ignore. Its objective was to take control of the entire Hudson River valley, the economic heart of the northern colonies, by a daring thrust from Lake Champlain—just as Carleton had tried to do months earlier. The reason for going after New England was obvious: as before, these colonies were considered the heart of the insurrection and the principal source of its manpower and supplies. By depriving Washington of his principal supply line, the rebellion would inevitably wither on the vine, and all revolutionary elements could be "cleansed" from the territory.

The man chosen to lead this expedition was one of the three senior generals on the scene, General "Johnny" Burgoyne. With ample troops at his disposal, Burgoyne was confident that he would finally inflict the decisive blow that the king and Parliament were demanding with rising impatience. And indeed, this expedition would mark the turning point in the war.

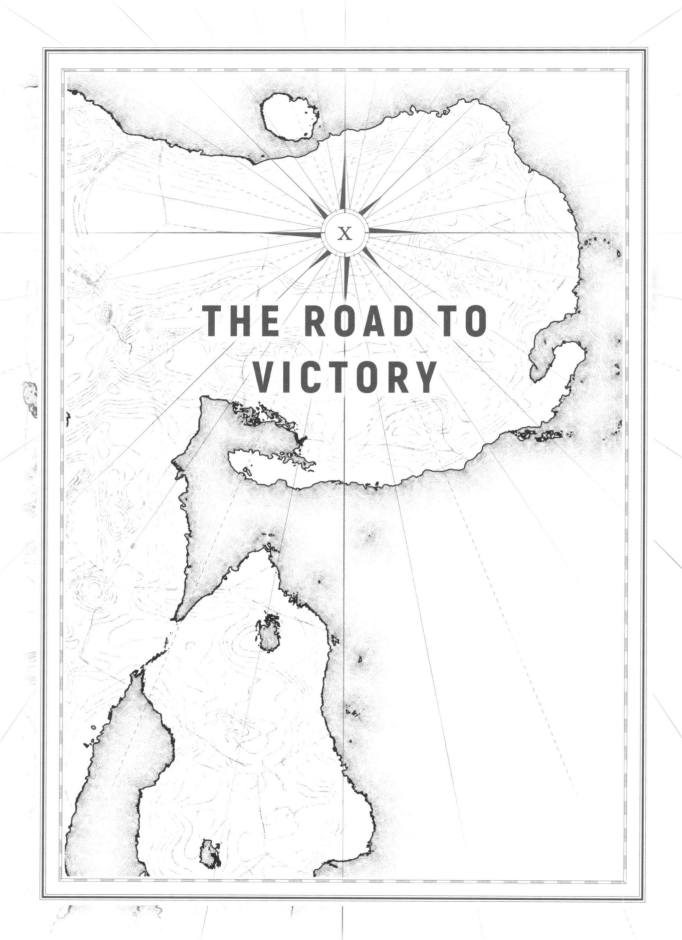

THE ROAD TO VICTORY

IN ONE IMPORTANT ASPECT, THE LOVELY SEVENTEENTH- AND EIGH-
teenth-century maps of North America made a crucial contribution to the
Continental cause in the Revolutionary War. It can be captured in one word:
scale. From the Golden Age of cartography to the royal British maps of the eighteenth century, most cartographers tried to show the colonies in their entirety,
from Quebec to the Chesapeake, or from the Hudson to the Florida peninsula.
Of course, this was motivated by the fact that these regions were the *only* ones
that had been charted, thus allowing the cartographers to illustrate them with
loving detail. Things were quite different west of the Mississippi, where the
continent faded into a strange, undiscovered terra incognita. Virtually all of
the maps that we have explored in preceding chapters share this unique quality
of trying to condense huge swaths of territory into a single map that could be
engraved, printed, and colored for a mass market.

The result was that most Europeans, and particularly the British, vastly
underestimated the actual size of the territories where the British Army was
now expected to fight. The eighteenth century produced many maps of Great
Britain, particularly after its absorption of Scotland, Ireland, and Wales. But
these maps depicted territory that could be measured in the hundreds of
square yards, rather than the thousands that maps of the American colonies
aimed to convey. For the eighteenth-century British officer, for whom printed,
hand-colored maps were a vital source of information, this difference was never
made explicit. Therefore, the British—from the king on down to his ministers,
officers, and infantry—subconsciously transferred their sense of scale from
the home maps they were familiar with to the maps of this new and unknown
territory where they were expected to fight.

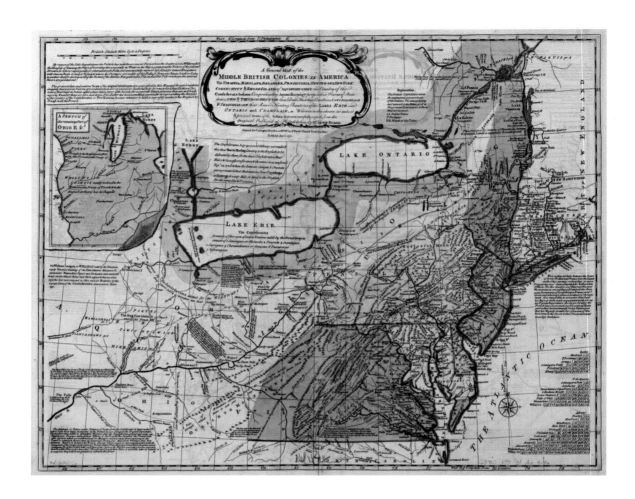

FIG. 127. A 1771 map of the "Middle British Colonies" of America. Britain's war leaders vastly underestimated the size of territories shown on maps such as these.

The problem was, North America was not a country. It was a vast continent, where the distance between Britain's forces in Quebec and those in the Carolinas was well over thirteen hundred miles. To think that any nation, British or otherwise, could subdue such a vast territory with just thirty thousand men was pure delusion. And yet, no British general ever truly grasped that simple fact.

Instead, the British soothed themselves into thinking that Washington's troops were not professional soldiers; that they were bands of irregular militia, farmers, and tobacco growers mostly, who could be dispatched in short order once properly herded into a killing field.

It is this idea that inspired the twin strategies adopted by the king's war council in the beginning of 1777. One was to launch the "northern campaign" from Quebec to New York, using the Quebec forces of General Guy Carleton, with the goal of isolating all of New England. Since Carleton's forces had previously dealt the Americans a stinging defeat in their attempt to capture British Canada, they were considered a highly trained and motivated force. By subduing New England and stopping the flow of men and matériel, the British believed they could starve the rebellion to death, not unlike the way the Pentagon believed in the late 1960s that the Vietnam insurgency would be strangled once the Ho Chi Minh trail was interdicted. Similarly, Burgoyne's New England campaign would seek to capture the principal routes in the Champlain–Hudson corridor, with the goal of cutting off supplies to Washington's army in New Jersey. A second campaign, commanded by Howe, would come up from the south and ultimately link up with Burgoyne's force in order to close the trap. Both maneuvers were expected to force Washington to come out in the open where he could be defeated.

Almost immediately, the plan went awry. Howe apparently misunderstood his orders from London and decided to march south on Philadelphia instead, believing that this would compel Washington to come to the defense of the city.[110] But when Washington refused to take the bait, Howe was confused and at loss for what he should do next. Like most other British officers, he did not know how to fight a guerilla insurgency that refused to adhere to the carefully scripted movements of eighteenth-century warfare. Instead, Howe decided to pull his army farther southward, to the Chesapeake, which eliminated any chance of his forces coming to the aid of Burgoyne's campaign.

General Burgoyne, who had traveled to London in the last weeks of 1776 to review his northern strategy in detail, planned to execute his campaign in two movements: his main force, which would travel down Lake Champlain, and a diversionary force led by Colonel Barry St. Leger, who would track along the Mohawk River. The idea was that both campaigns would protect each other's flanks and rendezvous in Albany. Having secured the approval of Lord Germain, the de facto minister for war, Burgoyne returned to British Canada and in June 1777 set out from Quebec with a force of eight thousand men, including regulars, militia, and German mercenaries. For the next few weeks they marched south from Montreal along Lake Champlain, exactly as planned, in the hope that St. Leger's force of two thousand men would likewise keep the pace by moving east down the Mohawk River.

At this point, Washington was wholly oblivious of this threat from the north. His focus was still on Howe and what he intended to do as soon as the fighting season started. As a result, the American garrisons in the Mohawk and Hudson valleys, including Fort Ticonderoga, were not reinforced, with the exception of a regiment sent to Fort Stanwix (near today's Rome, New York) and to Peekskill in Westchester County. The total Continental strength in the Hudson and Mohawk regions thus amounted to little more than eighty-five hundred soldiers and militia, though these were obviously distributed in pockets over a large area.

Initially, Burgoyne's northern thrust appeared to be doing well. On June 30, he easily captured Fort Crown Point, relying on Indians to screen his movements from any American troops in the area. Two days later he reached Fort Ticonderoga and proceeded to install his artillery on a hilltop known as Sugar Loaf, from where he could direct plunging fire on the fort's defenders. As soon as the commander of the American garrison, General Arthur St. Clair, realized what he was in for, he withdrew his troops, allowing Burgoyne to occupy the fort without a shot being fired. A Scotsman who had served in the British forces during the French and Indian War, St. Clair was loudly denounced for surrendering the fort without a fight and was promptly removed from his command.

Encouraged by this easy victory, Burgoyne ordered his advance formations to pursue the American retreat. The British troops caught up with them at the Battle of Hubbardton and the Battle of Fort Anne but were rudely surprised by the tough defense that the American garrison put up. While casualties were heavy, particularly on the American side, Burgoyne's force lost two hundred men. A further thirteen hundred had stayed back in order to occupy the captured fort. Nonetheless, Burgoyne wrote a glowing report to the king that depicted these skirmishes as a major victory. London promptly spread the news that the Americans were on the run, which of course was a gross exaggeration. But when the report reached Paris, it severely handicapped American diplomatic overtures to France, in the hope that she would enter the war.

Meanwhile, Burgoyne continued his advance, once again moving overland rather than by ship across the lake, in an effort to mop up any remaining American resistance. The American general in charge of this territory, Philip

Schuyler, was now fully alert to the danger from the north and decided to create a scratch force to stop or at least delay the approaching British forces. He rode hell-for-leather to Fort Edward, where he recruited some two thousand regulars and militia. These were put to work cutting down trees and stacking the trunks on Burgoyne's expected route. The gambit worked; the felled trees severely hampered Burgoyne's advance and at times forced him to carve out a new road through the wilderness. It did Schuyler little good, however, because like St. Clair he was sacked by Congress over the loss of Fort Ticonderoga and replaced by General Horatio Gates. Burgoyne soon found a way to circumvent the obstacles, and on July 29 he reached Fort Edward himself, now augmented by five hundred Indians from local tribes.

The Six Nations

The key role played by Native American tribes in this campaign was no accident. As an outflow of the French and Indian War, Britain had formally recognized the territory of Indians who had fought on the British side, including the confederation known previously as the Five Nations. This comprised the Seneca, Cayuga, Onondaga, Oneida, and Mohawk, who had united in this confederacy many centuries earlier, in 1200, long before the arrival of the Europeans. In 1722, the confederation admitted the Tuscarora nation as well, and it became known as the Six Nations.

Largely as a result of their animosity toward tribes allied with France, the Nations soon gravitated toward Britain, a rapprochement that was actively encouraged by Sir William Johnson, the British superintendent of Indian Affairs who had lived in the Mohawk Valley and had won the trust of the local tribes. In gratitude for their support during the French and Indian War, and with an eye on sustaining this alliance in the long term, the British Crown formally recognized the boundary lines of the Six Nations in the Treaty of Fort Stanwix of 1768. The Crown also made an effort to ensure that the Six Nations territory was included in all maps of North America, as shown in the 1777 map of Pennsylvania, New Jersey, and New York.

For these tribes, however, the internecine war between Britain and its former colonists was an entirely different affair. Most American Natives looked

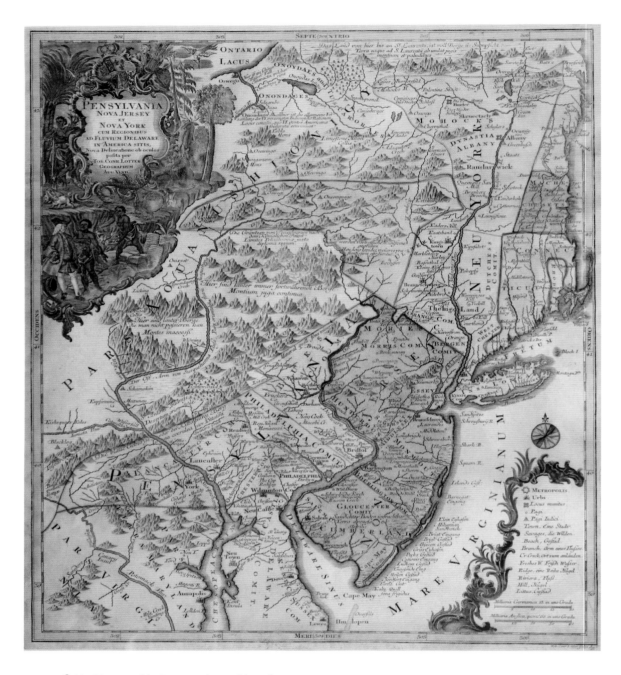

FIG. 128. The "Country of the Six Nations" west of the Delaware
River in a 1777 map by Matthew Lotter

on the conflict as a strange form of fratricide that could not fail to damage the confederacy by forcing it to split its allegiance. And in fact, that is exactly what happened. While a majority supported the British side, only a few nations—including the Oneida and the Tuscarora—went over to the Americans. George Washington never forgave the Six Nations for actively assisting the British military, as future events would show.[111]

John Burgoyne, on the other hand, leaned heavily on the British-Indian alliance to guide his troops through this territory, particularly since the Six Nations controlled the headwaters of the Ohio, Hudson, Delaware, Susquehanna, Chenango, Mohawk, and St. Lawrence rivers. He even placed the Indian units at the front of his troops, not only because they knew the lay of the land but also because he knew the sight of these indigenous warriors would strike terror in the hearts of the colonials. He was right: in many cases, the Continental militia simply faded away as soon as they saw these fearsome tribes come near. This was a source of great frustration to the Indian warriors who were itching to fight. Instead, they decided to vent their rage on any colonial families who remained in the area, even loyalist settlers, usually by scalping the men and enslaving the women and children. Burgoyne refused to intervene in these reprisals, in the belief that such terror could only help to discourage any remaining resistance along his path. But in fact, it had the opposite result. The terror tactics merely served to erode loyalist support for the British side and prompted many colonials to switch to the rebel cause. The killing of a young woman named Jane McCrea, a loyalist settler, at the hands of Huron Wendat warriors was particularly damaging to British interests. Needless to say, the murder was actively exploited by Congress in several gruesome prints as part of its global propaganda war against Great Britain.

Had there been a strong, central command of the English forces in North America, such crimes could have been prevented. But as we saw, there was no such central command, with Howe's authority constantly being undermined by Lord Germain in London or by other British generals in the theater.

In fact, the outcry over Jane McCrea's murder backfired and poisoned Burgoyne's relationship with his Indian allies. When public pressure mounted to denounce the Indians involved in the killing, Burgoyne had no choice but to comply, infuriating most of his Indian allies, who promptly decided to

FIG. 129. Henry Bryan Hall and Luigi Schiavonetti,
The Murder of Jane McCrea, ca. 1777

abandon him. This robbed the British general of his "eyes and ears," with dire consequences for the future of campaign.

Now bereft of his Indian scouts, Burgoyne proceeded more cautiously in his advance on Albany. On September 19, he stumbled across a hastily built defensive position some ten miles south of Saratoga, commanded by General Gates. As the British phalanx approached, Gates took command of the right flank, while placing Benedict Arnold in charge of the defense of the left, facing the Bemis Heights. This was the weakest position in the American line, as shown in William Faden's map, below, where the American positions are marked in gray and the British positions are shown in white and black. Faden's map is a typical example of a battle map, sketched on location and then rushed to London to be engraved and presented to George III and his war cabinet.

Arnold was aware that the British would soon discover the weakness of the left and would likely attack at this point. In response, he moved some of his forces to the far left, close to a position known as Freeman's Farm.

It so happened that some of Burgoyne's advance units were trying to occupy the same point as well, and a skirmish broke out that quickly developed into a fierce battle. After intense fighting with a ferociousness seldom witnessed in this war, the British carried the day but at the ruinous cost of six hundred casualties. The Americans had fought well, but ironically, Gates didn't see it that way. He scolded Arnold for his unauthorized move to the left, which led to a bitter argument between the two generals. Arnold thereupon threatened to resign. Fortunately, most of his senior officers rallied to his side, and the aggrieved general was persuaded to stay. But the episode would cast a long shadow, as we will see.

Indeed, the quarrel between the two officers was entirely unnecessary, for the sheer violence of the Battle of Freeman's Farm had shocked Burgoyne to the core. Like all other British generals, he had a low opinion of the Continentals' fighting skills and believed British military acumen would always triumph in the end. But "victories" such as these, which had cost 10 percent of his combat strength, he could ill afford. He therefore fell into the same apathetic stupor that Howe was prone to, and decided to stay put, while placing all his faith in reinforcements that General Clinton had vaguely indicated would be coming up from New York. Marooned and idled

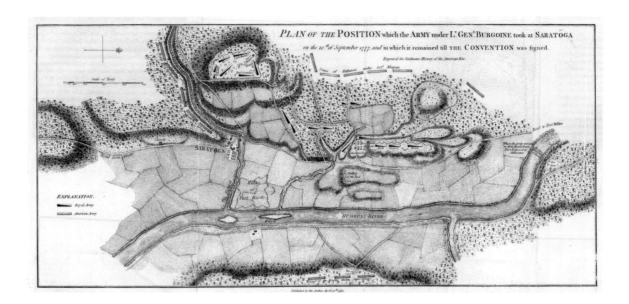

PLAN OF THE POSITION which the ARMY under L.ᵗ GEN.ᵗ BURGOINE took at SARATOGA on the 10.ᵗʰ of September 1777, and in which it remained till THE CONVENTION was signed.

FIG. 130. William Faden
and Charles Stedman, *Plan of
Burgoyne's Army at Saratoga*,
September 10, 1777

in Saratoga, and exposed to the elements, the British Army slowly bled out from lack of food, disease, and desertions. By contrast, news of the heroic stand at Freeman's Farm had quickly spread through the region, and Gates's army suddenly swelled with the arrival of thousands of militia, raising his battle strength to fifteen thousand men.

This did not go unnoticed on the English side, of course, and on October 3, Burgoyne decided to send out a reconnaissance force in strength to see what was happening. Once again, he planned to penetrate the American lines on their vulnerable left flank on the Bemis Heights. But before his assault could develop properly, Gates launched a counterattack, and once more a bloody clash ensued. This time, American arms prevailed. Burgoyne was forced to withdraw, leaving 900 men killed, wounded, or captured on the field, compared to only 150 casualties on the American side.[112]

One of the British officers killed was General Simon Fraser. In accordance with his wishes, he was buried the next day, in a spot just three miles above Stillwater, where the main British force had been encamped since September 20. When the Americans learned about the ceremony, they agreed to hold their fire so that the general's funeral could proceed with full honors. This remarkable event inspired the engraving below, which shows the British camp in startling detail, as well as the funeral cortege on the hill at right.

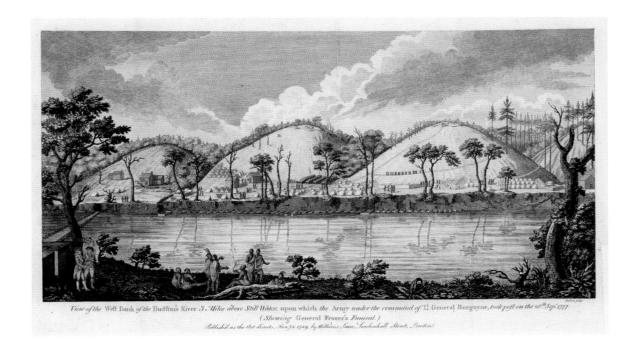

View of the West Bank of the Hudson's River 3 Miles above Still Water, upon which the Army under the command of L. General Burgoyne, took post on the 20th Sep. 1777.
(Showing General Frazer's Funeral.)
Published as the Act directs, Jan. 1. 1789, by William Lane, Leadenhall Street, London.

FIG. 131. William Lane, *View of the West Bank of the Hudson's River, Showing Gen. Frazer's Funeral,* 1789

In contrast to the idyllic mood of this picture, Burgoyne's army was now a mere shadow of itself. Defeated in the field, bereft of food and supplies, the general led the bedraggled survivors back to Saratoga, a two-day march in pouring rain that only added to the redcoats' misery. Gates followed close behind. As soon as the British were encamped, Gates used his superior forces to surround them and gradually tightened the noose. Burgoyne saw the writing on the wall, and on October 17, he formally surrendered to the Americans. He offered his sword to Gates, but as a sign of respect, Gates handed it back. Then, the British Army was ordered to march past in enfilade and stack its arms while the Continental band played "Yankee Doodle."

It was an astounding victory. Up to this point, the Continentals had sometimes bested their British foes in skirmishes and modest engagements such as Bunker Hill. But this was a triumph over an entire army, a large corps of British regulars some six thousand strong. Never before had a popular insurgency dealt such a humiliating blow to the world's most powerful military.

The timing couldn't have been better. On November 15, the Continental Congress had chosen to adopt "The United States of America" as the new name

FIG. 132. A gleeful French
depiction of the Surrender at
Saratoga, showing how "6040
well-disciplined troops lay down
their arms before the American
militia of farmers," drawn by
François Godefroy in 1784

SARRATOGA.

Le 17 Octobre 1777. le général Burgoine avec 6040 soldats bien disciplinés met bas les armes devant les milices Américaines nouvellement tirées de l'Agriculture et conduite par Horatio Gates.

of the confederated colonies. Overjoyed by the British surrender, Congress now declared December 18, 1777, to be a "day of solemn Thanksgiving and praise," as the new nation's first official holiday.

News of the surrender also reached Paris and the Continental envoy at the court of Versailles, Benjamin Franklin. A consummate diplomat, Franklin had been dispatched by Congress to broker an alliance with France and to find any way in which King Louis XVI would support the Revolutionary War. Louis, however, was on the fence. Obviously, the prospect of revenge for the humiliating terms of the 1763 Treaty of Paris had great appeal. If indeed the Americans were capable of defeating the British, then certainly France would lend its support. The problem was, that was a big "if." Up to this point, it seemed to the diplomatic corps in Paris that it was the British who had the momentum, given their powerful navy, their large forces, and their capture of New York. What's more, the French treasury was all but empty as a result of the ruinous wars of past decades. France could ill afford to support another belligerent and wound up on the losing side once more.

Franklin, however, embraced this challenge with his customary vigor. A showman through and through, he was aware of the romantic nostalgia with which Frenchmen viewed their lost territories in the New World, as illustrated by French maps and engravings of the period. He catered to that stereotype by dressing himself in a homespun brown suit and a fur cap, playing the slightly irreverent but always genial colonist from exotic lands.

As he wrote to his friend Emma Thompson, "[Imagine me] being very plainly dress'd wearing my thin gray strait hair, that peeps out from under my only coiffure, a fine Fur Cap, which comes down to my Forehead almost to my spectacles. Think how this must appear among the powder'd heads of Paris!"[113] Most Frenchmen at court assumed that Franklin's distinctive headwear was made of beaver pelts, a prime product of their former American trade. Franklin did nothing to dissuade them of that notion, but in fact his fur was made of simple untreated pelt.

FIG. 133. Benjamin Franklin wearing his fur cap in a 1777 engraving by C. N. Cochin

What's more, he not only spoke French but also the language of enlightenment, the ideals of *liberté, égalité, fraternité* ("liberty, equality, brotherhood") that were all the rage in the intellectual salons of Paris. As Friedrich Schlosser wrote, "Such was the number of portraits, busts, and medallions of him in circulation before he left Paris, that he would have been recognized from them by any adult citizen in any part of the civilized world."[114] It was an exaggeration, of course, but with a kernel of truth.

Thus it is due to Franklin's inestimable talents that the negotiations with the French foreign minister, Charles Gravier, Comte de Vergennes, continued even in the face of disastrous tidings from the war, such as Howe's capture of Philadelphia in September 1777. Vergennes had little patience for the high-flown principles of the Enlightenment that seemed to animate these American gentlemen, but like his sovereign he was thirsting for any opportunity to cut Britain down to size—literally. He just needed to be assured that he was betting on the right horse. And while France had no problem secretly providing the American insurgency with arms, cannons, and gunpowder, publicly proclaiming its support for the American cause—in effect, a declaration of war with Britain—was another matter entirely.

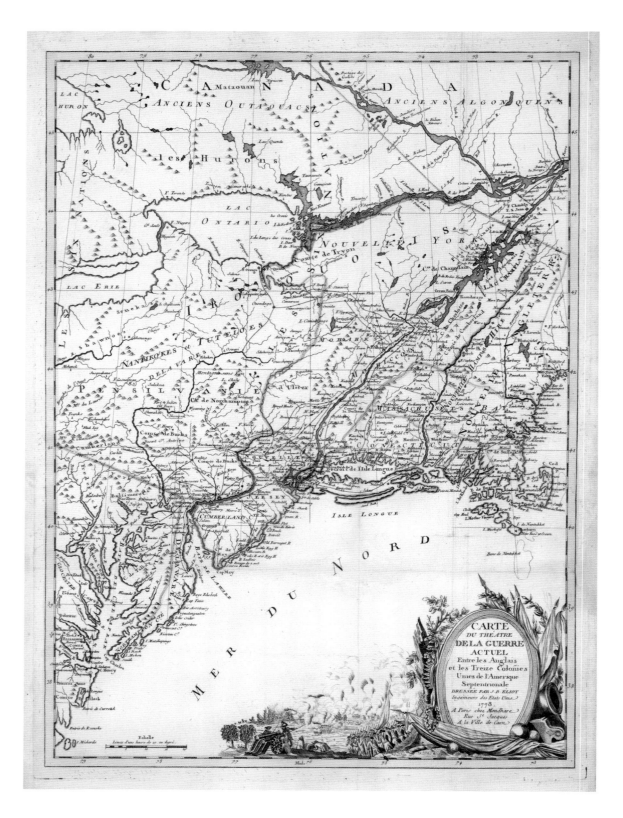

Then, news of the victory at Saratoga arrived on December 4, 1777, and in one fell swoop the mood at court changed. If these heroic militiamen could defeat some of George III's finest regiments, then clearly God was on their side. Two days later, King Louis XVI formally agreed to negotiations for an alliance. The terms of the treaty were hashed out with haste, and on February 6, 1778, the alliance between France and the United States was signed. To celebrate this momentous event, the American cartographer J. B. Eliot published a map in Paris that sought to illustrate the battlefield for the French public, now eager to follow the exploits of the heroic Americans.

Among others, the map clearly identifies St. Leger's unsuccessful expedition down the Mohawk Valley, Burgoyne's march from Crown Point to Albany, and Howe's campaign to take Philadelphia. All this suggests that Eliot, who is described as an aide-de-camp to General Washington but who is not otherwise known, must have had access to the freshest battlefield intelligence when he published it in 1778. There are only six known prints of this very important map, today valued at $25,000.

The war still had some four years to run, with many difficult battles ahead. But as the historian Richard Ketchum wrote, Saratoga was the turning point. From now on, the Revolutionary War would be fought between equals—and, crucially, with France on the side of the Americans.

From Valley Forge to Charlestown

On the face of it, then, there was ample reason for Washington and Congress to be optimistic. France was now in the war, which also meant that Spain had joined the conflict as a result of a treaty of mutual assistance between the two countries. On April 12, 1779, Spain made good on that promise by declaring war on Great Britain, in the hope of recovering its lost territories in Florida as well as Gibraltar and Menorca in the Mediterranean. Even the Dutch, England's traditional ally ever since William of Orange rose to the British throne as part of the "Glorious Revolution" of 1688, refused to come to her aid. Dutch merchants were too busy doing brisk business supplying the American revolution from Amsterdam.

As a result, Britain now found itself in a position that it had tried to avoid

FIG. 134. (*Opposite page*) J. B. Eliot, *Map of the Theater of War Between the British and the Thirteen United Colonies of North America,* 1778. This French map, printed to celebrate the alliance between France and the Continental Congress, is believed to be the first to bear the name *Etats Unis,* "United States."

FIG. 135. Jean-François
Hué, *La Bataille de Grenada
de 1779,* 1788

at all costs: a war on two fronts, both in America and Europe. This led to a
major diversion of British military forces back to the European continent, while
George III struggled to fend off challenges from the French, the Spanish, and
the Americans in what had become a truly global war. On top of that, British
overseas trade had suffered as a result of a French blockade of the sugar islands
of Jamaica and Barbados, depriving England of its most lucrative product. A
lengthy series of naval engagements in the Caribbean was the result, with both
sides pounding away until the French Comte d'Estaing dealt the British Navy a
crushing defeat at the Battle of Grenada of July 6, 1779. It was the worst British
naval defeat in more than a century.

All this should have been good news for the American cause, but the fact
of the matter is that by the winter of 1777, Washington's army was barely worthy of the name. Though nominally twelve thousand men strong, his troops
were spent. They were short of everything that a soldier, by rights, should
have: proper breeches, shirts, shoes, a hat, and a greatcoat against the biting
wind. Food was hard to come by, as was a dry place to sleep, preferably with a
fire to ward off frostbite. Washington's quartermaster warned him that three
thousand of his eleven thousand troops were "unfit for duty by reason of their
being barefoot and otherwise naked." How could he expect his men to fight
half-naked in the depth of winter, against a far superior foe?

"I am embarked on a wide ocean, boundless in its prospect," Washington
had written to his brother, John Augustine, shortly after his appointment as

FIG. 136. William Trego, *March to Valley Forge*, 1883

commander in chief of the Continental Army, "and from whence, perhaps, no safe harbor can be found." That safe harbor now seemed farther away than ever. True, after General Howe had invested the capital of the Continental Congress, Philadelphia—much to the embarrassment of the delegates—Washington had made a valiant attempt to relieve the city by attacking from the northwest, through a borough known as Germantown. But he failed to carry the day. He was repulsed, which convinced him that any further offensives in the depth of winter would be futile. He therefore decided to encamp among the rolling hills of Pennsylvania farmland, in a place called Valley Forge.

"My brave fellows, you have done all I asked you to do, and more than can be reasonably expected," Washington told his soldiers, "but your country is at stake, your wives, your houses, and all that you hold dear. You have worn yourselves out with fatigues and hardships, but we know not how to spare you."[115]

Brave words, but the fact of the matter was, his horses were dying for want of forage, and many troops were weak with hunger. He had beseeched Congress, now ensconced in York, to rush in new supplies, but if anything, these desperate pleas had worked against him. There were now several people in the assembly calling for his removal. It was time, they argued, to give Horatio Gates the supreme command. After all, *he* had scored a big victory, at the Battle of Saratoga,

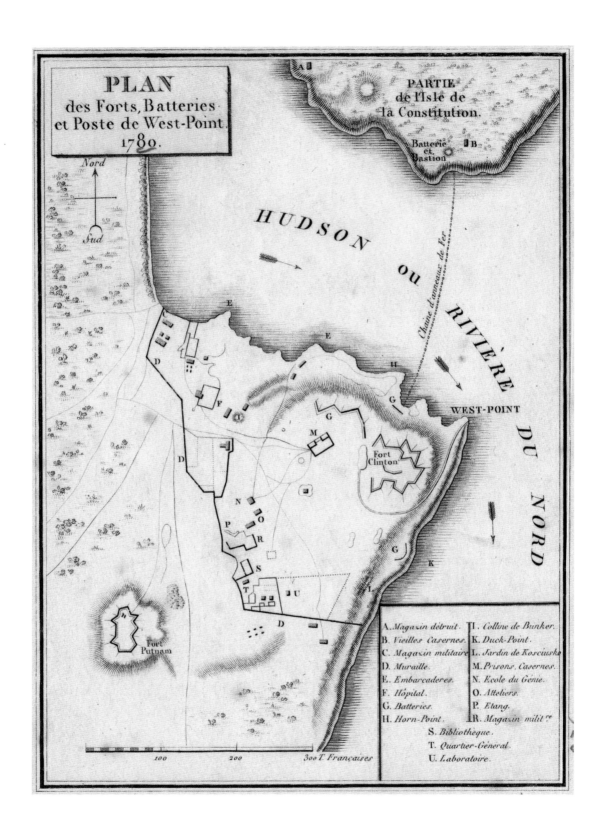

PLAN
des Forts, Batteries
et Poste de West-Point.
1780.

Nord

Sud

PARTIE
de l'Isle de
la Constitution.

A

Batterie
et
Bastion

B

HUDSON ou RIVIÈRE DU NORD

Chaîne d'anneaux de Fer

WEST-POINT

E

E

D

F

H

G

D

G

M

Fort
Clinton

N

O

P

R

G

S

K

T

H

U

D

Fort Putnam

A. Magazin détruit.   I. Colline de Bunker.
B. Vieilles Casernes.   K. Duck-Point.
C. Magazin militaire.   L. Jardin de Kosciusko.
D. Muraille.   M. Prisons, Casernes.
E. Embarcaderes.   N. Ecole du Génie.
F. Hôpital.   O. Atteliers.
G. Batteries.   P. Etang.
H. Horn-Point.   R. Magazin milit.re
          S. Bibliothèque.
          T. Quartier-Général.
          U. Laboratoire.

100   200   300 T. Françaises

while Washington was flailing about in Germantown to little effect. So far, these Congressional rebels had been kept at bay, but that wouldn't last long.

The problem was not the supplies themselves, as Washington well knew. There were storage depots all along the Eastern Seaboard piled high with clothing, provisions, and ammunition. The real problem was getting everything to Valley Forge, particularly now that rain and wet snow had turned the roads into quagmires.

There is a persistent legend that during one of his nighttime rides in the country, not too far from the camp, Washington got off his horse, doffed his hat, and knelt in the snow to pray. An eyewitness, Isaac Potts, later claimed to have heard the general in his devotions. If that is true, then in the months to come, Washington's prayers were finally heard. Convoys began to arrive that, while still inadequate, at least bolstered the morale of the troops. And on February 23, 1778, Washington got his best news yet: a Prussian officer named Friedrich von Steuben arrived to kick the Continental Army into something resembling a disciplined Prussian force.

Then, in March, British forces withdrew from Philadelphia to join Howe's army in New York City. And in July, a small American raiding party overran the British-held fort at Stony Point, killing 63 redcoats and taking another 543 prisoners, for the loss of only 15 Americans killed. It was the shot in the arm that the Continental Army needed.

Still, victory continued to elude Washington. The conflict had entered into a stalemate, with attritional warfare sapping the strength of both armies. General Clinton led a major assault on Connecticut, trying to force Washington into the type of open battle that the redcoats knew and craved, but Washington refused to oblige. A daring American naval raid on Maine known as the Penobscot Expedition failed miserably. In 1780, a force of six thousand Hessians led by General Wilhelm von Knyphausen invaded New Jersey but was defeated at Springfield. And so the seesaw continued.

Then, in October of 1780, shocking news arrived: General Benedict Arnold, the hero of Lake Champlain and Saratoga, had decided to defect. Never one to conform to military orthodoxy, Arnold had made many enemies, starting with General Gates, as well as with members of Congress. Repeatedly accused of financial wrongdoings, he was court-martialed, exonerated, and court-martialed again.

FIG. 137. (*Opposite page*) A 1780 map of the Fort at West Point, which Arnold used as a bargaining chip in his negotiations with the British

Prodded by his pretty wife, Peggy Shippen, daughter of a wealthy Philadelphia loyalist, Arnold was fed up with the American military leadership, who had never given him due credit for his victories. Thus, he secretly opened negotiations with the British. His opposite number was a close friend of Peggy's, named Major John André. As it happened, Arnold had been appointed to command the fort at West Point—as a peace offering by Washington, who considered Arnold a friend. Arnold, eager to sweeten the deal for the British, then came up with the astounding idea of surrendering the fort, lock, stock, and barrel, in exchange for £20,000 pounds. It was treason of the highest order. Some historians claim that as soon as Arnold took over the fort, he deliberately began to weaken its defenses so as to facilitate its capture by the British.

Unfortunately for Arnold, the plot was exposed when André was captured by American troops. He had unwisely decided to carry incriminating documents describing the West Point deal in the soles of his socks, of all places.[116] Major André was tried and hanged as a spy, but Arnold escaped, crossed the British lines, and fled to New York. There, he was granted a commission as a British officer and began fighting on the British side.

Not surprisingly, his defection doomed him in the eyes of history, and his reputation never recovered. Washington was deeply aggrieved when he heard the news. He had always tried to defend Arnold against his enemies and never hesitated to give him the credit that was his due for his heroic actions at Lake Champlain and Saratoga. That was one reason why Washington had given him the command of West Point, over the objections of many of his officers. Thus, Arnold's plan to surrender West Point on a silver platter rankled deeply, and Washington never forgave him.

Turncoats do not fare well, as plenty of examples in history have shown. After joining the Revolutionary War on the British side, Arnold was implicated in the massacre of Connecticut militia during the Battle of Groton Heights on September 6, 1781. This bloody incident cast a long shadow, and soon thereafter Arnold moved with his wife, Peggy, to London.

But London's social circles gave them the cold shoulder, and in 1785 they were on a ship once more, this time bound for Canada. Here, Arnold hoped to set up a business with his sons. Unfortunately, his various business dealings led to lawsuits, and in December 1791 Arnold and his family fled once more, back to London. Six months later, his pugnacious nature prompted a duel with the Earl of Lauderdale, a member of the House of Lords.

The French Revolution followed shortly thereafter. Arnold saw this as an opportunity. He moved to the West Indies in the hope of restoring his good name by defending British interests against French attacks. But he was already suffering from gout, and he died on June 14, 1801, at the age of sixty.

Modern historians have yet to initiate a rehabilitation of Arnold. His life has all the hallmarks of a Greek tragedy: a story of fierce devotion and poor character, of heroic deeds and abject betrayal. But in American culture, his name became a byword for traitor. To make that point, the victory monument at Saratoga has four niches. Three are occupied by statues of Generals Morgan, Schuyler, and Gates. But the fourth niche is empty.

FIG. 138. Daniel Gardner, Peggy Shippen Arnold with her daughter Sophia, ca. 1789

The Southern Strategy

In 1781, the British high command recognized that something needed to be done to bring the war to a close. Britain's military resources were being drained in too many conflicts around the world, while the country came to grips with what it took to police and govern a global empire. Loyalist exiles in London kept telling Parliament that there was strong sentiment in the South to remain in the union with the British Crown. In response, British war planners slowly gravitated toward a "Southern Strategy," one that would capitalize on the strong loyalist base in these regions by attacking the Continental Army through what Winston Churchill would have called its "soft underbelly." And indeed, the initial probes appeared promising. On December 29, 1778, a British expeditionary force from New York took Savannah with ease. A foray into Georgia near Brier Creek was successful as well, but the expedition faltered when the British tried to take Charleston in June 1779. Worse, the invading force engaged in an orgy of looting, which had the unique effect of unifying both loyalists and patriots in their protests. General Clinton merely shrugged and threw his forces against Charleston once more, finally besting the besieged city in May 1780.

The loss of Charleston marked one of the worst Continental defeats of the war. Over five thousand American soldiers were taken prisoner, virtually erasing Washington's forces in the south. To everyone, then, it seemed that the British southern strategy was working. That was also clear to the members of Congress, where the rebel faction, known as the Conway Cabal, now loudly clamored for General Horatio Gates to take over as supreme commander in the south. This motion was carried, and Gates gratefully traveled to Deep River, North Carolina, to take up his command.

Meanwhile, General Cornwallis was busy building up Charleston as a base from where to extend British control over all of South Carolina. Gates decided to stop him, but the resulting Battle of Camden of August 16, 1780, once more led to a catastrophic defeat for the Americans. Gates was relieved of his command and never again led troops in the field.

 Greatly encouraged, Clinton now decided to target Virginia. The man tapped to lead that attack was none other than Benedict Arnold, fresh from his defection and keen to demonstrate his bona fides to his new taskmasters. Clinton hoped that having an American in command of the invading forces would appeal to loyalists. He was not wrong. In January 1781, Arnold invaded Richmond with such ease that its governor, Thomas Jefferson, was only able to escape in the nick of time. Hardly a shot was fired, given that most of the local militia had melted away, leaving only two hundred soldiers to defend the city. Arnold sent a letter to Jefferson under flag of truce, offering to leave the city unharmed if Jefferson disclosed where its tobacco stores and military supplies could be found. Jefferson responded scathingly that he would not have anything to do with a turncoat. This so enraged Arnold that he ordered the city put to the torch. A spree of looting, pillaging, and destruction followed in that tragic city, further damning Benedict Arnold's reputation in American eyes.

Obviously, something had to be done to bolster American spirits in the South. In response, Jefferson's friend Colonel Sampson Mathews scraped together a force of two hundred soldiers that proceeded to harass Arnold's British Army at every turn. Using the now familiar guerilla tactics, they slowly bled Arnold's forces all the way along the James River. In retaliation, the British adopted a scorched-earth policy, burning plantations and private homes along the way. Slaves were freed and encouraged to join British troops. On January 19, 1781, Arnold led his bedraggled and exhausted troops into Portsmouth, and his expedition came to a close.

The British were ecstatic. The southern strategy had worked. Large Continental forces had been killed, wounded, or dispersed, and loyalist support was as strong as ever—or so it was believed. Worse, since Arnold was not reprimanded for his penchant for looting, other officers took their cue and began to launch punitive raids of their own, plundering to their heart's content. The war had sunk to new, unplumbed depths.

The Battle of Yorktown

The conflict now entered its final phase, even though the parties may not have been aware of it. The British firmly committed themselves to a southern strategy to defeat the revolution, and the man to lead that effort was General Cornwallis. This was somewhat of a surprise, since Cornwallis's effort to subjugate the Carolinas in October 1780 had been dealt a decisive check with the Battle of Kings Mountain. During this engagement, local patriot militia had defeated a loyalist force led by British major Patrick Ferguson. It was the largest all-American battle of the war, with loyalists battling revolutionaries, and the defeat of this detachment was a major morale boost for the Continental cause after the string of British victories. But Cornwallis's star had risen high in London, particularly since he had the confidence of the king.

In the meantime, Washington had looked for an officer to replace Gates in the south and settled on Nathanael Greene, the son of a Quaker family from Rhode Island. Greene had distinguished himself in the Boston and New Jersey campaigns and was at that time serving as Washington's quartermaster general. It was an inspired decision, for Greene combined military cunning and incisiveness with an absolute ruthlessness, key ingredients for the type of guerilla warfare that the southern army would need to conduct. Greene did not disappoint. Throughout 1781, he chipped away at Cornwallis's strength, inflicting heavy losses during clashes in Greensboro, North Carolina, as well as at Camden and Eutaw Springs, South Carolina. Thus, the British will to fight was slowly eroded, and eventually Greene was able to drive all British forces from the Carolinas, with the exception of its encampments in Charleston and Savannah.

Cornwallis searched for a way to defeat Greene's insidious guerilla attacks and fell back on the old strategy of strangling an army by cutting its supply line. As we saw, that ploy had been tried before, notably by General Burgoyne in the Hudson Valley. But Burgoyne's mission had failed because the British had once again underestimated the large distances involved, and the manpower needed to control it. Now, Cornwallis was going to try the same, based on intelligence that most of Greene's supplies were funneled through Virginia. The obvious solution, then, was a massive invasion of that colony, as he outlined in a letter to his nominal superior, General Clinton, and to Lord Germain in London. In his view, this would result in the wholesale collapse of the American southern forces and the defeat of the revolution. The problem with this idea was that Cornwallis had neither the men nor the arms to occupy and subdue a territory the size of Virginia, or any other colony for that matter. General Clinton realized that, too, and rejected Cornwallis's proposal, suggesting that he attack farther north, with a much narrower objective. Lord Germain, on the other hand, liked the plan and told Cornwallis to proceed, if for no reason other than that Clinton had yet to come up with a battle strategy of his own.

Events now slowly moved to their inevitable conclusion. Unbeknownst to the British high command, the French armed forces had been given the green light to begin major offensive operations with their American allies. On July 11, 1780, a division of fifty-five hundred French regulars had landed in Rhode Island, but its commander, Jean-Baptiste de Vimeur, Comte de Rochambeau, was under strict instructions not to expose this modest force to any undue risk. Nor was he to stray too far from the French fleet, which was ensconced in Narragansett Bay. As a result, the French troops sat around and did nothing while Washington and Rochambeau figured out what to do with this small but politically significant contribution from France. Washington wanted to attack the British in New York, but Rochambeau wanted to strike in Virginia instead. Both plans would depend on the active support of Admiral de Grasse, commander of the French fleet, so that its massive naval artillery could be brought to bear against the British fleet as well as British batteries ashore. Clinton got wind of these plans, however, and rushed reinforcements to New York, thus reducing his strength in the south where it was needed most.

Meanwhile, Cornwallis had come around and decided to move his army to Chesapeake Bay so as to interdict the flow of American supplies in due course. "I cannot help expressing my wishes that the Chesapeake may become the seat of war even (if necessary) at the expense of abandoning New York," Cornwallis wrote in a letter to Clinton. "The rivers of Virginia are advantageous to an invading army," he added hopefully.[117] Once again, Clinton disagreed with this plan, feeling that a campaign in Virginia posed a "great risk unless we are sure of a permanent superiority at sea," a prescient notion now that the French Navy was in play. But Clinton knew that Cornwallis was the current favorite at court, and so he grudgingly agreed to the plan, ordering his subordinate also to build a deepwater port as the base of the British strategy in the south.

Cornwallis rushed to launch his plan. His spies had told him that Nathanael Greene's troops posed no threat since he was still in the Carolinas and that the only opposing force he would face was the three thousand Continental regulars and militiamen commanded by the French general Marie-Joseph du Motier, better known as the Marquis de Lafayette. By contrast, Cornwallis had seventy-two hundred men at his disposal—more than double the American forces. Thus, as Cornwallis wrote to Clinton, "I shall now proceed to dislodge La Fayette (*sic*) from Richmond and with my light troops destroy any magazines or stores in the neighborhood." From there he would search for a place to build "a proper harbor and place of arms." He'd been looking at some maps and finally settled on one particular location. "I am inclined to think well of York," he wrote.[118]

Yorktown had much to recommend itself. It was ideally positioned on the York River, with a perfect anchorage for ships arriving from Chesapeake Bay. But to get there, Cornwallis knew he first had to defeat Lafayette's army, lest he suffer the same type of attritional guerilla warfare that had doomed his operations in the Carolinas. Unfortunately for him, Lafayette refused to be caught in the open. The French general withdrew his army from Richmond and then steadily shadowed Cornwallis's host as it ponderously made its way to Yorktown. Along the way, Lafayette made life miserable by sending out nuisance raids.

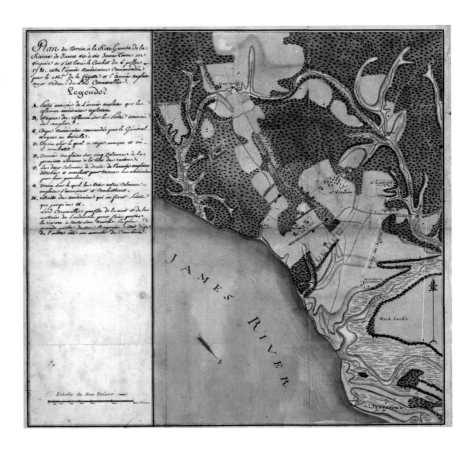

FIG. 139. Jean Nicholas
Desandroüins, *Map of the Left
Bank of the James River and the
Battle of Green Spring*, 1781

One of these produced the Battle of Green Spring, near the Virginian
plantation of Green Spring, where the American general "Mad" Anthony
Wayne, who had joined Lafayette with eight hundred militiamen, surprised
the far superior British forces with a bayonet charge.

By August, Cornwallis had finally secured his objective and settled down
to build a ring of fortifications in and around Yorktown. But Lafayette was
faster and quickly moved his forces to Malvern Hill, on the north bank of the
James River, some eighteen miles southwest of Richmond. From there, his
artillery could easily reach the British, who had orders to stay close to the river
so as to build an anchorage for British ships.

In the meantime, Washington and Rochambeau were still debating what
to do with their combined forces, including the fleet of Admiral de Grasse.
The American general kept pushing for a strong assault in New York, but
Rochambeau demurred. He knew that de Grasse, whose fleet was in the

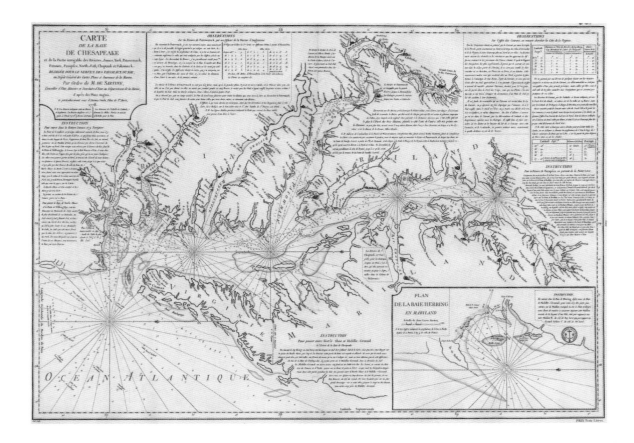

Caribbean at the time, would under no circumstance risk his precious fleet in a foolhardy attack on New York, where the British were well protected by the heavy firepower of the Royal Navy. Truth be told, the French admiral did not consider his involvement in the American Revolutionary War a priority. His real mission was to patrol the West Indies and protect French interests, and as far as he was concerned, the American Revolution was not a cause that mattered greatly to the French state. Thus, the debate between the French and American commanders was abruptly resolved when, on August 14, Washington received a letter from de Grasse, transmitted by Admiral Comte de Barras, the commander of the French naval forces in Rhode Island. It peremptorily informed him that de Grasse was sailing his twenty-nine warships from Santo Domingo up north, to anchor near Chesapeake Bay. This was exactly what Rochambeau had urged de Grasse to do, though of course Washington could not know that. For the French admiral, the move to the Chesapeake was principally motivated

FIG. 140. Admiral de Grasse used this chart of the Chesapeake Bay, prepared by the French *Depot de la Marine* in 1778, to plan his movements in support of the Franco-American forces on land.

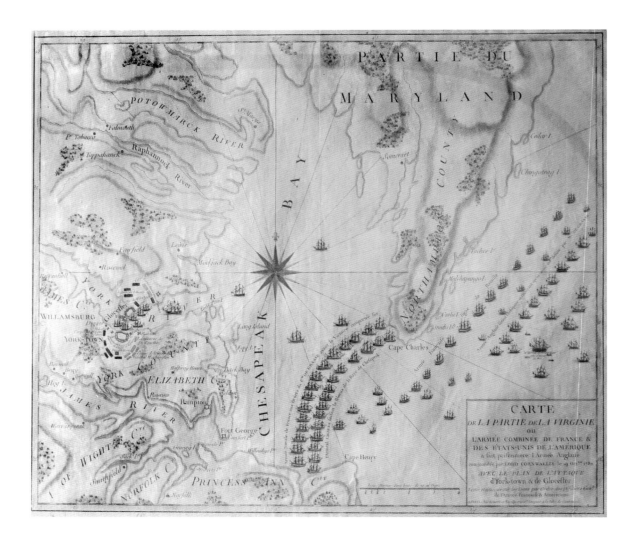

FIG. 141. French map showing the solid wall of de Grasse's French battleships blocking access to Cornwallis's besieged camp at Yorktown.

by considerations that had less to do with American military objectives. The hurricane season was upon them, and de Grasse needed a safe harbor to shelter his vessels—and the three thousand marines in its hold—before he sailed his fleet back to Europe in October, at the end of their rotation. Thus, by a stroke of pure luck, both the French and American forces were concentrating in the very area where Cornwallis had unwittingly decided to establish his base as well.

De Grasse's message prodded Washington into action. There was no time to lose if he was to exploit this window of opportunity of having the French fleet at his disposal. Leaving two thousand men to guard the fort at West Point and the Hudson, Washington took twenty-five hundred men and rushed down south, soon followed by Rochambeau's force of five thousand men. Fortunately, Clinton did not discover the combined Franco-American movement to Virginia until September 2, when it was too late to do anything about it. The only British officer who did get an inkling of what was afoot was Admiral Sir George Rodney, commander of the flotilla that had been shadowing de Grasse's French fleet in the Caribbean. When de Grasse suddenly set sail in August and headed north, Rodney surmised, correctly, that he was heading for the American coast in support of some form of offensive operations there. The problem was, Rodney was seriously ill, which clouded his judgment. Rodney somehow came to the conclusion that de Grasse was going to split his force: one group would sail north to drop the French marines in America, while the other sailed back to Europe forthwith. Secure in that conviction, Rodney dispatched only fourteen warships, led by Admiral Sir Samuel Hood, to follow de Grasse's fleet while he himself prepared to return to Britain for treatment. But Hood soon lost contact with his prey and wound up far up north, at Sandy Hook, just as de Grasse was dropping anchor near the Chesapeake.

It seemed, then, that at long last the tide was shifting in the Americans' favor and that fate was doing everything in its power to disperse the British forces, while concentrating everything that the French and Americans could throw at Cornwallis. Even better, Rochambeau was able to contact the French squadron in Rhode Island, led by Admiral Barras, and urged him to rush to the Chesapeake with all haste. Barras promptly mobilized his fleet and sailed down, miraculously avoiding all of the marauding vessels of the Royal Navy.

When the British finally discovered where everyone had run to, they gave chase. The combined fleet of both Samuel Hood and his superior, Admiral Graves, moved down and reached the Chesapeake Bay on September 5. But it was too late. De Grasse, now reinforced by Barras's warships, was waiting for him with a combined naval force of twenty-four ships of the line with eighteen hundred guns, versus nineteen English ships with fourteen hundred guns.[119] Undeterred, both fleets maneuvered into position, opened their gunports, and let loose a thundering volley of ball. The battle went on for two more days, inflicting heavy damage, until Graves decided that to press the attack any further would put British naval power at risk. Amazingly, on September 9 he raised

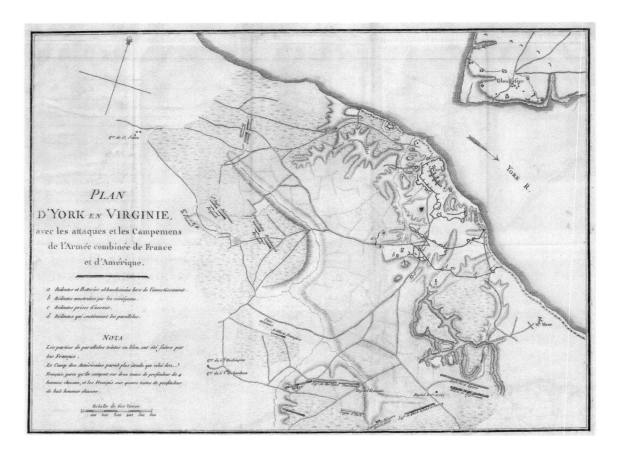

FIG. 142. Henri Soules, *Plan of the Battle of Yorktown*, 1787. This never-before-published map shows the positions of the French and American forces besieging the British fortifications.

anchor and sailed away, abandoning Cornwallis to his fate in Yorktown, exposed to whatever torments the French and Americans might wish to visit upon him.

Meanwhile, Washington had entered Philadelphia on September 2, eager to push on farther south, but his troops refused. They insisted on getting paid in coin first before they would take another step. Until now, they had been paid in Continental paper money, which had been devalued to the point that hardly any shops were prepared to accept it. Fortunately, Rochambeau generously lent Washington a portion of his stash of reals, Spanish gold coins, while a wealthy financier, Robert Morris, made up the balance. Thus satisfied, the troops resumed their march, reaching Williamsburg on September 14.

Two weeks later, all of the allied forces had safely arrived at the Chesapeake Bay and began to deploy. In addition to the seventy-eight hundred French troops delivered by Lafayette and the French Navy, Washington now commanded eight thousand Continentals as well as thirty-one hundred militiamen. For the first time, then, he led an overwhelmingly superior force of 18,900 men against a mere eight thousand British soldiers and sailors.

The funny thing was, General Cornwallis was still not duly concerned. He had built a ring of seven strongpoints, each bristling with artillery, and was confident that these powerful defensive works would rebuff whatever Washington planned to throw at him. And if push came to shove, he knew that the Royal Navy could always relieve him. Of Admiral Graves's abrupt departure, abandoning him to his fate, he was still blissfully unaware.

With the massive forces at their disposal, Washington and Rochambeau now studied the map of Yorktown shown here and agreed on the order of battle. They would throw a siege around the British by moving Rochambeau's troops to the left while Washington led his American troops to the right. In this manner, both commanders would gradually tighten the noose around Yorktown until the British were forced to give up the fight.

British reconnaissance parties soon detected these movements, and at long last, Cornwallis decided that some type of action was in order. He unleashed his artillery on September 29, vainly hoping that a strong bombardment would discourage the Americans from approaching his lines, but the Continentals had the scent of the fox and were eager to press their advantage. It was then that Cornwallis received the devastating news that the Royal Navy had departed from the scene. He immediately sent a frantic message to General Clinton, urging him to send a relief force, but he must have known in his heart of hearts that any force, whether by land or by sea, would arrive too late to make a difference. Washington had his blood up, and this time he meant to fight—the very set-piece battle that the British had craved for so long.

Back in New York, Clinton was utterly unaware of the growing crisis in Virginia until news of Cornwallis's plight arrived on September 23, stunning the high command. All this time, Clinton had still believed that Washington would strike at New York, secure in the knowledge that the fourteen British warships in port would easily defeat such an assault. But now the hammer would fall on Yorktown, rather than New York, and Clinton readily grasped the severity of the crisis. Once again he had been outfoxed, but this time on a scale he could scarcely imagine. Clinton grabbed a piece of paper and quickly scribbled a note to Cornwallis, promising that a relief force would be sent "within a week," but that was purely wishful thinking. Assembling such a force would take time, particularly since many ships had been laid up for urgent repairs after the action against de Grasse's fleet. The race against the clock was on.

Back in Yorktown, Cornwallis had come to the same conclusion. Having taken stock of his rapidly deteriorating situation, he pulled back from his outer defenses so as to concentrate his forces in a handful of strong points around Yorktown. Of course, as soon as the British vacated their outer perimeter, it was occupied by the French and American troops, which brought their artillery in range of the town proper. Cornwallis ordered a series of cannonades in response, but the attackers then built an elaborate network of trenches to shield them as they slowly moved closer to the British lines. Finally, at 3:00 p.m. on October 9, Rochambeau let loose a massive French barrage, joined two hours later by the full force of American artillery. According to one tradition, it was Washington who fired the first gun, and his shot struck the dining table of a group of British officers. They were probably dining on horsemeat; with the food supply perilously low, Cornwallis had ordered that most of the horses be slaughtered.

Over the next few days, the French and American forces slowly pushed forward, tightening the stranglehold around the British. Hard-pressed, Cornwallis received a letter from Clinton ordering him to stand firm, and that the rescue force was scheduled to sail from New York on October 12. Cornwallis shook his head and replied to the messenger that there was no way he could hold out for that long. He was right, for in the end, the British fleet did not depart from New York until a full week later, on October 19.

Outside British headquarters in Yorktown, heavy fighting continued. By October 14, the American position was within 150 yards of the last British defense line. Washington ordered a massive artillery attack, to be followed by a bayonet charge. The British fell back and tried to escape across the York River to Gloucester Point. Unfortunately for them, as soon as the first groups of pontoon boats pushed off, a huge storm broke over the bay as if by divine intervention, and the evacuation was aborted. The die had been cast. For Cornwallis, there was no turning back.

As dawn broke on the morning of October 17, two figures emerged from the mist and slowly made their way to the American lines. One was a drummer,

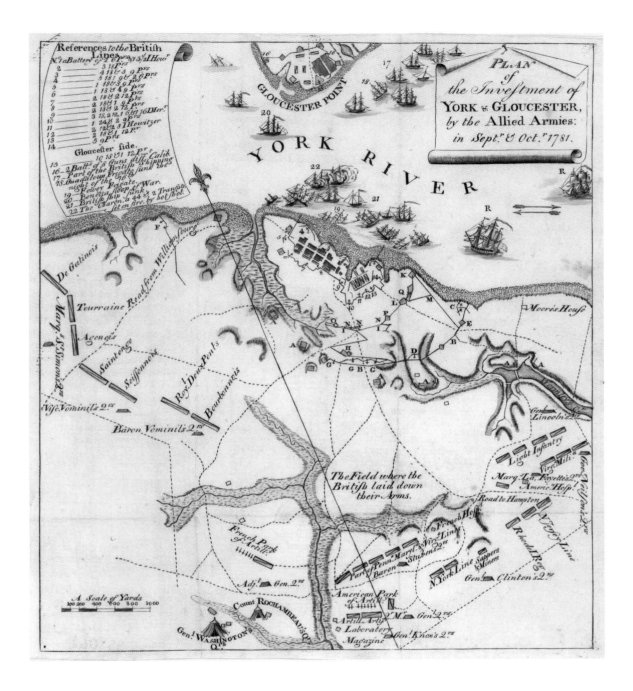

FIG. 143. The final act: The French and American stranglehold of Yorktown is vividly depicted in this rare map by the Charleston engraver Thomas Abernethie, 1785.

the other an officer waving a white handkerchief. It was done. Cornwallis had decided to throw in the towel.

Two days later, a scene unfolded that just eight months ago would have been unthinkable: Cornwallis's entire British Army of the South capitulated to the forces of the American Revolution. Dejected, Cornwallis asked to be allowed to march his army into captivity with flags flying and bayonets fixed, but Washington refused; a year before, after the siege of Charleston, those same honors of war had been denied to the defeated American army. What's more, he could never forgive the British for their campaign of terror: the indiscriminate raping and looting of innocent civilians, the bayonetting of wounded Americans, and the random burning of property. The British had not fought this war like the gentlemen they claimed to be; therefore, any honors befitting an honorable foe were denied. "From the former infatuation, duplicity, and perverse system of British Policy," Washington said in 1782, "I confess I am induced to doubt everything & to suspect everything."[120] He was talking about the peace negotiations in Paris, then continuing in fits and starts, but he might as well have been talking about the conduct of British troops throughout the war.

And so, in the end, the British Army was led out and forced to stack their arms in full view of the French and American troops. All told, the total haul amounted to eight thousand troops and sailors, 214 cannons, and twenty-four transport ships, plus thousands of muskets. It was an astounding victory, and one of the worst defeats in British military history.

Just five days later, Clinton's relief flotilla arrived in Yorktown. The place was empty. The only people on the scene were three fishermen, puttering about in the bay. When challenged, one of the men informed the English general that the British troops had surrendered. They were no more.

FIG. 144. John Trumbull, *The Surrender of Lord Cornwallis*, 1820

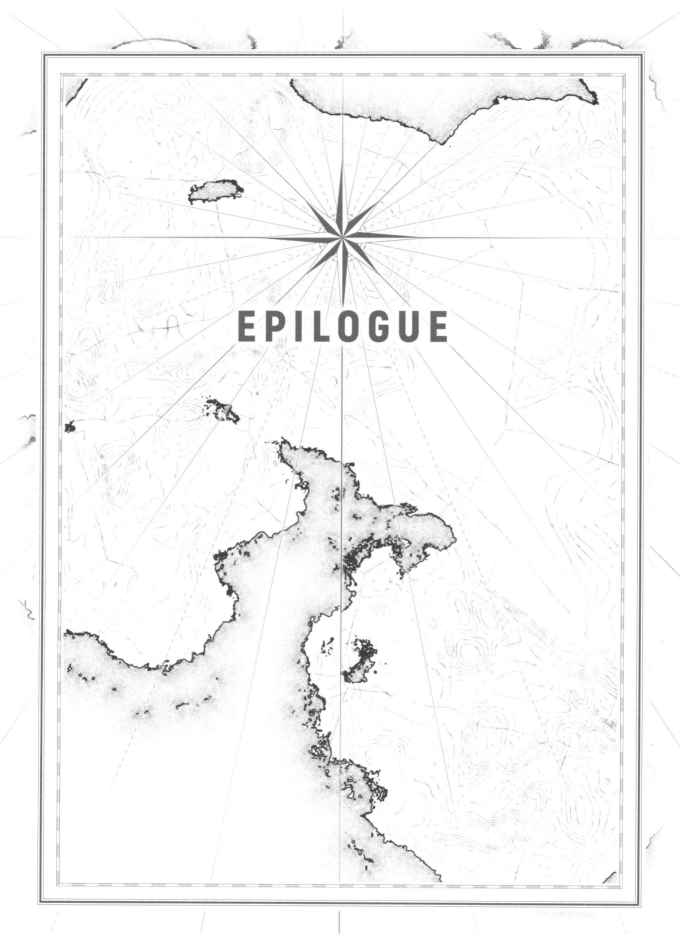

EPILOGUE

YORKTOWN WAS A CATASTROPHIC DEFEAT FOR THE BRITISH Crown, and not just on the war front. The repercussions were felt all the way in London as well. There, in the ornate halls of British Parliament in Westminster, the American victory gave the upper hand to the Whig party. The Whigs had long served as the peace party, opposing the pro-war Tories. Bitter disputes followed, but in early 1782, Parliament voted to end all offensive operations in North America. They had no particular love for the American cause, but the war in Europe continued unabated, and the state of the English treasury was by now truly appalling.

Not fighting didn't mean that peace had arrived, not yet. But in April of 1782, the British Navy was able to exact sweet revenge against de Grasse and his French fleet during the Battle of the Saintes near Guadeloupe. With honor thus restored, the British lion could finally agree to peace negotiations, with its head held high. That, too, took time, but in 1783, the Treaty of Paris was signed at last. The war was over. A new nation had risen on the other side of the Atlantic: the United States of America.

Naturally, this momentous development was celebrated in the one medium that had covered the birth of America from Columbus's voyage to the Revolutionary War: the colored map. Once again, it was the French, in this case Louis Brion de la Tour, who gave tribute to the young nation in a beautiful map that, as it happens, also contains one of the earliest depictions of the American flag.

With peace thus restored in the former British colonies, the main protagonists could leave the stage and get on with their lives.

By special permission from George Washington, General Cornwallis

FIG. 145. Louis Brion de la Tour, *Map of the United States and Operations of the Latest War*, 1784

was released on parole and returned to Britain on January 21, 1782. Much to his surprise, Cornwallis was welcomed as a hero upon his arrival. Indeed, he soon discovered that the surrender did not seem to have hurt his career, notwithstanding attempts by General Clinton to blame him for the failure of the southern campaign. Just three years later he was sent to Prussia as ambassador to Frederick the Great, and in 1786 he was made a Knight Companion of the Order of the Garter, one of the highest honors the king could bestow. Cornwallis then served as governor-general of India and died there on October 5, 1805.

John Burgoyne fell out of favor after his defeat in Saratoga, but he was restored to his rank in 1782 and made a colonel of the King's Own Royal Regiment. Since his wife had died in 1776, Burgoyne took a mistress, Susan Caulfield, and he had four children with her. One of these would later gain fame during the Napoleonic Wars as Field Marshal John Fox Burgoyne. On

August 3, 1792, John Burgoyne attended a theater performance in London and returned to his Mayfair home later that night. The next morning, quite unexpectedly, he was found dead.

Nathanael Greene continued to serve in the Continental Army after Yorktown and retired in 1783 to dedicate himself to growing a plantation in Chatham County, Georgia. But he soon fell into debt and died three years later, in 1786. Many modern historians believe he was the second best general of the American Revolutionary War, after George Washington.

Benjamin Franklin, who had played an outsized role in the story of America, continued to do so after his return from Paris. The man who in 1775 had been the first United States postmaster general before serving the revolutionary cause at the court of Louis XVI remained in his beloved Paris while the peace treaty was hashed out. On December 1, 1783, the American diplomat sat on a special dais in the Jardin des Tuileries, in an area reserved for VIPs, and watched open-mouthed as two French pilots took to the skies for the first time in human history, flying a hot-air balloon.

After his return to Pennsylvania in 1785, Franklin freed his slaves and became an ardent abolitionist, even accepting a post as the president of the Pennsylvania Abolition Society. Soon thereafter, the nation's leading men gathered once more in Philadelphia to debate the establishment of a Constitution. In a sense, it was an unprecedented idea for its time: to create a republic entirely based on the principles of a group of philosophers, the authors of the Enlightenment. Almost all nations of Europe were governed by hereditary monarchies—by dynasties of men and women who fervently believed they had been chosen by God to rule on this earth. But Jefferson and his fellow drafters thought differently. Greatly influenced by Montesquieu's *De l'Esprit des Loix* ("The Spirit of Laws," 1748), the Constitution that Jefferson, Franklin, and other founding fathers eventually agreed upon separated the government into three branches: legislative, judicial, and executive, with the last led by an elected president. Thus, the United States became the first nation on earth to be governed by the idea that every citizen had certain inalienable rights, including the right to life, liberty, and property. Franklin believed that freedom of speech was the greatest right of all. "Without freedom of thought there can be no such thing as wisdom," he wrote, "and no such thing as public liberty."[121]

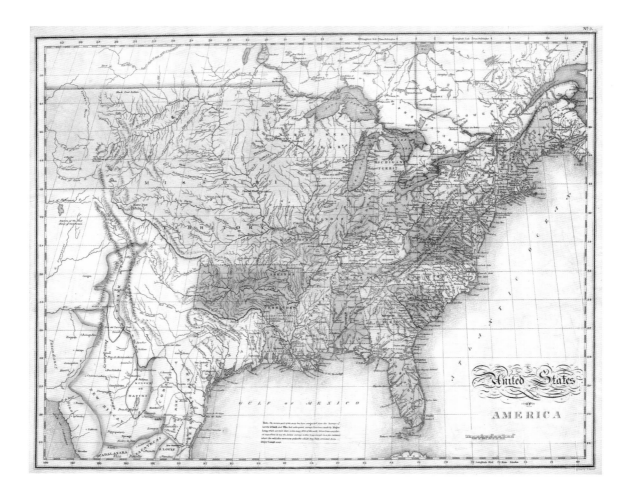

FIG. 146. John Melish,
Map of the United States with the
Contiguous British and Spanish
Possessions, 1822

Montesquieu's book also argued for an end to slavery, but it would take almost another century before this aspect of Enlightenment political theory would be written into American law as well.

The Constitution was adopted in 1787, making Franklin the only revolutionary figure who signed all four of the major documents establishing the United States: the Declaration of Independence, the Treaty of Alliance with France, the Treaty of Paris, and the Constitution. But Franklin was already advanced in years and suffered from a number of ailments, most of these brought on by obesity. He died at his Philadelphia home on April 17, 1790, aged eighty-four. After his death, numerous calls went up to grant him special honors. Among these was a curious drive to create a state in the Union named "Franklinland" or "State of Franklin." The idea was to carve its territory out of an existing state, something that North Carolina was more than willing to do in exchange for debt relief, since it owed large sums to the federal government as a result of the Revolutionary War. The "State of Franklin" was created in 1787 west of the Appalachian Mountains, in what is today northeastern Tennessee, with a capital in Jonesborough, soon thereafter moved to Greeneville. However, the state was never adopted into the Union, and after four and a half years it melted away to be absorbed once again into North Carolina.

After the peace treaty was concluded, George Washington looked forward to retirement, hoping to live out his years in the quiet life of a country gentleman at Mount Vernon. Of course, those happy thoughts came to naught when, six years after leaving his post as commander-in-chief, he was elected to be the first president of the United States. Eyewitnesses later reported that after Washington recited the oath of office, he spontaneously added the words "so help me God." A number of historians, including scholars at the Library of Congress, have argued that there is no documentation for that claim. Nevertheless, the custom continues to this day.

In 1811, a Scottish mapmaker who had traveled to the United States numerous times decided to move to Philadelphia and settle there. His name was John Melish. A year later, he published his *Travels through the United States of America, in the years 1806 & 1807, and 1809, 1810, & 1811,* documenting his voyages through his adopted homeland. He then conceived of the idea of creating a huge map that would depict all of America's territories. As we have seen, many cartographers had the same idea, from Waldseemüller to John Mitchell, and from the Dutch Golden Age to the rise of French cartography. But in several important aspects, Melish's map is radically different. He was the first to use new geographical data about the southwestern region, based on Stephen Long's expedition to the Rocky Mountains, as well as the expedition of Lewis and Clark. He also gathered information from the work of cartographers such as Benjamin Tanner and Mathew Cary. But the most important feature of Melish's map is that it did not stop at the boundaries of what had been explored at the time, as virtually all other mapmakers had done.

Instead, he envisioned a nation that ran uninterrupted from the Atlantic Coast to the Pacific Ocean, using green lines to chart American territory stretching from east to west, and from the thirty-eighth parallel (today's Marin

JOHN QUINCY ADAMS,
President of the United States

FIG. 147. *John Quincy Adams, President of the United States*, in an engraving after his official portrait by Thomas Sully, 1824

County) to beyond the forty-ninth parallel (today's Vancouver). The Great Plains, including areas outside the Louisiana Purchase, were shown to be part of the United States as well.

As such, the Melish Map was the first to project the idea of America's Manifest Destiny as a nation from sea to shining sea, long before that dream would become a political reality. To underscore that goal, Melish presented his map to Thomas Jefferson, the former US president (1801–1809), writing that "I have the pleasure of presenting You with a Copy of my new map and Description of the United States and Contiguous Countries, which I respectfully Submit to Your attention."[122] Jefferson was delighted. Whenever European diplomats visited him, he would show them this huge map, thus implying America's long-term purpose of becoming a continental nation without any foreign interference. He even sent copies to friends and allies in Europe.

In 1824, John Quincy Adams was elected president of the United States. Before taking office, Adams sat for his official portrait by Thomas Sully, which was subsequently engraved and printed for distribution across the country. In this picture, the president is seen sitting in his study surrounded by books, documents, and, most importantly, his maps. This was not by accident. Adam was involved in the development of the Chesapeake and Ohio Canal and would attend its groundbreaking in 1828. Most importantly, however, as then secretary of state serving under James Monroe, Adams had led the negotiations for the Adams-Onís Treaty with Spain of 1819, which established a formal boundary between the United States and New Spain following the Louisiana Purchase. As such, Adams was the man who took a great leap toward realizing the vision of the Melish map, which is why that map is prominently displayed to his left.

Not surprisingly, over the following decades the Melish map would be updated, revised, and improved in twenty-five known states—until America's Manifest Destiny became a reality at last.

FURTHER READING

The Renaissance

Bergreen, Laurence. *Columbus: The Four Voyages*. New York: Viking, 2011.

Birch, Thomas. *Memoirs of the Reign of Queen Elizabeth* (two vols.). London: A. Millar, 1754.

Brooke-Hitching, Edward. *The Golden Atlas: The Greatest Explorations, Quests and Discoveries on Maps*. New York: Simon & Schuster, 2018.

Columbus, Christopher. *The Log of Christopher Columbus,* translated by Robert H. Fuson. Camden: International Marine Publishing Co., 1987.

Edwards, Edward. *The Life of Sir Walter Raleigh* (two vols.). London: 1868.

Hannam, James. *The Genesis of Science: How the Christian Middle Ages Launched the Scientific Revolution*. Washington, DC: Regnery Publishing, 2014.

Isbouts, Jean-Pierre. *The Story of Christianity*. Washington, DC: National Geographic, 2013.

Marshall, Michael W. *Ocean Traders from the Portuguese Discoveries to the Present Day*. New York: Facts on File, 1990.

Morison, Samuel Eliot. *Admiral of the Ocean Sea: A Life of Christopher Columbus*. Boston: Little, Brown and Company, 1942.

Penrose, B. *Travel and discovery in the Renaissance, 1420–1620*. Cambridge: Harvard University Press, 1932.

Raleigh, Trevelyan. *Sir Walter Raleigh*. New York: Henry Holt & Co., 2002.

Schulten, Susan. *A History of America in 100 Maps*. Chicago: University of Chicago Press, 2018.

Colonial America

Bailyn, Bernard. *The Peopling of British North America*. New York: Alfred A. Knopf, 1986.

Gray, Edward G. *Colonial America: A History in Documents*. Oxford: Oxford University Press, 2003.

Greene, Jack P., and J. R. Pole (Eds.). *Colonial British America: Essays in the New History of the Early Modern Era*. Baltimore: The Johns Hopkins University Press, 1984.

Hawke, David Freeman (Ed.). *Everyday Life in Early America*. New York: Harper & Row, 1988.

Hughes, Robert. *American Visions: The Epic History of Art in America*. New York: Alfred A. Knopf, 1997.

Mackin, Anne. *Americans and Their Land: The House Built on Abundance*. Ann Arbor: University of Michigan Press, 2006.

Schlesinger, Arthur M. *The Birth of the Nation: A Portrait of the American People on the Eve of Independence*. New York: Alfred A. Knopf, 1968.

Stannard, David E. *American Holocaust: The Conquest of the New World*. Oxford: Oxford University Press, 1993.

Taylor, Alan. *American Colonies: The Settling of North America.* New York: Penguin Books, 2001.

Tillson, Albert H. *Gentry and Common Folk: Political Culture on a Virginia Frontier, 1740–1789.* Lexington: University Press of Kentucky, 1991.

Zinn, Howard. *A People's History of the United States: 1492 to Present.* New York: HarperCollins, 2009.

The Revolutionary War

Anderson, Mark R. *The Battle for the Fourteenth Colony: America's War of Liberation in Canada, 1774–1776.* Lebanon, NH: University Press of New England, 2013.

Atkinson, Rick. *The British Are Coming.* New York: Henry Holt & Co., 2019.

Axelrod, Alan. *The American Revolution: What Really Happened.* New York: Fall River Press, 2007.

Chernow, Ron. *Washington: A Life.* New York: Penguin Books, 2010.

Cook, Don. *The Long Fuse: How England Lost the American Colonies, 1760–1785.* New York: Atlantic Monthly Press, 1995.

Cook, Scott A., and William Earle Klay. "George Washington and Enlightenment Ideas on Educating Future Citizens and Public Servants," *Journal of Public Affairs Education*, Vol. 20: Washington, DC: Routledge, 2014.

Griffith, Samuel B. *The War for American Independence: from 1760 to the Surrender at Yorktown in 1781.* Champaign, IL: University of Illinois Press, 2002.

Hazelton, John H. *The Declaration of Independence: Its History.* New York: Da Capo Press, 1970.

Ketchum, Richard M. *Saratoga: Turning Point of America's Revolutionary War.* New York: Henry Holt & Co. 1997.

Lengel, Edward G. *General George Washington: A Military Life.* New York: Random House, 2005.

Lillback, Peter, and Jerry Newcombe. *George Washington's Sacred Fire.* King of Prussia, PA: Providence Forum Press, 2006.

Middlekauff, Robert. *Washington's Revolution.* New York: Alfred A. Knopf, 2015.

Miller, Nathan. *Sea of Glory: The Continental Navy Fights for Independence.* New York: David McKay, 1974.

O'Connell, Robert L. *Revolutionary: George Washington at War.* New York: Random House, 2019.

Sparks, Jared. *The Writings of George Washington.* Boston: American Stationers Co., 1838.

Treese, Lorett. *Valley Forge: Making and Remaking of a National Symbol.* University Park, PA: Penn State University Press, 1995.

Wood, Gordon S. *Revolutionary Characters: What Made the Founders Different.* New York: Penguin Books, 2006.

NOTES

Prologue

1   I am deeply grateful for Raleigh Trevelyan's masterful account of Sir Walter's last days in his book *Sir Walter Raleigh*, New York: Henry Holt & Co., 2002. Several citations in this prologue are taken from the chapter "Even Such is Time: 1618."

2   Bodleian Library, Tanner Collection, Ms 299:29.

3   Trevelyan, *Sir Walter Raleigh*, 541.

4   Birch, Thomas. *Memoirs of the Reign of Queen Elizabeth* (two vols.). London: A. Millar, 1754. Volume II, 97.

5   Trevelyan, *Sir Walter Raleigh*, 544.

6   Edwards, Edward. *The Life of Sir Walter Raleigh* (two vols.). London: 1868. Volume II, 413.

7   Trevelyan, *Sir Walter Raleigh*, 546.

8   "Monarchy of Man." British Library: the Harleian manuscripts, # 2228.

9   Trevelyan, *Sir Walter Raleigh*, 552.

10 Attar, Karen. "The decapitation of Sir Walter Raleigh: Villain or Victim?" in *Talking Humanities*, the School of Advanced Study, University of London; October 4, 2018. https://talkinghumanities.blogs.sas.ac.uk, retrieved on July 3, 2019.

11 Ellis, Joseph J. "Rick Atkinson's Savage American Revolution," in *The New York Times,* May 11, 2019. See https://www.nytimes.com/2019/05/11/books/review/rick-atkinson-the-british-are-coming.html.

1. The Dawn of the Renaissance

12 Atkinson, Rick. *The British Are Coming*. New York: Henry Holt & Co., 2019, 52, 54.

13 *The Log of Christopher Columbus,* translated by Robert H. Fuson. Camden: International Marine Publishing Co., 1987, 38.

14 *The Log of Christopher Columbus*, 52.

2. The Discovery of the Americas

15 However, in 1991 Oliver Dunn and James E. Kelly Jr. published an article that claimed that Columbus recorded his progress in two separate measurements for his own convenience: one tracking the mileage in ways he was used to as an Italian, and one using the standard of the Portuguese maritime tradition. See Oliver Dunn and James E. Kelley, Jr., "The Diario of Christopher Columbus's First Voyage to America 1492–93." *Renaissance Quarterly*, Vol. 44, No. 3. (Autumn 1991), 572–574.

16 *The Log of Christopher Columbus*, 71.

17 Of course, on the return, ships would typically move faster, given that the prevailing winds in the North Atlantic blow eastward. That is why a modern airliner today takes less time to fly from Boston to London than the other way around.

18 Zinn, Howard. *A People's History of the United States: 1492 to Present*. New York: HarperCollins, 2009, 3.

19 Bergreen, Laurence. *Columbus: The Four Voyages*. New York: Viking, 2011, 196–198.

20 Stannard, David E. *American Holocaust: The Conquest of the New World*. Oxford: Oxford University Press, 1993, 69.

21 Morison, Samuel Eliot. *Admiral of the Ocean Sea: A Life of Christopher Columbus.* Boston: Little, Brown and Company, 1942, 617.

22 *The Log of Christopher Columbus*, 237.

23 Bergreen, *Columbus: The Four Voyages*, 3.

24 Markham, C. R. "Introduction," in *The Letters of Amerigo Vespucci and Other Documents Illustrative of his Career.* London: Hakluyt, 1894.

25 *Lettera di Amerigo Vespucci delle isole nuovamente trovate in quattro suoi viaggi* ("Letter of Amerigo Vespucci concerning the isles newly discovered on his four voyages").

26 *Mundus Novus: Letter to Lorenzo Pietro Di Medici, by Amerigo Vespucci.* Translated by George Tyler Northrup. Princeton, NJ: Princeton University Press, 1916.

27 Schulten, Susan. *A History of America in 100 Maps.* Chicago: University of Chicago Press, 2018, 21.

28 Weare, G. E. *Cabot's Discovery of North America.* London: 1897, 116.

29 *Kurze Schirmred der Kunst der Astrologiae.* Joh. Grüninger, Straßburg 28. November 1520.

30 Ginzburg, Carlo. *Il nicodemismo.* Turin, Italy: Giulio Einaudi Editore, 1970, 30.

31 *Ein kurtze Schirmred der Kunst Astrologie, wider etliche unverstandene Vernichter, auch etliche Antwurt uff die Reden und Fragen Martini Luthers Augustiners, so er in seinen zehen Gebote[n] unformlich wider dise Ku[n]st getho[n] hat.* Abebooks.co.uk., retrieved on July 3, 2019.

3. The First European Settlements

32 Apparently, the bull was prepared by Cardinal Rodrigo Borgia, the future Pope Alexander VI, no doubt in exchange for the proper incentive. See Irene Plunkett, *Isabel of Castile.* New Rochelle, NY: The Knickerbocker Press, 1915, 78.

33 Raleigh, Sir Walter. "A Discourse of the Invention of Ships, Anchors, Compass, etc.," in *The Works of Sir Walter Raleigh, Kt.* 1829 (reprinted 1965), Vol. 8., 325.

34 Only two copies of the map are known to exist: one is at the Library of Congress, and the other is in the British Library.

35 Brooke-Hitching, Edward. *The Golden Atlas: The Greatest Explorations, Quests and Discoveries on Maps.* New York: Simon & Schuster, 2018, 104.

36 Taylor, Alan. *American Colonies: The Settling of North America.* New York: Penguin Books, 2001, 5.

37 Ibid., 101.

38 "The Charter to Sir Walter Raleigh of 1584," in *The Avalon Project, Documents in Law,* at the Lillian Goldman Law Library, Yale Law School, https://avalon.law.yale.edu/16th_century/raleigh.asp, retrieved on August 19, 2019.

39 Taylor, *American Colonies*, 130.

4. The Golden Age of Cartography

40 Penrose, B. *Travel and Discovery in the Renaissance, 1420–1620.* Cambridge, MA: Harvard University Press, 1932.

41 Manasek, F. J. "Frisland. Phantom Island of the North Atlantic," in *Mercator's World,* Vol. 2; No. 1. Jan./Feb. 1997, 14–18.

42 The coauthor of this book, Jean-Pierre Isbouts, is likewise a graduate of Leiden University and remembers taking class in the same building that Johannes De Laet would have frequented.

43 In the twentieth century, the Zuider Zee was dammed off and became a large lake, thus facilitating further land reclamations that are ongoing today.

44 The figure of sixty guilders appears in a letter by Pieter Janszoon Schagen. See "Peter Schaghen Letter with transcription," New Netherland Institute. November 7, 1626, retrieved on February 16, 2015.

5. The Eighteenth-Century Colonization of America

45 J. Hector St. John de Crèvecoeur, *Letters from an American Farmer*, 52.

46 Schlesinger, Arthur M. *The Birth of the Nation: A Portrait of the American People on the Eve of Independence*. New York: Alfred A. Knopf, 1968, 8.

47 J. Hector St. John de Crèvecoeur, *Letters from an American Farmer*, 53.

48 Knecht, R. J. *Richelieu*. Essex, England: Pearson Education Limited, 1991, 165.

49 Taylor, *American Colonies,* 371.

50 Landry, Yves. "Fertility in France and New France: The Distinguishing Characteristics of Canadian Behavior in the Seventeenth and Eighteenth Centuries." *Social Science History*. Winter 1993. 17 (4), 586.

51 Taylor, *American Colonies,* 386. My conversion of livres to dollars is based on the fact that 1 French livre in 1731 could buy 0.33 grams of gold. The price of 0.33 grams of gold in 2015 was about US $12.50. www.historicalstatistics.org.

52 Jackson, Robert H. "Epidemic Disease and Population Decline in the Baja California Missions, 1697–1834." *Southern California Quarterly* (1981), Vol. 63, No. 4, 308–341.

53 Tillson, Albert H. *Gentry and Common Folk: Political Culture on a Virginia Frontier, 1740–1789*. Lexington, KY: University Press of Kentucky, 1991, 20ff.

54 Rossiter, Clinton. *Seedtime of the Republic: The Origin of the American Tradition of Political Liberty* (1953), 106.

55 Schulten, *A History of America in 100 Maps*, 56.

56 Mackin, Anne. *Americans and Their Land: The House Built on Abundance*. Ann Arbor: University of Michigan Press, 2006, 29.

57 Edward Eggleston. *The Transit to Civilization*. New York: N. Appleton and Company, 1901.

6. Daily Life in the English Colonies

58 Schlesinger, *The Birth of the Nation*, 13.

59 See Marcia Zug, "The Mail Order Brides of Jamestown, Virginia" in *The Atlantic*, August 31, 2016.

60 George Alsop, 1666, as quoted in Ibid., 14.

61 *Letters from an American Farmer* became an instant success when it was published in London in 1782 and soon enjoyed publication in other languages as well.

62 Taylor, *American Colonies*, 302.

63 Marshall, Michael W. *Ocean Traders from the Portuguese Discoveries to the Present Day*. New York: Facts on File, 1990, 59–60.

64 Atkinson, *The British Are Coming,* 57.

65 Davis, Ralph. "English Foreign Trade, 1700–1774," in *Economic History Review,* Vol. 15 (1962), 300–301.

66 Schlesinger, *The Birth of the Nation,* 53.

67 See Alison M. Gavin, "In the King's Service: Hugh Finlay and the Postal System in Colonial America," in *Prologue Magazine,* National Archives, Vol. 41 (2), 2009.

68 Price, Jacob. "The Transatlantic Economy," in Jack P. Greene and J.R. Pole (Eds.), *Colonial British America: Essays in the new History of the Early Modern Era.* Baltimore: The Johns Hopkins University Press, 1984, 24–33.

69 Houston, Ron. *History of the World, Map by Map.* New York: Penguin Random House, 2018, 194.

70 "Letters and Papers of John Singleton Copley and Henry Pelham," 48. *Mass. Hist. Soc. Colls.,* Vol. LXXI (1914), 51.

71 McLanathan, Richard. *Gilbert Stuart.* New York: Harry N. Abrams, 1986, 147.

72 For more about the portrait see Elliot Bostwick Davis, et al., *American Painting.* Boston: MFA Publications, 2003.

73 Adkins, Leslie, and Roy A. Adkins. *Handbook to Life in Ancient Rome.* Oxford: Oxford University Press, 1994, 341.

74 Strayer, Joseph R. (Ed.). *Slavery, Slave Trade,* in *Dictionary of the Middle Ages,* Vol. 11. New York: Scribner, 1982.

75 Houston, Rob (Ed.). "The Atlantic Slave Trade," *History of the World, Map by Map.* Penguin Random House, 2018, 196–197.

76 See, for example, the statistics cited in David Stannard, *American Holocaust.* Oxford University Press, 1993.

77 Dunn, Richard S. "The Recruitment and Employment of Labor," in *Colonial British America,* 163–166.

7. Mapping the Prelude to War

78 Reinhartz, Dennis. *The Cartographer and the Literati: Herman Moll and His Intellectual Circle.* Lewiston, NY: Edwin Mellen Press, 1977.

79 *Library and Archive Catalogue of the Royal Society,* 1748.

80 O'Connell, Robert L. *Revolutionary: George Washington at War.* New York: Random House, 2019, 18.

81 Hughes, Robert. *American Visions: The Epic History of Art in America.* New York: Alfred A. Knopf, 1997, 70.

8. The Outbreak of Rebellion

82 Cook, Don. *The Long Fuse: How England Lost the American Colonies, 1760–1785.* New York: Atlantic Monthly Press, 1995.

83 Orr, Clarissa Campbell. "Marriage in a Global Context: Charlotte of Mecklenburg-Strelitz, Queen of Great Britain and Ireland," in Helen Watanabe-O'Kelly et al., *Queens Consort, Cultural Transfer and European Politics.* London: Taylor & Francis, 2016, 109.

84 Atkinson, *The British Are Coming,* 8.

85 Ibid.

86 Edmund Burke, "Speech on Conciliation with America," given in Parliament on March 22, 1775.

87 Alan Axelrod, *The American Revolution: What Really Happened,* 40.

88 Chaffin, Robert J. "The Townshend Acts Crisis, 1767–1770." *The Blackwell Encyclopedia of the American Revolution.* Jack P. Greene and J.R. Pole, eds. Malden, Massachusetts: Blackwell, 1991; reprint 1999.

89 Atkinson, *The British Are Coming,* 13.

90 Adolphus, John. *The History of England from the Accession of George III to 1783.* London: 1802, 135–136.

91 See *Proceedings of the Massachusetts Historical Society,* 1876, 242.

92 Known as the Olive Branch Petition and drafted by the Second Continental Congress on July 5, 1775, it was the last formal effort to avoid all-out war between the colonies and Britain. Reportedly, King George III even refused to read it, calling the colonists "traitors."

93 Atkinson, *The British Are Coming,* 24.

9. The Battle for Independence

94 Atkinson, *The British Are Coming,* 247.

95 Griffith, Samuel B. *The War for American Independence: From 1760 to the Surrender at Yorktown in 1781.* Champaign, IL: University of Illinois Press, 2002, 234.

96 Atkinson, *The British Are Coming,* 246.

97 Cook, *The Long Fuse,* 233.

98 Anderson, Mark R., *The Battle for the Fourteenth Colony: America's War of Liberation in Canada, 1774–1776.* Lebanon, NH: University Press of New England, 2013.

99 Hazelton, John H. *The Declaration of Independence: Its History.* New York: Da Capo Press, 1970, 19.

100 Isbouts, Jean-Pierre. *The Story of Christianity.* National Geographic, 2013, 273–282.

101 Wood, Gordon S. *Revolutionary Characters: What Made the Founders Different.* New York: Penguin Books, 2006, 577.

102 Lengel, Edward G. *General George Washington: A Military Life.* New York: Random House, 2005, 146.

103 Ibid., 154.

104 Miller, Nathan. *Sea of Glory: The Continental Navy Fights for Independence.* New York: David McKay, 1974, 179.

105 O'Connell, *Revolutionary: George Washington at War,* 152.

106 Nathan Miller, *Sea of Glory,* 178.

107 O'Connell, *Revolutionary: George Washington at War,* 137.

108 Ibid., 163.

109 Chernow, Ron. *Washington: A Life.* New York: Penguin Books, 2010, 283.

10. The Road to Victory

110 Historians have endlessly debated the confusion around Howe's orders that spring. However, in a letter from Germain to Howe dated May 18, 1777, the minister made clear that the Philadelphia expedition should "be executed in time for you to co-operate with the army ordered to proceed from Canada and put itself under your command." While that gave Howe considerable latitude, it also clearly specified that the northern campaign was to be supported in every aspect, even if it was led by his subordinate, John Burgoyne.

111 See "The Six Nations Confederacy During the American Revolution," https://www.nps.gov/fost/learn/historyculture/the-six-nations-confederacy-during-the-american-revolution.htm.

112 Ketchum, Richard M. *Saratoga: Turning Point of America's Revolutionary War*. New York: Henry Holt & Co., 1997, 400.

113 Benjamin Franklin to Emma Thompson, February 8, 1777, in Digital Ben Franklin Project, Yale University with The Packard Humanities Institute, http://franklinpapers.org/franklin/framedVolumes.jsp?vol=23&page=296c.

114 Walter Isaacson. *Benjamin Franklin: An American Life*. New York: Simon & Schuster, 2004, 229–230.

115 Isbouts, Jean-Pierre. "George Washington's Prayer," in *Ten Prayers That Changed the World*. New York: Random House, 2017.

116 Cook, *The Long Fuse*, 329.

117 Lengel, Edward G. *General George Washington: A Military Life*. New York: Random House, 2005, 329.

118 Ibid., 330.

119 Cook, *The Long Fuse*, 345.

120 Middlekauff, Robert. *Washington's Revolution*. New York: Alfred A. Knopf, 2015, 286.

Epilogue

121 Franklin, Benjamin. *Silence Dogood No. 8*, 1722.

122 John Melish to Thomas Jefferson, November 23, 1816, *Founders Online*, National Archives. https://founders.archives.gov/documents/Jefferson/03-10-02-0407, retrieved on April 11, 2019.